READING
EXPLORER

PAUL MACINTYRE • DAVID BOHLKE

Second Edition

NATIONAL GEOGRAPHIC LEARNING

CENGAGE Learning

Australia • Brazil • Japan • Korea • Mexico • Singapore • Spain • United Kingdom • United States

Reading Explorer 4
Second Edition

Paul MacIntyre and David Bohlke

Publisher: Andrew Robinson

Executive Editor: Sean Bermingham

Senior Development Editor: Derek Mackrell

Associate Development Editor:
Michelle Harris

Director of Global Marketing: Ian Martin

Product Marketing Manager: Lindsey Miller

Senior Director of Production:
Michael Burggren

Senior Content Project Manager: Tan Jin Hock

Manufacturing Planner: Mary Beth Hennebury

Compositor: Page 2, LLC.

Cover/Text Design: Creative Director:
Christopher Roy, Art Director: Scott Baker,
Senior Designer: Michael Rosenquest

Cover Photo: Ray Chui/Your Shot/National
Geographic Creative

For permission to use material from this text or product,
submit all requests online at **cengage.com/permissions**
Further permissions questions can be emailed to
permissionrequest@cengage.com

Student Book with Online Workbook:
ISBN-13: 978-1-305-25449-7

Student Book:
ISBN-13: 978-1-285-84692-7

National Geographic Learning
20 Channel Center Street
Boston, MA 02210
USA

Cengage Learning is a leading provider of customized learning solutions with office locations around the globe, including Singapore, the United Kingdom, Australia, Mexico, Brazil, and Japan. Locate your local office at:
international.cengage.com/region

Cengage Learning products are represented in Canada by Nelson Education, Ltd.

Visit National Geographic Learning online at **NGL.Cengage.com**

Visit our corporate website at **www.cengage.com**

Printed in the United States of America
Print Number: 06   Print Year: 2017

Contents

Scope and Sequence

Unit	Theme	Reading
1	The Power of Image	**A:** The Visual Village **B:** My Journey in Photographs by Annie Griffiths
2	Love and Attraction	**A:** Love: A Chemical Reaction? **B:** Feathers of Love
3	Food and Health	**A:** How Safe is Our Food? **B:** Genetically Modified Foods
4	Design and Engineering	**A:** Design by Nature: Biomimetics **B:** The Future of Fashion: Dreamweavers
5	Human Journey	**A:** The DNA Trail **B:** Fantastic Voyage
6	Conservation Challenges	**A:** Racing to Rescue Koalas **B:** For the Love of Elephants
7	Ritual Lives	**A:** A Crowd in Harmony **B:** Why We Celebrate
8	Investigations	**A:** Who Killed the Emperor? **B:** In the Lab with Marcella and Alphonse
9	Rediscovering the Past	**A:** Virtually Immortal **B:** In Search of Genghis Khan
10	Earth and Beyond	**A:** Black Holes **B:** The Threat from Space
11	Green Concerns	**A:** Water Worries **B:** Technology as Trash
12	Living Longer	**A:** Genes, Health, and Lifespan **B:** In Search of Longevity

Reading Skill	Vocabulary Building	Video
A: Understanding Words with Multiple Meanings **B:** Scanning for Specific Details	**A:** Word Partnership: *profound* **B:** Thesaurus: *thus*	A Photographer's Life
A: Distinguishing Facts from Theories **B:** Recognizing Figurative Language	**A:** Usage: *chance* **B:** Thesaurus: *absurd*	Singing Mice
A: Understanding Cause and Effect Relationships **B:** Understanding Arguments For and Against an Issue	**A:** Word Link: *-wide* **B:** Thesaurus: *diminish*	The Smelliest Fruit
A: Recognizing Collocations **B:** Understanding Synonyms and Antonyms	**A:** Word Partnership: *vital* **B:** Word Link: *fore-*	Kinetic Sculpture
A: Understanding Relative Clauses (I) **B:** Synthesizing Information	**A:** Word Partnership: *proof* **B:** Thesaurus: *stubborn*	Journey of Discovery
A: Recognizing Conditional Relationships **B:** Sequencing Information	**A:** Word Partnership: *vibrant* **B:** Word Partnership: *chaos*	A Match Made in Africa
A: Understanding Words from Context **B:** Understanding Word Roots and Affixes	**A:** Word Link: *gress* **B:** Thesaurus: *striking*	Festival of Lights
A: Evaluating Theories **B:** Understanding Idiomatic Expressions	**A:** Usage: *grand* **B:** Word Link: *leg*	Frog Licker
A: Recognizing the Use of Ellipsis **B:** Understanding Relative Clauses (II)	**A:** Word Partnership: *virtual* **B:** Word Partnership: *exception*	Secrets of Stonehenge
A: Visualizing from an Author's Description **B:** Understanding References to Things Beyond the Text	**A:** Thesaurus: *preposterous* **B:** Word Link: *di-*	Solar System
A: Identifying Sources of Information **B:** Understanding a Writer's Attitude and Bias	**A:** Thesaurus: *leak* **B:** Word Partnership: *substance*	Your Water Footprint
A: Identifying Reasons **B:** Understanding Quantitative and Qualitative Data	**A:** Word Link: *gen* **B:** Word Partnership: *relief*	The Science of Stress

Welcome to Reading Explorer!

In this book, you'll travel the globe, explore different cultures, and discover new ways of looking at the world. You'll also become a better reader!

What's new in the Second Edition?

New and updated topics

Explore the power of crowds, the mystery of black holes, and discover the secrets to living longer.

New Reading Skill section

Learn how to read strategically—and think critically as you read.

WHY WE CELEBRATE

Before You Read

A. **Scanning.** Scan the text and photos on pages 123–127 and match the photographers (1–5) to the image descriptions (a–e).

1. _____ Reza   a. music festival to raise funds
2. _____ Joel Sartore   b. a traditional dance ritual
3. _____ Chris Johns   c. people in fancy costumes and masks
4. _____ Sam Abell   d. a religious pilgrimage
5. _____ Jason Edwards   e. carnival rides and booths

B. **Predict.** Historically, what reasons do you think first caused humans to gather in public and celebrate? With a partner, discuss your ideas. Then read the passage and check your ideas.

Reza's photograph of Muslim pilgrims surrounding the Ka'aba in the Al-Haram mosque in Mecca, Saudi Arabia

Unit 7B 123

Expanded Viewing section

Apply your language skills when you watch a specially adapted National Geographic video.

Now you're ready

to explore your world!

THE POWER OF IMAGE

Photographer Bill Hatcher ascends Trango Tower, in the Karakoram Mountains, Pakistan.

Warm Up

Discuss these questions with a partner.

1. What famous photographs do you know? What made them famous?

2. What factors are important for a great photograph?

3. What can a photograph do that words cannot?

Before You Read

A. Matching. Read the information and match each word in **bold** with its definition.

The dramatic **shot** you see above was taken on July 13, 2011 as a tornado approached Aurora, Colorado, U.S.A. Magazines and newspapers often rely on local **amateur** photographers to **document** the impact of natural disasters like this one. With the availability of smartphone camera **apps**, uploading photos to the Internet has become a faster way of delivering breaking-news images to online readers.

1. _____document_____ : to record

2. _____amateur_____ : not professional

3. _____shot_____ : a photograph

4. _____apps_____ : a type of software

This photo was taken by Geoff Ridenour as a supercell tornado hovered over the western landscape in Aurora, Colorado, U.S.A.

B. Skim. Skim the first two paragraphs of the reading passage. Circle the statement the author would probably most agree with. Then read the rest of the passage.

a. The quality of smartphone photos is far below that of digital cameras, but no one cares.

b. Smartphones, apps, and the Internet have allowed anyone to be a photographer.

c. Professional photographers are sharing and commenting on more amateur photos.

THE VISUAL VILLAGE

Since = because
since = from until now

1 **BEFORE THE AGE OF THE SMARTPHONE**, aspiring photographers had to learn how to use high-tech cameras and photographic techniques. Not everyone had cameras, and it took skill
5 and a good eye to capture and create a great photograph. Today, with the huge range of camera apps on our smartphones, we're all **amateur** photographers, and pretty good ones at that, since the **quality** of smartphone images
10 now nearly equals that of digital cameras.

→ a desire for food

The new ease of photography has given us a **tremendous** appetite for capturing the magical and the ordinary. We are **obsessed** with documenting everyday moments, whether it's
15 a shot of our breakfast, our cat—or the cat's breakfast. And rather than collect pictures in scrapbooks, we share, like, and comment on them with friends and strangers around the globe. Even photojournalists[1] are experimenting
20 with mobile phones because their near invisibility makes it easier to capture unguarded moments.[2] And the Internet allows them to avoid traditional media, to act as their own publishers—reaching huge audiences via social media sites such as
25 Instagram. A photograph taken in New York can get a response from someone in Lagos within seconds of being uploaded.

In the past, magazines published unforgettable photos of important people and global events
30 that captured our imaginations. These photos had the power to change public opinion and even the course of history. But if there are fewer memorable images today, it's not because there are fewer good images. It's because there
35 are so many, and no one image gets to be special for long.

unguarded = un prepare
natural pic

---

1 A **photojournalist** is a reporter who presents news stories primarily through photographs.
2 If you do something in an **unguarded moment**, you do it carelessly and without thinking.

↑ Will van Overbeek took this photograph of the Botanical Gardens in Quebec, Canada, during the Magic of Lanterns festival.

The act of carefully watching →

Cameras are everywhere—a situation that is transforming the way we experience dramatic events. With surveillance cameras observing

40 most urban centers, have we gotten to the point where cameras don't need photographers and photographers don't even need cameras? When there are political events or natural disasters, it is ordinary citizens with cell

45 phones—not photojournalists—who often provide the first news images. Quality still matters, but it's less important than what's **relevant** and **instantly** shared.

As people everywhere embrace photography

50 and the media make use of citizen journalists,[3] professional standards appear to be shifting. Before digital images, most people trusted photographs to accurately reflect reality. Today, images can be altered in ways the naked eye

to change or make different

55 might never notice. Photojournalists are trained to accurately represent what they witness. Yet any image can be altered to create an "improved" picture of reality. The average viewer is left with no way to assess the accuracy of an image

60 except through trust in a news organization or photographer.

The question of the accuracy of images gets even trickier when photojournalists start experimenting with camera apps—like Hipstamatic or

65 Instagram—which encourage the use of filters. Images can be colored, brightened, faded, and scratched to make photographs more artistic, or to give them an antique look. Photographers using camera apps to cover wars and conflicts have

70 created powerful images—but also **controversy**.

argument

---

3 A **citizen journalist** is an average or amateur person gathering and sharing the news.

Cameras are everywhere—
a situation that is
transforming the way
we experience dramatic
events.

radical =original- fundational -primary

The increase in the number of photographs
90   and photographers might even be good for
democracy itself. Hundreds of millions of
potential citizen journalists make the world
smaller and help keep leaders honest. People
can now show what they are up against,
95   making it increasingly difficult for governments
to hide their actions. If everyone has a camera,
Big Brother[5] isn't the only one watching.

Who knows? Our obsession with
documentation and constantly being connected
100   could lead to a radical change in our way
of being. Perhaps we are witnessing the
development of a universal visual language,
one that could change the way we relate to
each other and the world. Of course, as with
105   any language, there will be those who produce
poetry and those who make shopping lists.

It's not clear whether this flowering of image-
making will lead to a public that better
appreciates and understands images—or simply
110   numb[6] us to the **profound** effects a well-made
image can have. But the change is irreversible.
Let's hope the millions of new photographs
made today help us see what we all have in
common, rather than what sets us apart.

Critics worry that antique-looking photographs
romanticize war, while distancing us from those
who fight in them.

Yet photography has always been more subjective
75   than we assume. Each picture is a result of a series
of decisions—where to stand, what lens[4] to use,
what to leave in and what to leave out of the
frame. Does altering photographs with camera
app filters make them less true? There's something
80   powerful and exciting about the experiment the
digital age has forced upon us. These new tools
make it easier to tell our own stories—and they
give others the power to do the same. Many
members of the media get stuck on the same
85   stories, focusing on elections, governments, wars,
and disasters, and in the process, miss out on the
less dramatic images of daily life that can be
as revealing.

---

4 A **lens** is a thin, curved piece of glass or plastic used in things
   such as cameras, telescopes, and eyeglasses.
5 From the name of the head of state in George Orwell's
   novel *1984*, **Big Brother** means a person or an organization
   exercising total control over people's lives.
6 If an event or experience **numbs** you, you can no longer
   think, feel, or react normally.

Reading Comprehension

Multiple Choice. Choose the best answer for each question.

Detail

1. According to the author, why are there fewer memorable photographs today?
   a. Because the quality of many images is still poor.
   b. Because most images are not interesting to a global audience.
   c. Because traditional media refuse to allow amateur photos.
   d. Because there are so many good images these days.

Detail

2. What kinds of images does the author think matter most these days?
   a. images that are important to people and that can be shared quickly
   b. images that are of a high quality that help show dramatic events
   c. images that reflect reality but are presented in a traditional way
   d. images that can be altered to improve one's sense of reality

Purpose

3. Why does the author put the word *improved* in quotation marks in paragraph 5 (starting line 49)?
   a. The writer is using the exact word from another source.
   b. The writer wishes to stress that the picture of reality is greatly improved.
   c. The writer believes it is arguable whether the picture is truly improved.
   d. The writer is not sure the reader understands the word, so draws attention to it.

Inference

4. Who does the author criticize in this reading?
   a. citizen journalists
   b. people who use surveillance cameras
   c. some members of today's media
   d. people who alter photos

Main Idea

5. What is the main idea of paragraph 8 (starting line 89)?
   a. Big Brother is no longer watching us.
   b. Democratic governments are the only governments that allow cameras.
   c. People with cameras can help show how things really are in the world.
   d. More governments are trying to ban the use of cameras in their countries.

Paraphrase

6. When referring to visual language, what does the author mean by *as with any language, there will be those who produce poetry and those who make shopping lists* (lines 104–106)?
   a. It will be most useful for shopping and for writing beautiful poetry.
   b. It will be better because it can be used for a wide variety of things.
   c. We can do the same thing with visual language as written language.
   d. Some people will use it for everyday things and others for more creative things.

Cohesion

7. The following sentence would best be placed at the end of which paragraph?
Such images may be more useful in communicating how the person behind the camera felt than in documenting what was actually in front of the camera.
   a. 2 (starting line 11)   b. 6 (starting line 62)
   c. 9 (starting line 98)   d. 10 (starting line 107)

Evaluating: Do you think news photographers should be allowed to use filters and other techniques to alter photos? Why, or why not?

Discussion: Are you aware of all the photos of yourself that have been uploaded? What would you do if you found out someone was uploading photos of you without your permission?

imply past implied v implication (n)

Understanding Words with Multiple Meanings

Many words have more than one meaning. These words may be different parts of speech and have meanings that are very different (e.g., a **slip** of paper, to **slip** on the ice), or the words may be closer in meaning (e.g., a distance of one **foot**, my right **foot**). In either case, it may be necessary to use a dictionary to understand a word's exact meaning.

A. Multiple Choice. Read each excerpt from the reading. Choose the sentence in which the underlined word has the same meaning as the **bold** word.

1. Before the **age** of the smartphone . . . (line 1)
   a. I want to travel before I reach a certain <u>age</u>.
   b. We are now living in the digital <u>age</u>.

2. . . . with the huge **range** of camera apps . . . (lines 6–7)
   a. It's the longest mountain <u>range</u> in the world.
   b. The store has a small <u>range</u> of new appliances.

3. . . . a tremendous **appetite** for capturing the magical . . . (line 12)
   a. She has an <u>appetite</u> for learning about new cultures.
   b. She has a big <u>appetite</u>, so I hope you made lots of food.

4. . . . and even the **course** of history. (line 32)
   a. I had to take a history <u>course</u> in college.
   b. One never knows what <u>course</u> to follow.

5. As people everywhere **embrace** photography . . . (line 49)
   a. She wanted to <u>embrace</u> her son after he was found.
   b. It was not easy for her to <u>embrace</u> married life.

6. . . . people trusted photographs to accurately **reflect** reality. (lines 52–53)
   a. His novel doesn't <u>reflect</u> his actual views.
   b. The water pools <u>reflect</u> light beautifully.

7. Photographers using camera apps to **cover** wars . . . (lines 68–69)
   a. The exam will <u>cover</u> everything that's been taught so far.
   b. It was a huge accomplishment to have his work featured on the <u>cover</u> of the magazine.

8. . . . a result of a **series** of decisions . . . (lines 75–76)
   a. There has been an unusual <u>series</u> of events.
   b. What is the most popular comic book <u>series</u>?

9. . . . and what to leave out of the **frame**. (lines 77–78)
   a. The <u>frame</u> of his bicycle was destroyed.
   b. Look in the camera <u>frame</u> and tell me what you see.

Vocabulary Practice

A. Completion. Complete the information by circling the correct word in each pair.

Photographing Cities

A radical change has happened in photography. The wide availability of smartphones means that ordinary people can now take **1. (quality / obsessed)** photographs of the world around them. **2. (Amateur / Controversial)** photographers are **3. (instant / obsessed)** with capturing and documenting the world around them, especially the cities in which they live in.

When and where a photograph is taken can have a(n) **4. (instant / profound)** effect on what the viewer feels. To bring a city to life, look for a mid-level view. It's still close enough to feel the experience of the city without looking down on it. In any city, there will be publicly accessible places that let you look into the city. New York City, especially, has a unique geography. Since Manhattan is an island, the city has had to grow tall. That height, surrounded by water with its bridges, makes New York a **5. (tremendous / romanticized)** place to photograph.
amazing

B. Words in Context. Complete each sentence with the correct answer.

1. A **controversy** involves _____ among people.
   a. agreement   b. disagreement

2. If a movie **romanticizes** an event in history, it shows it _____ than it really was.
   a. worse   b. better

3. In a **democracy**, citizens _____ the right to vote.
   a. have   b. don't have

4. If the ideas in an old book are **relevant** today, they _____.
   a. still matter   b. no longer matter

5. If something happens **instantly**, it happens _____.
   a. without delay   b. after a long delay

⌃ lower Manhattan at dusk

> **Word Partnership**
> Use **profound** with:
> (*n.*) profound **effect**,
> profound **influence**,
> profound **impact**,
> profound **image**,
> profound **experience**.

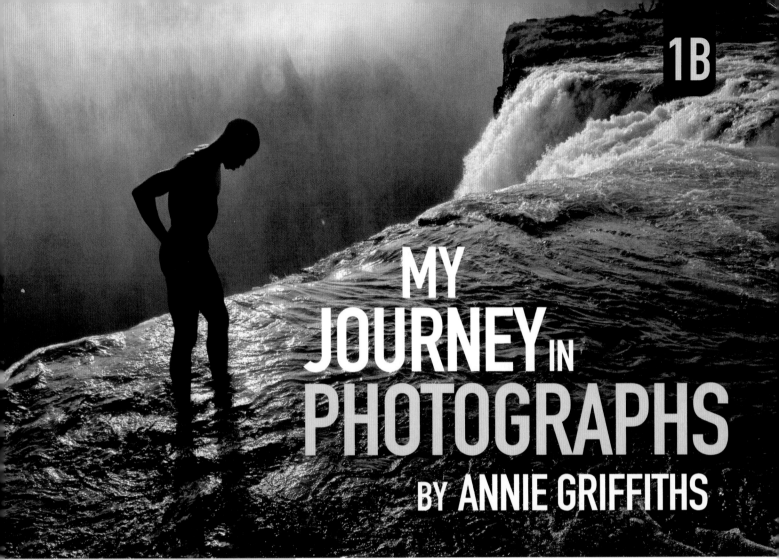

MY JOURNEY IN PHOTOGRAPHS
BY ANNIE GRIFFITHS

Before You Read

A. Matching. You are going to read about award-winning photographer Annie Griffiths. Below are some expressions she uses (**1–7**) in the reading. Match them to the definitions (**a–g**) on the left.

1. _e_ am knee-deep in
2. _f_ by some miracle
3. _c_ like a master class
4. _g_ of very few words
5. _b_ put at ease
6. _a_ small talk
7. _d_ top-notch

a. light conversation
b. make people feel comfortable
c. excellent training
d. first-class
e. have more than enough
f. incredibly lucky
g. not speaking very much

Annie Griffiths took this photograph of a swimmer standing at the top of a hidden pool, Victoria Falls, South Africa.

B. Discuss. What do you think are the challenges of being a professional photographer? Check your ideas as you read the passage.

I'm over my head to do homework

Two portraits by ➤ Annie Griffiths: (Left) A child peers between her sisters' robes in southern Pakistan (Right) An old aborigine man and child

1 **I GOT MY FIRST REAL JOB AT AGE 12**, as a waitress. I am convinced that I learned more as a waitress than I ever did in a classroom. It certainly was more interesting. And when I went
5 on to college, it paid for tuition and housing and, eventually, a camera. It allowed me to rent an apartment and feed myself (chicken pot pies, four for a dollar!). But best of all, being a waitress taught me to quickly assess and understand all
10 kinds of people. I learned how to make small talk and how to quickly put people at ease— great training for a journalist. Waiting tables also taught me **teamwork** and service and humor. For the first eight years, I loved it. For the final
15 two years, I just wanted to be a photographer.

From the moment I picked up a camera, I was hooked. I lost interest in other studies, and all I wanted to do was take pictures for the university newspaper, the *Minnesota Daily*. The paper at
20 that time was one of the largest in the state and was produced by young journalists who went on to work at every major magazine in the country. In six months, I was able to get a lot of great experience. The week I finished college, I was
25 contacted by the *Worthington Daily Globe*, a regional daily newspaper in southern Minnesota with a history of excellence in photography. It was wonderfully printed with fantastic photographs. By some miracle I was hired, and the two-year
30 experience that followed was like a master class in photojournalism.

Jim Vance was the top-notch publisher of the *Globe*. He had very high **expectations** of all the staff. With little or no instruction from him,
35 writers and photographers were expected to fill the paper with stories that were important to our readers. I didn't know it at the time, but this independent reporting was perfect training for my future career at *National Geographic*.

They are not very friendly

40 Among the most important things I learned at the *Globe* was that if you can make friends with a shy Norwegian farmer and be invited to his kitchen table, you can probably do well in any culture on Earth. I worked with a wonderful

45 writer named Paul Gruchow. Together we would search the farming communities for stories. Paul had grown up on a farm himself and lived through personal tragedy, so he was able to **project** warmth and understanding to anyone

50 he met. Farmers would invite us into their homes and willingly share their personal thoughts with us. From Paul I learned how to be a patient listener as well as the importance of giving each subject time and sincere attention.

true

55 It was while I was working at the *Globe* that I happened to answer the phone one morning. A man's voice asked, "You a photographer?" When I replied that indeed I was, the voice

without a doubt certainly

60 responded, "This is Bob Gilka. *National Geographic*. I need a hail[1] damage picture. You guys get a big hailstorm last night?" I **overcame** my nervousness and said, "Yes, sir." When he asked if I could take the picture for him, I again said, "Yes, sir." **Thus** began

65 one of the most important relationships of my life, with the legendary Director of Photography at *National Geographic*, Bob Gilka.

unreal

impressed = to affect strongly

Bob was always looking for talented

70 photographers to join his team, and he was not easily impressed. As he used to say, "I am knee-deep in talent, but only ankle-deep in ideas. I want people with ideas!" He was a man of very few words, so every word was heard.

75 **Praise** from Bob meant as much to most photographers as a Pulitzer Prize.

---

1 **Hail** is small balls of ice that fall from the sky like rain.

↳ *icy rain*

... if you can make friends with a shy Norwegian farmer and be invited to his kitchen table, you can probably do well in any culture on Earth.

surveys = to look

My little picture of hail damage in southern Minnesota was well received, and a year later, I was working for Bob. I was the youngest photographer working for *National Geographic* when I arrived in 1978, and I spent at least a decade just trying not to make mistakes. While I was grateful for the opportunity, it was very difficult for me. With each new assignment came the fear that this was going to be the one where they figured out that I couldn't do the job.

On many assignments, the most challenging part **turned out** to be the transportation. Over the years, I traveled by horse, car, train, truck, and all sorts of old vehicles. I traveled by mule[2] in Mexico, by ship along the Indian Ocean, by fishing boat in the Sea of Galilee, by moped[3] in Bermuda, by sailboat in Sydney. I flew in helicopters chasing bears in the Arctic. Twice, while flying in light planes, pilots have had to make emergency landings far from any airport. But there were also wonderful experiences. In Africa I traveled by balloon, ultralight aircraft, and elephant. In a rubber raft off the west coast of Mexico, I was suddenly lifted out of the water on the back of a friendly whale.

ultra = very

Wherever I traveled in the world, taking beautiful pictures was always my goal. However, later in my career, I also wanted my pictures to make a real difference in people's lives. That is why each spring I tour two or three developing countries, shooting **portraits** of people whose lives are better because of the dedicated workers who care about them. The photos are used in a variety of fund-raising[4] products. The other issue that stole my heart was the environment. With support from the National Geographic Expeditions Council, I have traveled all over the United States to photograph the last one percent of wilderness left here.

wild areas

I am deeply grateful for my life in photography and the amazing lessons it has taught me. I have learned that women really do hold up half the sky; that language isn't always necessary, but touch usually is; that all people are not alike, but they do mostly have the same hopes and fears; that judging others does great harm, but listening to them **enriches**; and that it is impossible to hate a group of people once you get to know one of them as an individual.

---

2 A **mule** is a hybrid between a horse and a donkey.
3 A **moped** is a type of lightweight motorcycle.
4 **Fund-raising** is collecting or earning money for a charity, a school, a political party, etc.

6 = dedicated spending a great deal of one's time and energy on a subject

A Bedouin surveys the view around Petra, Jordan. ⌄

Reading Comprehension

Multiple Choice. Choose the best answer for each question.

Purpose
1. What is the purpose of the first paragraph?
   a. to describe what life was like working as a waitress
   b. to explain how waitressing helped prepare Griffiths for life as a photographer
   c. to compare Griffiths' life before and after becoming a waitress
   d. to complain about how working as a waitress affected Griffiths' university studies

Vocabulary
2. In lines 16–17, the expression *I was hooked* is closest in meaning to _____.
   a. I was hurt
   b. I was employed
   c. I was addicted
   d. I was successful

Sequence
3. What happened after Griffiths graduated from college?
   a. She picked up a camera for the first time.
   b. She got a job at the *Minnesota Daily.*
   c. She got a job at the *Worthington Daily Globe.*
   d. She started taking photos for the university newspaper.

Detail
4. Which sentence does NOT describe Griffiths' job at the *Globe*?
   a. She received detailed instructions from her publisher.
   b. She learned to be a patient listener and give people attention.
   c. The job prepared Griffiths well for a job at *National Geographic.*
   d. She and the writers were expected to fill the paper with stories that were important to readers.

Detail
5. What first brought Griffiths to the attention of *National Geographic*?
   a. a photo she had published in the *Globe*
   b. a photo that *National Geographic* had asked her to take for them
   c. a photo she secretly sent to *National Geographic*
   d. a photo of hers sent by a college friend to *National Geographic*

Detail
6. What did Griffiths find especially challenging when on assignments?
   a. the weather
   b. wild animals
   c. the transportation
   d. being away from home

Detail
7. According to the passage, what has life as a *National Geographic* photographer taught Griffiths?
   a. that language is important
   b. that people have different hopes and fears
   c. that judging people does great harm
   d. that one can never really know people as individuals

Critical Thinking

Interpreting: Griffiths says she has learned that "women really do hold up half the sky." What do you think she means by this?

_____

Discussion: What do you think would be Griffiths' advice for someone who wanted to get a job as a professional photographer?

Reading Skill

Scanning for Specific Details

When you scan to find specific details, such as dates, names, amounts, or places, you need to have a clear idea of the kind of information you are looking for. If possible, have one or two key words in mind. Then quickly read through the material, looking only for these words or related words. Don't try to read every word and don't worry about understanding everything. When you find the relevant word(s), read the surrounding context to check how the information relates to the rest of the text.

A. Scanning. Use content words (names, places, dates, etc.) in each sentence below to help you quickly locate the section of the reading it relates to. Then mark the sentences **T** (True) or **F** (False). All information is in paragraphs 1–5.

1. _F_ The best thing about being a waitress was that it allowed Griffiths to buy a camera.

2. _F_ Griffiths worked at the *Worthington Daily Globe* for two years and six months.

3. _T_ The *Worthington Daily Globe* was wonderfully printed with fantastic photographs.

4. _T_ Jim Vance was the publisher of the *Worthington Daily Globe.*

5. _F_ Paul Gruchow was a Norwegian farmer she took photographs of.

6. _T_ Griffiths' first photo for *National Geographic* was a picture of hail.

B. Scanning. Use content words (names, places, dates, etc.) in each sentence below to help you quickly locate the section of the reading it relates to. Then complete the sentences. All information is in paragraphs 6–10.

1. Griffiths compares getting praise from Bob Gilka to receiving a ___Pulitzer___ Prize.

2. Griffiths got a job with *National Geographic* a ___year later___ after sending them her photo.

3. Griffiths describes traveling by ___mule___ and in a ___rubber raft___ while on assignment in Mexico.

4. Griffiths has had to make ___two___ emergency landings while flying.

5. Griffiths wants to take photos that make a ___real difference___ in people's lives.

6. According to Griffiths, language is not always necessary, but ___touch___ usually is.

Vocabulary Practice

A. Completion. Complete the information with the correct form of words from the box. Two words are extra.

enrich	expectation	overcome	portrait
project	staff	teamwork	thus

National Geographic photographers often have to
1. _overcome_ great difficulties to get the shots
they need. The **2.** _expectation_ of quality are very
high. In order to get the best results, they understand that "the
photograph is never taken—it is always given." The photo is
3. _thus_ an outcome of **4.** _teamwork_
between two people on either side of the lens.

The magazine's most iconic photograph is not of anyone or
anything historic. Rather, it's a(n) **5.** _portrait_
of Sharbat Gula, a young Afghan girl at a refugee camp in
Pakistan. What her intense green eyes **6.** _project_
from the cover of *National Geographic's* June 1985 issue was
truth—the harsh reality of a war-torn country.

B. Definitions. Match the definitions to words from the box.

Sharbat Gula, the young girl who was featured on the National Geographic Magazine cover of the June 1985 issue

enrich	expectation	portrait	praise
project	staff	teamwork	turn out

1. _turn out_ : to happen in a particular way

2. _enrich_ : to improve or enhance the quality of something

3. _project_ : to have or show a quality that can be seen by others

4. _praise_ : words about the good qualities of someone or something

5. _staff_ : a group of people who work for a company or business

6. _teamwork_ : the effort of people working together to get something done

7. _expectation_ : strong hope or belief that something will happen

8. _portrait_ : a photo or drawing of a person that usually only includes the person's head and shoulders

Thesaurus thus
also look up:
(*adv.*) *so, hence,
consequently, as a
result, for this reason*

VIEWING | A Photographer's Life

Before You Watch

A. Discussion. You are going to watch an interview with the photographer Annie Griffiths. First, look at some of her photos. Then discuss the questions below with a partner.

1. What kinds of things do you think Griffiths likes to photograph?
2. How would you describe the photographs above?
3. Choose one photograph above. What do you think she is trying to say with the photo?

While You Watch

A. True or False. Watch the video. Read the sentences and circle **T** (True) or **F** (False).

1. Annie Griffiths has always wanted to be a photographer.   **T**   **F**
2. Griffiths' children spent time with local children when she traveled for work.   **T**   **F**
3. Griffiths says the challenge for a photographer is that almost everything has been photographed before.   **T**   **F**
4. To Griffiths, the best part of traveling is immersing yourself in a culture.   **T**   **F**
5. Griffiths says one of the most inspirational parts about photography is seeing your photographs published.   **T**   **F**

B. Completion. Use words from the box to complete each quote. Then check your answers as you watch the video again. One word is extra.

artistically	available	communication	creative	dark
flexible	flexibility	inspirational	terrible	wonderful

Annie Griffiths on Becoming a Photographer

". . . there was something . . . being in that kind of **1.** _____ wonderful place watching images come up that touched me, and . . . and I realized that that's what I wanted to do."

The Gift of Traveling

". . . what I've learned from my kids is how delightful **2.** _____ is, and how naturally **3.** _____ most kids are, as long as they've got the basics . . ."

Changing Perspectives in Photography

"It's a(n) **4.** _____ **5.** _____ job because you get this opportunity to go out and do it, but then you're supposed to do it better than it's ever been done before."

Immersion in Different Cultures

"What traveling has taught me is that once you, you know, step into another culture and you allow yourself to really immerse yourself in another culture, and be **6.** _____ to them, **7.** _____ happens very quickly . . ."

Finding Inspiration in Photography

". . . to have a career where . . . I get to be **8.** _____, I'm immersed in really interesting situations, and I continue to grow **9.** _____—what's better than that?"

After You Watch

A. Discussion. Discuss these questions with a partner.

1. Griffiths says she had always planned to be a writer until she took a photography class. Have you ever had a class affect you strongly, either positively or negatively?

2. Griffiths describes her job as "wonderful terrible." What does she mean? Can you think of something you would describe the same way?

3. Griffiths describes her children's travel experience as very positive. What do you think might have been something negative they experienced?

LOVE AND ATTRACTION

Lovebirds mate for life, and mating pairs are often seen sitting close together for long periods of time.

Warm Up

Discuss these questions with a partner.

1. What are some things that animals do to attract a mate?

2. What is it that makes one person attractive to another?

3. In what ways do you think science might explain feelings of love?

25

Before You Read

A. Discussion. Check (✓) whether you agree or disagree with the following statements about love. Then explain your answers to a partner.

	Agree	Disagree
1. The idea of romantic love is a modern one.		✓
2. The feeling of love is caused by chemicals in the brain.	✓	
3. Attitudes about love are basically the same in all cultures.		✓
4. The feeling of romantic love usually only lasts a short time.		✓
5. Arranged marriages are likely to last longer than ones started in romance.		✓

B. Scan. You are going to read about some specialists' beliefs about love. Quickly scan the reading on pages 27–29. Then match the people on the left with their professions on the right.

1. __d__ Thomas Lewis   **a.** Swiss university professor

2. __a__ Claus Wedekind   **b.** Italian university professor

3. __b__ Donatella Marazziti   **c.** American anthropologist

4. __c__ Helen Fisher   **d.** American psychiatrist

LOVE: A CHEMICAL REACTION?

Newlyweds dressed in Han-dynasty costumes face each other during a traditional group wedding ceremony in Xi'an, China.

1 **SOME ANTHROPOLOGISTS**[1] **ONCE THOUGHT** that **romance** was a Western idea, developed in the Middle Ages.[2] Non-Western societies, they thought, were too occupied with social and
5 family relationships for romance. Today, scientists believe that romance has existed in human brains in all societies since prehistoric[3] times. In one study, for example, men and women from Europe, Japan, and the Philippines were asked to
10 fill out a survey to measure their experiences of passionate love. All three groups said that they felt passion with the same extreme intensity.

But though romantic love may be universal, its cultural expression is not. To the Fulbe people of
15 northern Cameroon, men who spend too much time with their wives are insulted[4] and looked down on. Those who fall deeply in love are thought to have fallen under a dangerous spell. For the Fulbe, to be controlled by love is seen
20 as shameful.

In India, marriages have traditionally been arranged, usually by the bride's and groom's parents, but today love marriages appear to be on the rise, often in **defiance** of parents'
25 wishes. The victory of romantic love is celebrated in Bollywood films. However, most Indians still believe arranged marriages are more likely to succeed than love marriages. In one survey of Indian college students, 76 percent said they
30 would marry someone with all the right qualities even if they weren't in love with the person. Marriage is considered too important a step to leave to **chance**.

1 An **anthropologist** studies people, society, and culture.
2 The **Middle Ages** was the period in European history between about 500 A.D. and about 1500 A.D.
3 **Prehistoric** people and things existed at a time before information was written down.
4 If someone **insults** you, they say or do something that is rude or offensive.

Finding the Right Person

35 Some psychiatrists,[5] such as Thomas Lewis from the University of California, hypothesize that romantic love is rooted in experiences of physical closeness in childhood—for example, how we felt in our mother's arms. These feelings of comfort
40 and affection are written on our brain, and as adults, our constant **inclination** is to find them again. According to this theory, we love whom we love not so much because of the future we hope to build, but rather because of the past we hope
45 to live again. The person who "feels right" has a certain look, smell, sound, or touch that activates very deep memories.

Evolutionary psychologists explain, however, that survival skills are **inherent** in our choice of a mate.
50 According to this hypothesis, we are attracted to people who look healthy—for example, a woman with a 70 percent waist-to-hip ratio is attractive because she can likely bear children successfully. A man with rugged features probably has a
55 strong immune system[6] and therefore is more likely to give his partner healthy children.

On the other hand, perhaps our choice of a mate is a simple matter of following our noses. Claus Wedekind, a professor at the University of
60 Lausanne in Switzerland conducted an interesting experiment with sweaty[7] T-shirts. He asked 49 women to smell T-shirts previously worn by a variety of unidentified men. He then asked the women to rate which T-shirts smelled the best
65 and which the worst.

He found that women preferred the smell of a T-shirt worn by a man who was the most genetically different from her. This genetic difference means that it is likely that the man's
70 immune system possesses something hers does not. By choosing him as the father of her children, she increases the chance that her children will be healthy.

---

5 A **psychiatrist** is a doctor who treats people with a particular mental condition or illness.
6 The body's **immune system** protects it from diseases of all kinds.
7 **Sweat** is the salty, colorless liquid that comes through your skin when you are hot, sick, or afraid.

Is It All Just Chemicals?

75 According to other researchers, love may be caused by chemicals in the body. Donatella Marazziti, a professor at the University of Pisa in Italy, has studied the biochemistry[8] of lovesickness.[9] Having been in love twice herself and felt its overwhelming
80 power, Marazziti became interested in exploring the similarities between love and obsessive-compulsive disorder (OCD).[10]

Marazziti examined the blood of 24 people who had fallen deeply in love within the past six
85 months, and measured their levels of serotonin. Serotonin is a powerful chemical in the brain and body that is connected with our moods, emotions, and **desires**. She found that their levels of serotonin were 40 percent lower than normal
90 people—the same results she found from people with OCD. Her conclusion was that love and mental illness may be difficult to tell apart.

Another scientist, anthropologist Helen Fisher, from Rutgers University, U.S.A., has been looking at love
95 with the aid of an MRI machine.[11] She **recruited** subjects who were "madly in love," and once they were inside the MRI machine, she showed them two photographs, one neutral, the other of their loved one.

100 What Fisher saw fascinated her. When each subject looked at his or her loved one, the parts of the brain linked to reward and pleasure "lit up." Love "lights up" these areas using a chemical called dopamine. Dopamine creates intense energy,
105 exhilaration, focused attention, and motivation to win rewards. Dopamine levels do eventually drop, though, and studies around the world confirm that a decrease in passion is the norm.

Fisher has suggested that relationships frequently
110 break up after about four years because that's

---

8 **Biochemistry** is the study of the chemical processes that occur in living things.
9 A **lovesick** person experiences overwhelming feelings of love.
10 **Obsessive-compulsive disorder (OCD)** is a mental illness that involves repeating actions or thinking about certain things too much.
11 An **MRI machine** uses a magnetic field and radio waves to create detailed images of the body.

A couple poses for a portrait a few days before their wedding in Delhi, India.

about how long it takes to raise a child through infancy.[12] Passion, that wild feeling, turns out to be practical after all. A couple not only needs to bring a child into this world; they also
115 need a bond that continues long enough to raise a helpless human infant.

Maintaining Love

Eventually, all couples find that their passion declines over time. For relationships that get
120 beyond the initial stage of passion to have a real chance of lasting, a chemical called oxytocin may be the key. Oxytocin is a hormone our body produces that promotes

mutual feelings of connection and bonding.
125 It is produced when we hug our long-term partners or our children. In long-term relationships that work, oxytocin is believed to be **abundant** in both partners. According to Helen Fisher, couples who want their
130 relationship to last should make an effort to keep a close physical relationship. Through frequent physical contact, they can **trigger** the production of more oxytocin—and in this way feel closer to each other.

---

12 **Infancy** is the period of your life when you are a baby or very young child.

Reading Comprehension

Multiple Choice. Choose the best answer for each question.

Gist

1. Another title for this reading could be _____.
   a. Science Can Conquer Passion
   b. The Right Way to Choose a Mate
   c. Explaining Why We Fall in Love
   d. The Case for Arranged Marriage

Detail

2. How do the Fulbe people of Cameroon feel about love?
   a. Everyone falls in love in the same way.
   b. The men's wives don't want them around.
   c. It is shameful to be controlled by love.
   d. Men can fall in love, but women cannot.

Reference

3. Which choice best expresses the meaning of *this theory* in line 42?
   a. Marriage is too important to leave to chance.
   b. Without the approval of family, romantic love rarely succeeds.
   c. Romantic love is based on pleasant memories that we try to find again.
   d. Memories of comfort and affection can satisfy our need for romantic love.

Detail

4. According to evolutionary psychology, why would a woman choose a man with rugged features?
   a. to improve her immune system
   b. to have healthier children
   c. to protect her from animals and other threats
   d. because he is more likely to have a 70 percent waist-to-hip ratio

Inference

5. Why did Marazziti probably choose to study similarities between love and OCD?
   a. She wanted to better understand her own experiences.
   b. She had naturally low serotonin levels.
   c. Other researchers felt it was an important area to study.
   d. She suffered from a mental illness.

Detail

6. According to researchers, which chemical is most closely related to successful long-term relationships?
   a. dopamine
   b. oxytocin
   c. serotonin
   d. none of the above

Inference

7. What advice would Helen Fisher probably give to couples who want a long-term relationship?
   a. Hug each other often.
   b. Avoid having children.
   c. Keep your partner's photo in your wallet.
   d. Spend time apart so you appreciate each other when you're together.

Critical Thinking

Discussion: Evolutionary psychologists suggest we are attracted to healthy people because they are more likely to have healthy children. Do you think this "survival skills" theory is still true today? What qualities do people look for in a mate these days?

Relating: The author writes that a particular chemical may be the key to lasting relationships. How do you feel about relationships relying on a chemical?

Distinguishing Facts from Theories

Scientific texts often contain a mix of facts and theories. Facts are ideas that are known to be true, or can be proven. Theories and hypotheses are ideas that have not been proven to be true or false. Words and phrases that may indicate a theory include *think, believe, hypothesize, may, might, possibly, likely, suggest,* and *according to this theory/hypothesis.*

A. Scanning. Look back at the reading on pages 27–29. Find and underline the following information.

1. _____ Romance has existed in human brains in all societies since prehistoric times. (lines 6–7)

2. _____ The cultural expression of love is not universal. (lines 13–14)

3. _____ Arranged marriages in India are more likely to succeed than love marriages. (lines 27–28)

4. _____ Romantic love is rooted in experiences of physical closeness in childhood. (lines 37–38)

5. _____ We love whom we love because of the past we hope to live again. (lines 42–45)

6. _____ We are attracted to people who look healthy. (lines 50–51)

7. _____ In one study, women preferred the smell of a T-shirt worn by a man who was the most genetically different from her. (lines 66–68)

8. _____ Love is caused by chemicals in the body. (lines 75–76)

9. _____ Serotonin is a powerful chemical in the brain and body that is related to our moods, emotions, and desires. (lines 86–88)

10. _____ Love and mental illness are difficult to tell apart. (lines 91–92)

11. _____ The reason relationships often break up after four years is that it takes that long to raise a child through infancy. (lines 109–112)

12. _____ All couples find that their passion declines over time. (lines 118–119)

13. _____ In long-term relationships that work, oxytocin is abundant in both partners. (lines 126–128)

B. Fact or Theory. Which of the statements above are facts and which are theories? Write **F** (Fact) or **T** (Theory) next to each statement. Then circle the words in the reading that indicate the theories.

Vocabulary Practice

A. Matching. Read the information below and match each word in **red** with its definition.

The Origins of Valentine's Day

Although Valentine's Day may seem like a modern event, its roots go back over 2,000 years.

Around 270 A.D., Roman Emperor Claudius II, seeking to **recruit** more soldiers for his army, prohibited young men from marrying. Valentine was a priest who performed marriages in secret despite the ban. As the story goes, Valentine was killed—on February 14—for his **defiance** of the emperor. When the emperor Constantine made Christianity the official religion of the Roman Empire in 313 A.D., February 14 was celebrated as a day to remember Saint Valentine.

Over time, it became widely recognized as a day of **romance** and a celebration of love. The first Valentine's Day card was sent in 1415 from France's Duke of Orléans to his wife to express the love and **desire** he felt for her while he was held prisoner in England. Today, lovers all around the world exchange cards, chocolates, and gifts as a sign of their love for each other.

1. _____ : behavior showing you are not willing to obey
2. _____ : the actions and feelings of people who are in love
3. _____ : a very strong want or wish
4. _____ : to select or persuade someone to join an organization

St. Valentine is looked upon as the guardian saint of lovers.

B. Completion. Complete the sentences using the correct form of words from the box.

abundant	chance	inclination	inherent	mutual	trigger

1. Chocolate may be _____ romantic—it contains chemicals that cause you to feel like you're in love.
2. However, chocolate, which may cause feelings of love in some people, can _____ severe headaches for others.
3. By exchanging gifts, a person in love sometimes discovers that the love is _____ , and that his or her feelings are returned.
4. According to a recent scientific study, women with large chins have a greater _____ to cheat in relationships.
5. A(n) _____ of certain chemicals in the brain causes the racing heart, blushing, and sweaty palms of someone in love.
6. In the natural world, there is an element of _____ in winning a mate.

> **Usage** Use **chance** to mean events that happen when they are not planned or controlled.

FEATHERS OF LOVE

Before You Read

A Wilson's bird of paradise displays his elaborate tail feathers. Like other birds of paradise, male Wilson birds are more colorful than their female counterparts.

A. Quiz. Guess the answers to the questions below. Then use the captions, maps, and images on pages 33–37 to check your answers.

1. Most birds of paradise live in Australia.	**Yes**	**No**
2. The female birds of paradise are more colorful than the males.	**Yes**	**No**
3. The male bird of paradise dances to attract females.	**Yes**	**No**
4. Most birds of paradise live at altitudes below 2,000 m.	**Yes**	**No**

B. Predict. Look again at the title, headings, photos, and captions on pages 33–37. Check (✓) the information about birds of paradise you think you'll read about.

- ☐ what they eat
- ☐ their commercial uses
- ☐ why they have such beautiful feathers
- ☐ how they attract a mate

1 **COVERED IN SOFT, BLACK FEATHERS,** the **noble** performer bows deeply to his audience. From the top of his head grow several long feathers that tap the ground as he begins his dance. This 5 dancing bird is Carola's parotia, just one of the fascinating and unique birds of paradise that live on the island of New Guinea. What is the reason for the dance show? This male bird is attempting to impress a row of females that are watching 10 him from a branch above.

Keeping the females' attention isn't easy, so he really gives it his all. He pauses for dramatic effect, and then **commences** his dance again. His neck sinks and his head moves up and 15 down, head feathers **bouncing.** He jumps and shakes his feathers until his performance attracts the attention of one of the females— the one that will be his mate.

An Amazing Performance

20 In the dense and humid jungle of New Guinea is nature's most **absurd** theater, the very special mating game of the birds of paradise. To attract females, males' feathers are costumes worthy of the stage. The bright reds, yellows, and blues of 25 their feathers stand out sharply against the green of the forest. It seems that the more extreme the male's costume and colors, the better his chance of attracting a mate.

Not only do most male birds of paradise have 30 extremely beautiful feathers, they know how to use them. Each species has its own type of display behavior. Some dance remarkably complex dances on the ground, in areas that they have cleared and prepared like their own 35 version of a dance floor.[1] Others perform their display high in the trees.

The male red bird of paradise shows off his delightful red and yellow feathers in a display sometimes called a "butterfly dance." He 40 spreads and moves his wings intensely like some giant butterfly. The male Carola's parotia has at least six different dance moves. These include one in which he spreads out his feathers like a dress in a move called the "ballerina[2] dance." 45 While some birds of paradise perform alone, others, like Goldie's birds of paradise, often perform together, creating an eye-catching performance that female birds find impossible to resist. Hanging from nearby branches, male 50 Goldie's birds **prominently** display the clouds of soft red feathers that rise from their backs as they flap[3] their wings with great energy. Excited females soon arrive to choose the one that pleased them the most.

---

1 A **dance floor** is an area where people can dance.
2 A **ballerina** is a woman who dances ballet, a type of artistic dance.
3 If a bird or an insect **flaps** its wings, the wings move quickly up and down.

PACIFIC OCEAN

MOLUCCAS

Puncak Jaya
16,024 ft
4,884 m

Foja
Mountains

3,000 m

PAPUA NEW GUINEA
INDONESIA

INDONESIA

PAPUA

NEW GUINEA

Mt. Wilhelm
PAPUA
NEW GUINEA

2,000 m
1,000 m

NEW GUINEA

Arafura
Sea

CRATER
MOUNTAIN
WILDLIFE
MANAGEMENT
AREA   Port★
Moresby

BIRD OF PARADISE
RANGE

NEW GUINEA

AUSTRALIA
0 mi   1,000
0 km   1,000

0 mi   100
0 km   100

The island of New Guinea is home to 38 species of birds of paradise, more than anywhere else in the world. Most birds of paradise, including the Red bird of paradise (above), live within a single mountain range and altitude.[4] This isolation reduces the flow of genes between populations, allowing the birds to evolve separately into their wonderful varieties.

genes = DNA

4 A location's **altitude** is its height above sea level.

3,000 m

Stephanie's
astrapia
(*Astrapia
stephaniae*)

Brown
sicklebill
(*Epimachus
meyeri*)

King of Saxony
bird of paradise
(*Pteridophora
alberti*)

2,000 m

Superb
bird of paradise
(*Lophorina
superba*)

Western
parotia
(*Parotia
sefilata*)

Buff-tailed
sicklebill
(*Drepanornis
albertisi*)

1,000 m

Raggiana
bird of paradise
(*Paradisaea
raggiana*)

Magnificent
bird of paradise
(*Cicinnurus
magnificus*)

Magnificent
riflebird
(*Ptiloris
magnificus*)

King
bird of paradise
(*Cicinnurus
regius*)

Curl-crested
manucode
(*Manucodia
comrii*)

Twelve-wired
bird of paradise
(*Seleucidis
melanoleuca*)

ART BY JOHN NORTON
SOURCES: CLIFFORD B. FRITH, BRUCE M. BEEHLER

species = variety
(*تنوع*)

The Evolution of Color

55 These brilliantly colored birds of paradise have evolved over millions of years from ancient birds whose feathers were dark and boring in comparison. Of today's 43 brightly colored birds
60 of paradise species, most live only on the island of New Guinea. These birds of paradise invite us to solve a mystery of nature. It seems to be a contradiction[5] that such extreme feathers and colors could have been favored by the process of
65 evolution. After all, these same brightly colored feathers that attract mates also make them much more noticeable to predators[6] and slow the birds down, making fleeing from those predators more difficult. The answer lies in the safe environment
70 in which the birds live, and a process of evolution known as "sexual selection."

"Life here is pretty comfortable for birds of paradise. The island's unique environment has allowed them to go to extremes unheard of
75 elsewhere," says biologist Ed Scholes. Under *hard* **harsher** conditions, he says, "evolution simply wouldn't have come up with these birds." Fruit and insects are abundant all year in the forests of New Guinea, and predators are few. The result is a
80 perfect environment for birds.

Sexual selection has thus been the driving force in the evolution of birds of paradise. Freed of other pressures, birds of paradise began to specialize in attracting mates. Over millions of years, they have
85 slowly **undergone** changes in their color, feathers, and other talents. Characteristics that made one bird more attractive than another were passed *improve* on and enhanced over time. "The usual rules of survival aren't as important here as the rules of
90 successful mating," Scholes adds.

The diversity of New Guinea's birds also springs from its varied environments: from humid coastal plains to high-elevation cloud forests, from swamps[7] to mountains rising as high as 5,000
95 meters (16,000 feet). The landscape has many physical barriers that isolate animal populations, allowing them to develop into separate and distinct species.

Two birds of ❯ paradise dancing as part of a mating ritual

Bird Performers, Human Dancers

100 The people of New Guinea have been watching the displays of the birds of paradise for centuries. "Locals will tell you they went into the forest and copied their **rituals** from the birds," says anthropologist Gillian Gillison of the University of
105 Toronto, who lived among New Guinea tribes for more than a decade. At local dance performances, now more tourist entertainment than true ritual, the painted dancers still **evoke** the birds with their movements and beautiful costumes. "By wearing
110 the feathers," Gillison says, ". . . you capture the animal's life force. It makes you a warrior."

In the past, demand for the birds' beautiful feathers resulted in a huge amount of hunting. At the peak

---

5 If an aspect of a situation is a **contradiction**, it is completely different from other aspects and makes the situation confusing.

6 A **predator** is an animal that kills and eats other animals.

7 A **swamp** is an area of very wet land with wild plants growing in it.

of the trade, in the early 1900s, 80,000 skins
115 a year were exported from New Guinea for
European ladies' hats. However, surprisingly
few birds die for these costumes nowadays.
Ceremonial feathers are passed down from
generation to generation. Local people are still
120 permitted to hunt birds of paradise for traditional
uses. However, hunters usually target older
male birds, leaving younger males to continue
breeding.

There are more serious threats to the birds'
125 welfare. An illegal market in feathers still exists.
Large farms use up thousands of hectares of
forest where birds of paradise once lived, as does
large-scale industrial logging.[8] Oil prospecting
and mining[9] also present dangers to New
130 Guinea's wildest forests. Meanwhile, human
populations continue to grow. Land is owned by
different local families whose leaders disagree
about which areas should be protected.

David Mitchell, a conservationist, is using local
135 villagers to record where the birds display and what
they eat. He hopes not only to gather data, but
also to encourage protection of the birds' habitat.
The strategy seems to be working. "I had come to
cut down some trees and plant yam vines,"[10] says
140 Ambrose Joseph, one of Mitchell's farmers. "Then
I saw the birds land there, so I left the trees alone."
For millions of years, these impressive birds have
danced to find their mates. They'll keep dancing
for as long as the forest offers them a stage.

---

8 **Logging** is the business of cutting down trees for use as wood.
9 **Mining** is the business of digging deep into the earth to
obtain valuable materials.
10 A **yam** is a root vegetable, like a potato, that grows in tropical
areas. A **vine** is a plant that grows up or over things.

Reading Comprehension

Multiple Choice. Choose the best answer for each question.

Main Idea

1. Why do birds of paradise dance and display their feathers?
   a. to frighten away predators
   b. to attract a mate
   c. to exercise and clean their bodies
   d. to show possession of an area

Vocabulary

2. In line 12, the phrase *gives it his all* is closest in meaning to _____.
   a. tries as hard as possible
   b. gives everything away
   c. stops paying attention
   d. starts to lose hope

Detail

3. Which type of bird dances in a group?
   a. male Carola's parotia
   b. female Carola's parotia
   c. male Goldie's bird of paradise
   d. female Goldie's bird of paradise

Detail

4. Which factor is NOT mentioned as a reason for the birds' unusual characteristics?
   a. widespread availability of fruit and insects
   b. variety of environments
   c. lack of predators
   d. the island's geographical location

Cause and Effect

5. Why did so many birds of paradise die in the early 1900s?
   a. There was a high demand for feathers to use in European ladies' hats.
   b. Local people hunted the birds for traditional uses.
   c. Large scale deforestation to make way for industrial development.
   d. Illegal logging drastically reduced the birds' habitat.

Inference

6. Why do local people continue to hunt birds of paradise?
   a. to eat them
   b. to sell them to tourists
   c. to make traditional costumes
   d. to keep their numbers down

Cohesion

7. The following sentence would best be placed at the beginning of which paragraph? *However, there may be some good news for the birds.*
   a. 5   (starting line 37)
   b. 9   (starting line 91)
   c. 12 (starting line 124)
   d. 13 (starting line 134)

Critical Thinking

Inference: Why does the author include the quote from Ambrose Joseph in the last paragraph?

_____

Discussion: Besides the feathers of birds of paradise, what other animal characteristics might sexual selection be responsible for?

Recognizing Figurative Language

Figurative language is a creative way to use language to describe someone or something. Writers use it to create an image in the reader's mind. Examples include similes, metaphors, and personification.

A **simile** compares two different things using *like* or *as*.

Her skin was as cold as ice.

A **metaphor** says one thing *is* another thing.

The road during rush hour is a parking lot.

Personification gives humanlike qualities to something nonhuman.

Lightning danced across the sky.

A. Analyzing. Look at these examples from the reading. Mark each one as an example of a simile (**S**), a metaphor (**M**), or personification (**P**). Some have more than one answer.

1. __P__ Covered in soft, black feathers, the noble performer bows deeply to his audience. (lines 1–2)

2. __M__ To attract females, males' feathers are costumes worthy of the stage. (lines 22–24)

3. __S__ He spreads and moves his wings intensely like some giant butterfly. (lines 39–41)

4. __S__ These include one in which he spreads out his feathers like a dress. (lines 42–44)

5. __P__ For millions of years, these impressive birds have danced to find their mates. (lines 142–143)

B. Analyzing. Work with a partner. Complete each of these figurative sentences.

1. He eats like a ___h___ .   a. bedroom
2. Her ___g___ is like silk.   b. book
3. She is a walking ___f___ . knows many words   c. cake
4. His ___i___ is a bottomless pit. keep eating   d. camera
5. His ___a___ is a disaster zone. very messy   e. door
6. The ___d___ loves the model.   f. dictionary
7. The ___e___ protested as I forced it open.   g. hair
8. That ___b___ flew off the shelves. very popular   h. horse
9. The last piece of ___c___ was calling my name.   i. stomach
10. The flowers were begging for ___water j___ .   j. water

Vocabulary Practice

A. Completion. Complete the information using the correct form of words from the box. Five words are extra.

[handwritten annotations: un reasonable ○غير, jump, (v), أطلقت, to cause or produce, noticeable ○غير, feel go through]

absurd	bounce	breed	commence	evoke
harsh	noble	prominent	ritual	undergo

Jennifer Holland is a writer who went to Papua New Guinea to do research for an article on birds of paradise. She later shared her experiences there.

Jennifer Holland's favorite species of bird of paradise is Carola's parotia. Its dance **1.** _____commence_____ includes motions such as bowing, flapping, and **2.** _____bounce_____ to move the heavy and **3.** _____evoke_____ wirelike feathers on its head, in hopes of winning one of the watching females. "Its mating dance is so **4.** _____absurd_____ that I could hardly keep from laughing."

For a couple of nights, Holland stayed in a tiny village with a local family. It is the custom of the local people to build a fire pit in the center of the room. Because she was not accustomed to the smoke, it was very **5.** _____harsh_____ on her eyes and lungs. "My eyes watered constantly, I coughed like a new smoker, and I had to step outside regularly to get fresh air—much to the delight of the local kids who sat on the steps waiting for us to emerge."

∧ A male Carola's parotia displays his courting ritual to a female.

B. Definitions. Match the definitions to words from the box in **A**.

1. _____breed_____ : to mate and have babies (for animals)

2. _____commence_____ : to begin

3. _____harsh_____ : to have something necessary or unpleasant happen to you

4. _____evoke_____ : to cause a particular memory, idea, emotion, or response to occur

5. _____noble_____ : grand or magnificent *[handwritten: نبيل]*

6. _____absurd_____ : ridiculous or not making sense

7. _____prominent_____ : easily visible; obvious

8. _____ritual_____ : something done in a particular situation and in the same way each time

> **Thesaurus**
> **absurd** Also look up: (adj.) *ridiculous, ludicrous, crazy, foolish*

VIEWING Singing Mice

Before You Watch

A. Definitions. Look at the picture and read the caption. Then match each word in **bold** with its definition.

❮ During **courtship**, living creatures do all sorts of things to impress the opposite sex. Some even **break into song**. Researchers have discovered that the **vocalizations** of mice sound like songs. In the lab, these **ultrasonic** mice **tunes** are recorded and played back in **frequencies** that can be detected by the human ear.

1. _____: musical notes in a series
2. _____: sound vibrations per unit of time
3. _____: to suddenly start to sing
4. _____: sounds made by voice
5. _____: too high for the human ear to hear
6. _____: behavior that leads to mating

B. Discussion. Discuss these questions with a partner.

1. Do you think that male mice sing to females, or females sing to males?
2. What other animals can sing?
3. Besides singing, what other methods do animals use to court the opposite sex?

While You Watch

A. Fact or Theory. Watch the video. Mark if these statements are fact or theory.

	Fact	Theory
1. Older humpback whales teach popular tunes to younger whales.	☐	☐
2. Singing is most often a masculine pursuit in the natural world.	☐	☐
3. A male mouse sings because it is courting a female mouse.	☐	☐
4. When a male mouse sings, it enhances its mating success with a female.	☐	☐

B. Completion. Complete each caption with the correct words from the box.

bolder	complex	future	genes
mammals	mate	opposite	researchers

Many species of birds sing to attract a
1. _____, but only a handful of
2. _____ have been known to sing.

Gibbons make loud, long, and **3.** _____
vocalizations during mating season. This is considered singing
by **4.** _____ .

It's usually the female that gets to choose a mate, and the
male must demonstrate that his **5.** _____
are worth passing along to **6.** _____
offspring.

When it comes to pursuing the **7.** _____
sex, a timid creature may be **8.** _____
than we ever imagined.

After You Watch

A. Discussion. In addition to singing, some other human traits have been observed in the animal world. Read the information below. Which information surprises you? What are some other examples of humanlike behavior in other species?

Naming their young

Dolphins, monkeys, and parrots use unique calls to get the attention of their offspring. This shows that some animals have the equivalent of their own names.

Playing with dolls

Female chimps take sticks, bark, and vines and hold them as if they are dolls. They have been observed putting their "dolls" to bed and even building separate nests for them.

Using correct grammar

Some birds have grammar rules when it comes to songs. When a song is played back out of order, the birds get very annoyed. Is it the equivalent of a *there/their/they're* mistake?

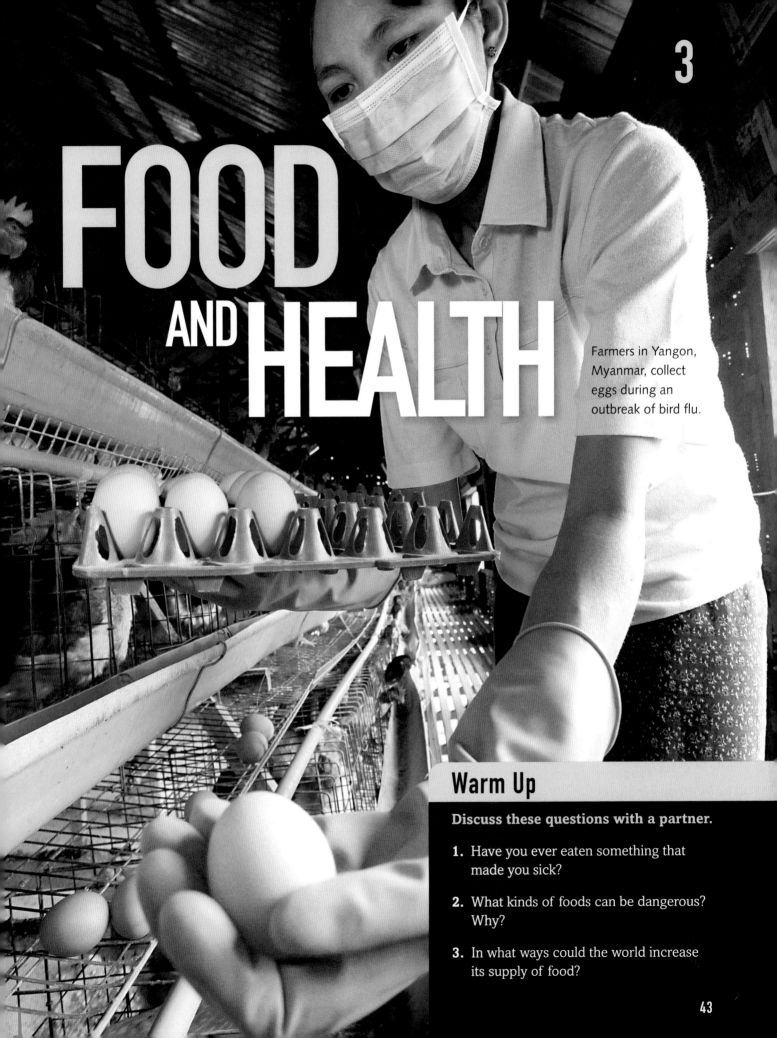

FOOD
AND HEALTH

Farmers in Yangon, Myanmar, collect eggs during an outbreak of bird flu.

Warm Up

Discuss these questions with a partner.

1. Have you ever eaten something that made you sick?

2. What kinds of foods can be dangerous? Why?

3. In what ways could the world increase its supply of food?

Before You Read

A. Definition. Read the information below and match each word in **bold** with its definition.

Whether people are getting sicker from food today than they were 50 years ago is a matter of debate. What is different is that certain types of **bacteria** have become more dangerous than they used to be. **Toxins** produced by these bacteria pose severe health risks, and people with weakened **immune systems** are the most vulnerable. Advances in processing and sanitation have diminished some **foodborne** threats, but new hazards come with changes in lifestyle and food production.

Workers in a seafood processing plant are required to wear protective coats, gloves, and hairnets, to ensure the food does not get contaminated during the packaging process.

1. _____Toxins_____ : poisonous substances created by an organism
2. _____bacteria_____ : very small organisms that can cause disease
3. ___immune systems___ : parts and processes of the body that fight illness
4. _____foodborne_____ : carried into our bodies in the things we eat

B. Skim. Skim the first two paragraphs of the reading passage. What incident caused the U.S. government to take foodborne illness more seriously?

HOW SAFE IS OUR FOOD?

A WEEK BEFORE CHRISTMAS, 1992, Lauren Beth Rudolph ate a cheeseburger from a fast-food restaurant in California. On Christmas Eve, suffering from severe stomach pain, Lauren was admitted to the hospital. There, she endured three heart attacks before eventually dying on December 28. She was six years old.

The burger Lauren ate was **contaminated** with the **virulent** bacteria E. coli O157:H7. Her death was the first in an outbreak[1] that caused 732 illnesses in five states and killed four children. The E. coli bacteria are so virulent that it takes no more than a few of them to cause a deadly infection. "We used to think of foodborne illness as little more than a stomachache," says Joseph Levitt of the U.S. government's Food and Drug Administration. "After the [Rudolph case], we realized this was no issue of stomachaches, but a serious and compelling[2] public health problem."

Bacteria to Blame

There is more risk involved in our everyday activity of eating than you might think. It is estimated that each year in the United States, 76 million people suffer from foodborne diseases; 325,000 of them are hospitalized, and 5,000 die. In the developing world, contaminated food and water kill almost two million children a year. In most cases, virulent types of bacteria are to blame.

---

1 If there is an **outbreak** of something unpleasant, such as violence or a disease, it happens suddenly.
2 A **compelling** reason is one that convinces you that something is true, or that something should be done.

30 Bacteria are an **integral** part of a healthy life. There are 200 times as many bacteria in the colon[3] of a single human as there are human beings who have ever lived. Most of these bacteria help with **digestion**, making vitamins,
35 shaping the immune system, and keeping us healthy. Nearly all raw food, too, has bacteria in it. But the bacteria that produce foodborne illness are of a different, more virulent kind.

powerful, strong, deadly

Many of the bacteria that produce foodborne
40 illnesses are present in the intestines of the animals we raise for food. When a food animal containing dangerous bacteria is cut open during processing, bacteria inside the animal can contaminate meat. Fruits and vegetables
45 can pick up the dangerous bacteria if washed or watered with contaminated water. A single bacterium, given the right conditions, divides rapidly enough to produce colonies of billions over the course of a day. This means that even
50 only lightly contaminated food can become highly infectious. The bacteria can also hide and multiply on sponges, dishtowels, cutting boards, sinks, knives, and kitchen counters, where they're easily transferred to food or hands.

55 Changes in the way in which farm animals are raised are also affecting the rate at which dangerous bacteria can spread. In the name of efficiency and economy, fish, cattle, and chickens are raised in giant "factory" farms,
60 which **confine** large numbers of animals in tight quarters. Cattle, for example, are so crowded together under such conditions that even if only one animal is contaminated with *E. coli* O157:H7, it will likely spread to others.

65 Tracking the Source

Disease investigators, like Patricia Griffin, are working to find the sources of these outbreaks and prevent them in the future. Griffin, of the U.S. CDC (Centers for Disease Control and
70 Prevention), has worked in the foodborne-disease business for 15 years. Outbreaks like the incident that killed Lauren Beth Rudolph turned her attention to the public food safety threat that exists in restaurants and in the food

75 production system. Food safety is no longer just a question of handling food properly in the domestic kitchen. "Now," Griffin says, "we are more aware that the responsibility does not rest solely with the cook. We know
80 that contamination often occurs early in the production process—at steps on the way from farm or field or fishing ground to market."

Griffin's job is to look for trends in food-related illness through analysis of outbreaks. Her
85 staff tries to identify both the food source of an outbreak and the contaminating bacteria. To link cases together, the scientists use a powerful tool called PulseNet, a network of public health laboratories connected by
90 computer that matches types of bacteria using DNA.[4] PulseNet allows epidemiologists[5] to associate an illness in Nebraska, say, with one in Texas, tying together what might otherwise appear as unrelated cases. Then it's the job
95 of the investigators to track down what went wrong in the food's journey to the table. This allows them to determine whether to recall[6] a particular food or to change the process by which it's produced.

100 In January 2000, public health officials in Virginia noted an unusual group of patients sick with food poisoning from salmonella. Using PulseNet, the CDC identified 79 patients in 13 states who suffered infection from the
105 same type of salmonella bacteria. Fifteen had been hospitalized; two had died. What was the common factor? All had eaten mangoes during the previous November and December. The investigation led to a single large mango
110 farm in Brazil, where it was discovered that mangoes were being washed in contaminated water containing a type of salmonella bacteria. Salmonella contamination is a widespread problem, and in the following years, other

---

3 Your **colon** is part of your intestines—the tubes in your body through which food passes when it has left your stomach.

4 **DNA** is a material in living things that contains the code for their structure and many of their functions.

5 **Epidemiologists** are scientists who study outbreaks of disease.

6 When sellers **recall** a product, they ask customers to return it to them.

115 salmonella cases were detected. In the spring of 2001, for example, almonds from a farm in California infected 160 Canadians with salmonella.

120 The mango and almond outbreaks had a larger lesson: we no longer eat only fruits and vegetables in season and that are grown locally, as we once did. Instead, we demand our strawberries, peaches, mangoes, and lettuce year-round. As a result, we are depending
125 more and more on imports. Eating food grown elsewhere in the world means depending on the soil, water, and sanitary[7] conditions in those places, and on the way their workers farm, harvest, process, and transport the products.

Reducing the Risk

130

There are a number of success stories that provide hope and show us how international food production need not mean increased risk of contamination. Costa Rica has made
135 sanitary production of fruits and vegetables a **nationwide** priority. Produce is packed carefully in sanitary conditions; frequent hand washing is **compulsory**, and proper toilets are provided for workers in the fields. Such changes have
140 made Carmela Velazquez, a food scientist from the University of Costa Rica, **optimistic** about the future. "The farmers we've trained," she says, "will become models for all our growers."

In Sweden, too, progress has been made in
145 reducing the occurrences of foodborne disease at an early stage. Swedish chicken farmers have virtually eliminated salmonella from their flocks[8] by **diligently** cleaning up their chicken houses and by using chicken feed that has undergone
150 heating to rid it of the dangerous bacteria. Now the chickens that Swedes buy are salmonella-free. The success of these pioneers suggests that it is indeed **feasible** for companies and farms to produce safe and sanitary food, while
155 still turning a profit.

---

7 **Sanitary** means concerned with keeping things clean and healthy.
8 A **flock** of birds, sheep, or goats is a group of them.

∧ Dishes containing colonies of campylobacter, a disease-causing bacteria found in chickens tested at the University of Arkansas, U.S.A.

Reading Comprehension

Multiple Choice. Choose the best answer for each question.

Gist

1. What is the reading mainly about?
- a. avoiding foodborne bacteria by eating at home, not in restaurants
- b. poor sanitary conditions in restaurants and farms around the world
- c. dangerous foodborne bacteria, their sources, detection, and control
- d. the importance of advanced technology in the fight against foodborne bacteria

Inference

2. What is Joseph Levitt's opinion about the government's attitude before the Rudolph case?
- a. It already took foodborne illness very seriously.
- b. It was concerned about the number of stomachaches in California.
- c. It didn't see foodborne illness as a serious public health problem.
- d. It focused too much on disease outbreaks in fast-food restaurants.

Detail

3. Why is even a single disease-causing bacterium dangerous?
- a. It can mix with other bacteria.
- b. It can become billions in a day.
- c. Just one can kill a six-year-old child.
- d. It can move more rapidly alone.

Purpose

4. What is PulseNet used for?
- a. to match types of bacteria using DNA
- b. to identify restaurants with poor sanitary conditions
- c. to connect patients with foodborne illness to doctors
- d. to catalog sanitary food production methods

Detail

5. According to the article, why are people eating more imported food?
- a. We want to have certain foods year-round.
- b. Imported foods are usually cheaper.
- c. Imported foods are usually safer.
- d. Consumers don't realize their food is imported.

Paraphrase

6. What does Carmela Velazquez mean when she says, "The farmers we've trained will become models for all our growers"?
- a. The farmers will go on TV to talk about what they learned from her.
- b. More farmers will adopt the habits that were taught to the other farmers.
- c. Both farmers and growers will now work together to assure food safety.
- d. Farmers need to listen to the growers to learn and decide what works for them.

Reference

7. In line 152, *these pioneers* refers to _____.
- a. international food producers who can still turn a profit
- b. people who improve sanitary conditions in Costa Rica and Sweden
- c. scientists who create new bacteria-resistant foods
- d. journalists who write stories about outbreaks of foodborne illness

Critical Thinking

Inferring: Why do you think the sanitary practices in Costa Rica and Sweden are not more widely practiced worldwide?

_____

Discussion: What do you think can be done to protect ourselves from foodborne illnesses?

Reading Skill

Understanding Cause and Effect Relationships

A cause is an action or a condition that makes something happen. An effect is a result of that action. Some texts use words that indicate cause and effect relationships, such as *caused*, *as a result*, *because*, *so*, *due to*, *consequently*, *thus*, and *the reason*. In other cases, a writer may imply a cause-effect relationship without using these words. As you read, try to make connections between events by asking *What caused . . . ?* and *What was the result of . . . ?* questions.

A. Analyzing. Read the sentences below. In each sentence, underline the cause and double-underline the effect.

[handwritten: effect]

1. I didn't go to the doctor because I forgot about the appointment. *[handwritten: cause]*

[handwritten: cause]

2. The medicine in our cabinet was old, so we threw it out. *[handwritten: effect]*

3. The reason I didn't go to school was that I had a stomachache. *[handwritten: cause]*

[handwritten: cause]

4. The scientist published her findings. Consequently, she was able to help many people.

5. Due to new health guidelines, all food will be removed from the staff fridge on weekends.

[handwritten: cause]

6. Investigators believe improper hand washing led to the disease outbreak at the school. *[handwritten: not proper]*

B. Matching. Look back at the reading on pages 45–47. Match each cause with its effect.

Causes		Effects
1. cutting open food animals in processing	*c*	**a.** greater dependence on imports
2. the use of "factory" farms	*e*	**b.** salmonella-free chickens
3. all-year demand for fresh vegetables	*a*	**c.** meat is contaminated by bacteria
4. improving sanitary conditions on farms	*d*	**d.** fewer cases of contaminated produce
5. heating of feed	*b*	**e.** bacteria easily spread from animal to animal

Vocabulary Practice

A. Matching. Read the information below and match the correct form of each word in **red** with its definition.

In late 2008 to early 2009, a food **contamination** scare occurred in the United States involving one of the country's most beloved foods—the peanut. It was reported that nine people died and almost 700 people **nationwide** were affected by salmonella poisoning.

The cause of the salmonella outbreak was found to be peanut products. Peanuts are used in a wide variety of products and are an **integral** part of health bars, cookies, ice cream varieties, and even dog biscuits. Although the Food and Drug Administration (FDA) does not have the authority to order a **compulsory** recall, stores across the country voluntarily removed peanuts and peanut products from their shelves.

Using DNA technology, the FDA traced the exact type of salmonella back to a company called Peanut Corporation of America, that was likely not **diligent** enough in its testing and cleanliness. The company has since gone out of business.

∧ According to the Alabama Peanut Producers Association, Americans consume 1.5 kilograms of peanut butter per person every year.

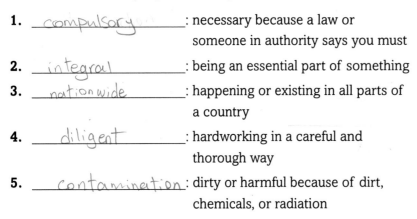

1. ___compulsory___ : necessary because a law or someone in authority says you must

2. ___integral___ : being an essential part of something

3. ___nationwide___ : happening or existing in all parts of a country

4. ___diligent___ : hardworking in a careful and thorough way

5. ___contamination___ : dirty or harmful because of dirt, chemicals, or radiation

B. Words in Context. Complete each sentence with the correct answer.

1. If contamination is **confined**, it _____.
   a. occurs within a certain area   b. has spread to many areas

2. The body's **digestive** system primarily _____.
   a. fights disease   b. takes nutrients from food

3. If a project is **feasible**, it _____ be done.
   a. can   b. can't

4. An **optimistic** person believes that the future will be _____ than today.
   a. worse   b. better

5. If something is **virulent**, it is extremely _____.
   a. poisonous or deadly   b. mild and pleasant

> **Word Link**
> The suffix **-wide** has the meaning of "extending throughout," e.g., *citywide, nationwide, worldwide.*

GENETICALLY MODIFIED FOODS

Before You Read

A. Discussion. Read the information below. What benefits and risks might be associated with the examples mentioned?

In recent years, scientists have been busy altering the genes of the animals and plants we use for food. The genes of corn have been altered to create new varieties that are resistant to insects and to herbicides.[1] A new golden-colored rice, high in vitamin A, is also the product of genetic alteration. While these "biotech" varieties seem to offer clear benefits, critics continue to point out the risks of genetic alteration of foods.

B. Predict. The following three questions are headings in the reading passage. What answers do you think will appear in the passage? Read the passage to check your ideas.

1. Are biotech foods safe for humans?

2. Can biotech foods harm the environment?

3. Can biotech foods help feed the world?

A non-genetically modified variety of eggplant that has been attacked by the fruit and shoot borer insect (left) compared to a genetically modified variety (right) that is resistant to the insect attack

1 **Herbicides** are chemicals that are used to kill plants.

Two 18-month-old coho salmon show the ❯ difference genetic engineering can make. The top fish has been given a modified gene that allows it to grow faster than the unmodified fish below.

The Battle for Biotech Foods

Genetic engineering of crops and animals through the manipulation of DNA is producing a **revolution** in food production. It is also starting
5 a battle between those who believe in its promise and critics who doubt and fear it. The potential to improve the quality and **nutritional** value of the vegetables and animals we eat seems unlimited. Such potential benefits **notwithstanding**, critics
10 fear that genetically engineered products, so-called biotech foods, are being rushed to market before their effects are fully understood.

Q: What exactly are biotech foods?

Biotech foods are produced from animals and
15 plants that have been genetically altered. Genetic alteration is nothing new. Humans have been altering the genetic **traits** of plants for thousands of years by keeping seeds from the best crops and planting them in following years, and by
20 breeding varieties to make them taste sweeter, grow bigger, or last longer. In this way, we've transformed the wild tomato from a fruit the size of a small stone to the giant ones we have today. From a plant called teosinte with an
25 "ear" barely an inch long have come our foot-long[1] ears of sweet white and yellow corn.

On the other hand, the techniques of genetic engineering are new, and quite different from **conventional** breeding. Conventional
30 breeders always used plants or animals that were related, or genetically similar. In so doing, they transferred tens of thousands of genes. By contrast, today's genetic engineers can transfer just a few genes at a time between species that

---

1 One inch = 2.54 cm; one **foot** = 12 inches (30 cm).

resist = to fight against

to involve

35 are distantly related or not related at all. There are surprising examples: Rat genes have been inserted into lettuce plants to make a plant that produces vitamin C, and moth genes have been inserted into apple trees to add disease

40 resistance. The purpose of conventional and modern techniques is the same—to insert a gene or genes from an organism that carries a desired trait into an organism that does not have the trait. Several dozen biotech food crops are

45 currently on the market, among them varieties of corn, soybeans, and cotton. Most of these crops are engineered to help farmers deal with age-old[2] farming problems: weeds,[3] insects, and disease.

Q: Are biotech foods safe for humans?

50 As far as we know. So far, problems have been few. In fact, according to Steve L. Taylor, of the Department of Food Science and Technology at the University of Nebraska, "None of the current biotech products have been implicated[4]

55 in **allergic** reactions or any other healthcare problem in people." Some biotech foods might even be safer than conventional varieties. Corn damaged by insects often contains high levels of

poison = toxin

fumonisins, toxins[5] that are carried on the backs

60 of insects and that grow in the wounds of the damaged corn. Lab tests have linked fumonisins with cancer in animals. Studies show that most corn **modified** for insect resistance has lower levels of fumonisins than conventional corn

65 damaged by insects.

---

2 An **age-old** story, tradition, or problem has existed for many generations or centuries.

3 A **weed** is a wild plant that grows in gardens or fields of crops and prevents the plants that you want from growing properly.

4 If someone is **implicated** in a crime or bad situation, they are involved in it or responsible for it.

5 A **toxin** is any poison produced by an animal, a plant, or bacteria.

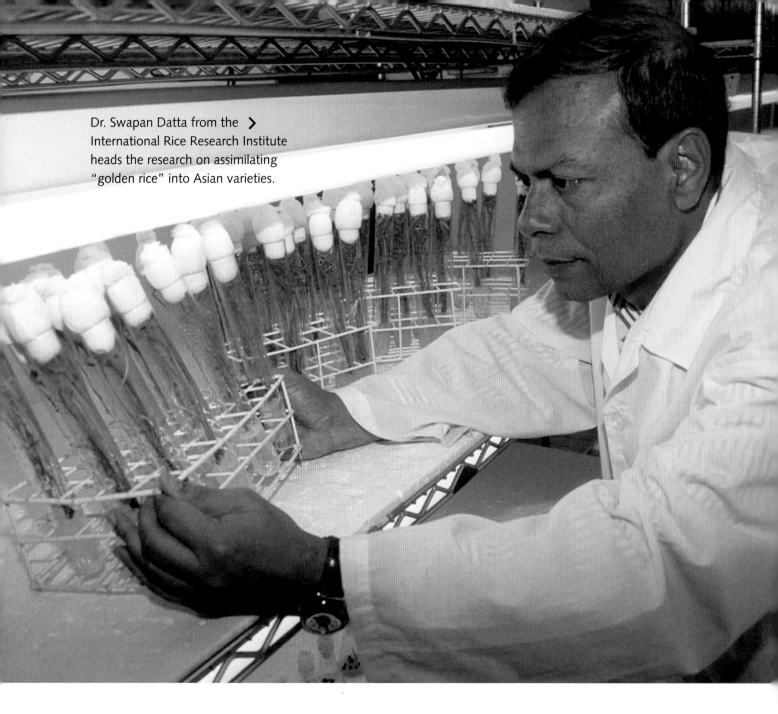

Dr. Swapan Datta from the ›
International Rice Research Institute
heads the research on assimilating
"golden rice" into Asian varieties.

However, biotech foods have had problems in
the past. One problem occurred in the mid-
1990s when soybeans were modified using genes
from a nut. The modified soybeans contained a
70 protein[6] that causes reactions in humans who are
allergic to nuts. While this protein was discovered
before any damage was done, critics fear that
other harmful proteins created through genetic
modification may slip by undiscovered. The
75 technique of moving genes across dramatically
different species, such as rats and lettuce, also
makes critics nervous. They fear something
could go very wrong either in the function of the

inserted gene or in the function of the host[7] DNA,
80 with the possibility of unexpected health effects.

Q: Can biotech foods harm the environment?

Most scientists agree that the main safety issues
of genetically engineered crops involve not people
but the environment. Allison Snow is a plant
85 ecologist at Ohio State University known for her

---

6 **Protein** is a substance found in food like meat, eggs,
or milk that you need to be healthy.
7 The **host** is the animal or plant into which the foreign DNA
is inserted.

The potential of biotech foods is enormous, yet they carry risks.

potential = possible

research on "gene flow," the natural movement of plant genes from one population of plants to another. She worries that genetically engineered crops are being developed too quickly and
90 released before they've been adequately tested. On the other hand, advocates of genetically engineered crops argue that some genetically modified plants may actually be good for the land, by offering an environmentally friendly alternative
95 to pesticide,[8] which tends to pollute water and harm animals.

Far less pesticide needs to be applied to cotton plants that have been genetically modified to produce their own natural pesticide. While applied
100 chemical pesticides kill nearly all the insects in a field, biotech crops with natural pesticide only harm insects that actually try to eat those crops, leaving the rest unharmed.

Q: Can biotech foods help feed the world?

105 "Eight hundred million people on this planet are malnourished,"[9] says Channapatna Prakash, a native of India and a scientist at the Center for Plant Biotechnology Research at Tuskegee University, "and the number continues to
110 grow." Prakash and many other scientists argue that genetic engineering can help address the urgent problems of food shortage and hunger by increasing crop quantities and nutritional value, offering crop varieties that resist **pests** and
115 disease, and providing ways to grow crops on land that would otherwise not support farming.

According to the World Health Organization, for example, between 100 million and 140 million children in the world suffer from vitamin A
120 deficiency.[10] Some 500,000 go blind every year because of that deficiency, and half of those

children die within a year of losing their sight. "Golden rice," a biotech variety named for its yellow color, is thought by some to be a potential
125 solution to the suffering and illness caused by vitamin A deficiency.

Skeptics, however, claim that golden rice is little more than a public relations exercise[11] by the biotechnology industry, which they
130 say has exaggerated its benefits. "Golden rice alone won't greatly **diminish** vitamin A deficiency," says Professor Marion Nestle of New York University. "Beta-carotene,[12] which is already widely available in fruit and vegetables,
135 isn't converted to vitamin A when people are malnourished. Golden rice does not contain much beta-carotene, and whether it will improve vitamin A levels remains to be seen."

Q: What's next?

140 Whether biotech foods will deliver on their promise of eliminating world hunger and bettering the lives of all remains to be seen. Their potential is enormous, yet they carry risks. If science proceeds with caution, testing new
145 products thoroughly and using sound judgment, the world may avoid the dangers of genetic modification while enjoying its benefits.

---

8 **Pesticides** are chemicals used to kill harmful insects.
9 Someone who is **malnourished** is weakened from not eating enough or the right kinds of food.
10 **Deficiency** in something, especially something that your body needs, is not having enough of it.
11 A **public relations exercise** is an activity that is intended to make people have a good opinion about something.
12 **Beta-carotene**, a natural substance found in red or orange fruit and vegetables, is used in the body to create vitamin A.

Reading Comprehension

Multiple Choice. Choose the best answer for each question.

Purpose

1. What is the author's purpose in writing the passage?
   a. to make biotech foods seem as attractive as possible
   b. to show both sides of the biotech foods issue
   c. to convince the reader that biotech foods are dangerous
   d. to explain why biotech foods will probably not be successful

Detail

2. Which of the following is NOT practiced by conventional breeders?
   a. using related organisms to breed   → To produce
   b. altering the genetic traits of organisms
   c. creating organisms with desired traits
   d. transferring just a few genes at a time

Paraphrase

3. In line 50, the phrase *As far as we know* could be replaced by _____.
   a. As a matter of fact
   b. As we have said before
   c. To the best of our knowledge
   d. Since we are discussing this topic

Inference

4. What is the danger of fumonisins?
   a. They might cause cancer in humans.
   b. They could cause insect resistance to modified corn.
   c. They might cause insects to damage corn plants.
   d. They could decrease the numbers of insects.

Detail

5. Which of these is NOT mentioned as a worry of some scientists?
   a. Genetically engineered crops are being developed too quickly.
   b. Something could go wrong when moving genes across dramatically different species.
   c. Genetically engineered crops are being released before they've been adequately tested.
   d. Genetically engineered species will pollute water and harm animals.

Detail

6. According to the World Health Organization, about how many children die within a year of going blind from vitamin A deficiency?
   a. 140 million   b. 100 million   c. 500,000   d. 250,000

Main Idea

7. What is the main idea of the final paragraph?
   a. With care, the potential of biotech foods could possibly be realized.
   b. The risks of biotech foods seem to outweigh any possible benefits.
   c. The world has already seen great advances due to biotech foods.
   d. Biotech food development has been slowed by the many risks involved.

Critical Thinking

Evaluating: What is your opinion of biotech foods? Which arguments presented in the text do you think are the strongest?

Discussion: Would you eat food that has been genetically modified? Why, or why not?

Reading Skill

Understanding Arguments For and Against an Issue

> Writers sometimes present two sides of an argument—giving reasons for and against an idea. Understanding both sides is a useful way to consider an issue. It can also help you decide on your own opinion. To evaluate a writer's arguments, it can be useful to list the reasons for and against in two columns, like in a T-chart.

A. Scanning. Look back at the reading on pages 52–55. Find and underline arguments for biotech foods. Find and double-underline arguments against biotech foods

B. Completion. Complete the chart using no more than three words from the reading in each blank.

Reasons for biotech foods	Reasons against biotech foods
There is nothing new about humans altering the **1.** _genetic_ traits of plants. We've been doing it for thousands of years.	Even though we try to catch them all, harmful proteins created through genetic modifications may still **5.** _may slip by undiscovered_
Not one current biotech food has been linked to **2.** _allergic_ reactions or health problems in people.	Something could go wrong when genes are moved across different species, with the possibility of unexpected **6.** _health effects_ .
Insect-resistant biotech plants offer an environmentally safe alternative to **3.** _pesticide_ .	Genetically engineered crops are sometimes released into the environment before they have been **7.** _adequately tested_
Genetic engineering can provide ways to **4.** _grow crops_ on land that would otherwise not support farming.	The benefits of golden rice are exaggerated. It is little more than a(n) **8.** _public relations exercise_

(handwritten note next to item 3: choice of second Possibility)

Vocabulary Practice

A. Completion. Complete the information using words from the box.
Three words are extra.

allergic	**conventional**	**diminished**	**modified**
notwithstanding	**nutritional**	**pests**	**revolutionary**
skeptics	**traits**		

to make to appear greater

According to a study, Chinese farmers growing rice that has been
genetically **1.** __modified__ to enhance insect resistance *build up*
reduced their pesticide use by 80 percent. In addition, the genetically
modified (GM) rice seed boosted crop production by almost 10
percent. There has been resistance to using GM grains as food crops—
but some think this news from China may signal an important and
possibly **2.** __revolutionary__ change. *to change or make different*

For the study, two types of rice were genetically altered to resist two
common insect **3.** __pests__, which usually require
heavy use of pesticides to control. During the study, the amount of
pesticide used by farmers **4.** __diminished__ because they
saw less need for it.

However, there are still many **5.** __skeptics__ who don't
trust GM foods. They worry that there could be unexpected and
possibly life-threatening **6.** __allergic__ reactions to them
in humans. Such fears and concerns **7.** __notwithstanding__,
proven examples of problems with GM foods have been quite rare.

Farmers in China are
benefiting from the use
of genetically modified
rice seed.

B. Definitions. Match the definitions to the correct form of words from
the box in **A**.

1. __Diminish__ : to reduce in size, importance, or intensity
2. __traits__ : a characteristic that someone or
   something has
3. __modified__ : to make partial or minor changes to
   something
4. __notwithstanding__ : despite
5. __allergic__ : a reaction whereby you become ill when
   you eat, smell, or touch something
6. __nutritional__ : food that can be absorbed by the body
   for growth and health
7. __revolutionary__ : a very great change in the way that
   something is done or made
8. __conventional__ : usually used

> **Thesaurus diminish**
> Also look up: (*v.*) *decline,
> decrease, lessen, recede,
> shrink, subside, wane*

VIEWING The Smelliest Fruit

Before You Watch

A. Discussion. Discuss these questions with a group.

1. The durian fruit is considered one of the world's smelliest foods. It is very popular in Southeast Asia. Have you ever seen one? Have you ever tasted one? If so, what did it taste like?

2. Can you think of foods that are both hated and loved for their unique taste and smell? Look at the examples below.

3. What food do you like that you think people from other cultures may not like?

Chou tofu is tofu that has been soaked in a mixture of sour milk, vegetables, and meat juices. It means "smelly tofu" in Chinese.

Natto is a traditional Japanese breakfast food made of sticky, slimy, fermented[1] soybeans.

Stilton, *Roquefort*, and *Gorgonzola* are moldy[2] "blue" cheeses widely eaten in Europe.

Surströmming is fish that has been fermented for several months, and then put into cans for a year. Popular in northern Sweden, people usually eat it outdoors.

1 When food is **fermented**, chemicals are broken down by microorganisms.

2 Something that is **moldy** is covered in fungus due to decay.

While You Watch

A. Noticing. Circle the words and phrases that the narrator uses to describe durian.

precious	smelly	natural
strange	bad for business	unique
king of fruit	spiky	tasty

B. Completion. Complete the summary using words from the box. Four words are extra.

compulsory	confined	contaminated	diligently
diminishes	feasible	integral	modified
notwithstanding	optimistically		

In Malaysian Borneo, hotels are involved in a battle with guests over a very smelly fruit called the durian. The smell of the durian is hard to describe, and has been compared to rotten fish or a garbage dump. This is why it is
1. _____ for durians to be kept outside the hotel. Hotel staff must **2.** _____ keep watch for this food because guests often try to smuggle it in.

When the fruit is in season, hotel managers in Kuching must work harder to keep it out. A hotel that smells of durian will find that the number of guests visiting it quickly **3.** _____. But since it's not **4.** _____ to check every single guest entering the hotel, a certain number of durians inevitably get through. There are several ways to clean a room that has been
5. _____ by a durian's smell. One is charcoal, which absorbs the odor slowly. Another way is to use a machine called an ionizer, which can remove the smell in three hours or less.

Its offensive smell **6.** _____, the durian is loved by people all over Southeast Asia and is commonly regarded as the "King of Fruits."

After You Watch

A. Discussion. Discuss these questions with a partner.

1. What do you think is the natural purpose of the durian's strong smell?

2. What do you think should happen to someone who is caught smuggling durians into a hotel room?

3. Are there other foods that should be banned in public?

DESIGN AND ENGINEERING

4

Australian swimmer Matt Walsh tests out the new Speedo Fastskin FS II. The suit mimics the design of sharkskin.

Warm Up

new changes

Discuss these questions with a partner.

1. What are some examples of recent fashion innovations?

2. How have the materials used to make clothes changed over the years?

3. What will clothes be made of in the future?

Before You Read

A. Matching. Read the information below and match each phrase in **bold** with its definition.

Biomimetic engineers have a **concrete purpose** in mind: to create designs that **have the potential** to change our everyday lives. These engineers **draw inspiration** from designs found in nature, many of which are **unimaginably complex**. They then apply the design principles in order to improve existing technologies or create entirely new ones. Recent applications of biomimetic research include new technologies used in engineering, medicine, and many other fields.

1. ___draw inspiration___ : to get ideas
2. ___unimaginably complex___ : extremely difficult to understand
3. ___have the potential___ : to possess the capability
4. ___concrete purpose___ : a definite goal or aim

> The Australian thorny devil can drink water through its foot. It moves water to its mouth using channels between its scales.

B. Skim. Skim the first paragraph of the reading passage to answer these questions.

1. Who is Andrew Parker? He's an evolutionary biologist
2. What special ability does the thorny devil have? can drink water through its food
3. What does Parker want to do with the knowledge he has obtained?

DESIGN BY NATURE: BIOMIMETICS

1 **ONE CLOUDLESS MIDSUMMER DAY,** Andrew Parker, an evolutionary biologist, knelt in the baking red sand of an Australian desert and gently placed the right back leg of a thorny
5 devil into a dish of water. The thorny devil, a small lizard that has learned to survive in the intense heat of the Australian desert, has a secret that fascinated Parker. "Look, look!" he exclaimed. "Its back is completely drenched!"[1]
10 Sure enough, in less than a minute, water from the dish had traveled up the lizard's leg, across its skin, and into its mouth. It was, in essence, drinking through its foot. The thorny devil can also do this when standing on damp
15 sand—a **vital** competitive advantage in the desert. Parker had come here to solve the **riddle** of precisely how it does this, not from purely biological[2] interest, but with a concrete purpose in mind: to make a **device** to help
20 people collect water in the desert.

---

1 If something is **drenched**, it is completely wet.
2 **Biological** processes occur in the bodies of living things.

From Natural Wonder to Useful Tool

Parker is a leading scientist in the field of biomimetics—applying designs from nature
25 to solve problems in engineering, materials science, medicine, and other fields. His studies of the body coverings of butterflies and beetles have led to brighter screens for cell phones. He sometimes draws inspiration from nature's past:
30 While visiting a museum in Warsaw, Poland, he noticed a 45-million-year-old fly trapped in amber[3] and observed how the shape of its eye's surface reduced light reflection. This shape is now being used in solar panels.[4] As the next
35 phase in his plan to create a water-collection device inspired by the lizard, Parker sent his observations and experimental results to Michael Rubner and Robert Cohen, two

---

3 **Amber** is a hard yellowish-brown substance used for making jewelry.
4 A **solar panel** is a device used to collect electrical energy from the sun.

∧ Cockleburs have hooked spines
that stick to fur or clothing.

colleagues at the Massachusetts Institute of
40 Technology. On the one hand, Parker is full of
inspiration and enthusiasm about the many
possibilities of biomimetics. On the other,
Rubner and Cohen are much more practical
and focus on the ideas that actually have
45 a chance of being applied successfully.
This combination of biological **insight** and
engineering pragmatism[5] is vital to success in
biomimetics, and has led to several promising
technologies.

50 Though Rubner and Cohen are certainly
impressed by biological structures, they consider
nature merely a starting point for innovation.
Cohen says, "The natural structure provides
a clue to what is useful . . . But maybe you
55 can do it better." Ultimately, they consider
a biomimetics project a success only if it has
the potential to make a useful tool for people.

"Looking at pretty structures in nature is not
sufficient," says Cohen. "What I want to know
60 is can we actually transform these structures into
[something] with true utility[6] in the real world?"

Unlocking Nature's Secrets

The work of Parker, Rubner, and Cohen is
only one part of a growing global biomimetics
65 movement. Scientists around the world are
studying and trying to copy a wide variety of
nature's design secrets, with the goal of using
them to create something useful. In the United
States, researchers are looking at the shape
70 of humpback whale fins in order to improve
windmills that generate electric energy. The
shape of the body of a certain fish has inspired
designers at Mercedes-Benz to develop a more

---

5 **Pragmatism** means dealing with problems in a practical way.

6 The **utility** of something is its usefulness.

∧ Swiss engineer Georges de Mestral invented Velcro after being
inspired by cockleburs (left) that stuck to his dog's fur.

efficient car design. By analyzing how termites[7]
keep their large nests at the right temperature
and humidity, architects in Zimbabwe hope to
build more comfortable buildings. And in Japan,
medical researchers have developed a painless
needle that is similar in shape to the proboscis[8]
of a mosquito.

The Bio-Inspired Robot

Potentially, one of the most useful applications
of biomimetics is the robot. Robots can perform
tasks that might be too boring or dangerous
for humans, but such robots are extremely
difficult to build. Professor Ronald Fearing of the
University of California is creating a tiny robot
fly that can be used in surveillance[9] or rescue
operations. Fearing's fly is a much simplified
copy of the real thing. "Some things are just
too mysterious and complicated to be able to

replicate,"[10] he says. It will still be years before
his robot fly can perform anything like an actual
fly, but Fearing is confident that over time he
will close the **gap** between nature and human
engineering.

At Stanford University in California, Mark
Cutkosky is working on a robot gecko. As
long ago as the fifth century B.C., the Greek
philosopher Aristotle was amazed at how this
small lizard "can run up and down a tree in

---

7 **Termites** are small insects that eat wood.
8 A **proboscis** is a long mouth part, usually of an insect.
9 **Surveillance** is the careful watching of someone, especially
   by an organization such as the police or the army.
10 If you **replicate** something, you make a copy of it.

any way, even with the head downward."
Cutkosky studied the extremely small structures on the gecko's feet that allow it to run up

105 and down **vertical** walls as easily as humans run down the street. He applied what he learned to create Stickybot, a robot that can walk up and down smooth vertical surfaces

110 made, for example, of glass or plastic. The U.S. **military**, which funds the project, hopes that one day Stickybot will be able to climb up a building and stay there for

115 days, monitoring the area below. Cutkosky hypothesizes a range of non-military uses as well.

‹ Gecko toes have special adaptations that enable them to adhere to most surfaces.

"I'm trying to get robots to go places where they've never gone before," he says. For now,

120 Stickybot only climbs very clean and smooth surfaces quite slowly—quite unlike a real gecko, which can run up just about any surface very quickly.

However, despite the promise of the field, and the

125 brilliant people who work in it, biomimetics has led to surprisingly few business successes. Perhaps only one product has become truly famous—Velcro, which was invented in 1948 by Swiss engineer Georges de Mestral, who copied the way seeds

130 called cockleburs stuck to his dog's fur. Some blame industry, whose short-term expectations about how soon a project should be completed and become profitable conflict with the time-consuming nature of biomimetics research. But the main reason

135 biomimetics hasn't yet been a business success is that nature is inherently and unimaginably complex. For the present, engineers cannot hope to **reproduce** it.

Nonetheless, the gap with nature is **gradually**

140 closing. Researchers are using more powerful microscopes, high-speed computers, and other new technologies to learn more from nature. A growing number of biomimetic materials are being produced. And although the field of biomimetics

145 has yet to become a very successful commercial industry, it has already developed into a powerful new tool for understanding nature's secrets.

⌃ A prototype of a wall-walking robot, based on the movements of a gecko, in the hands of Nancy Smith at the headquarters of iRobot in Bedford, Massachusetts, U.S.A.

Reading Comprehension

Multiple Choice. Choose the best answer for each question.

Gist
1. Another title for this reading could be _____.
   a. The Life of the Thorny Devil
   b. Why Biomimetics Can't Succeed
   c. Technology Inspired by Nature
   d. Andrew Parker's Scientific Career

Detail
2. Why did Andrew Parker go to the Australian desert?
   a. to capture and bring back a thorny devil
   b. to understand how the thorny devil collects water
   c. to provide water to thirsty thorny devils
   d. to discover water in the Australian desert

Detail
3. What has the study of termite nests inspired?
   a. more comfortable buildings
   b. improved windmills
   c. a more efficient car design
   d. a painless needle

Reference
4. In line 90, what does *things* refer to?
   a. abilities
   b. robot flies
   c. copies
   d. rescue operations

Detail
5. According to the article, which is a limitation of Stickybot?
   a. It can't climb up rough surfaces.
   b. It can move forward but not backward.
   c. It's too heavy to stay on a wall for long.
   d. The military won't let others use the technology.

Main Idea
6. What is the main idea of paragraph 8 (starting line 124)?
   a. Velcro is the greatest business success biomimetics has ever had.
   b. Biomimetics would be more successful if industry were less demanding.
   c. Nature's complexity is why biomimetics has had few business successes.
   d. Today's engineers are unable to copy nature as well as de Mestral could.

Detail
7. Which of these statements about biomimetics is NOT true?
   a. Parker hopes to create a water-collection device inspired by the thorny devil.
   b. Studying humpback whale fins may be useful for improving windmills.
   c. The body of a fish inspired a car design.
   d. Stickybot is perhaps the most famous biomimetic creation so far.

Critical Thinking

Evaluating:
The writer says that the "combination of biological insight and engineering pragmatism is vital to success in biomimetics." Why do you think the writer makes this claim?

Discussion: Which feature of an animal or a plant not mentioned in the reading do you think would be useful to replicate? Can you think of a practical use for it?

Recognizing Collocations

A collocation is two or more words that naturally go together. For example, we say, "make the bed" and "make a mistake" but not "make my homework" or "make a break." Here are some of the most common types, with examples:

Verb + noun	*take responsibility*
Adjective + noun	*innovative design*
Adjective + preposition	*concerned about*
Noun + noun	*design concept*
Adverb + adjective	*highly original*
Adverb + verb	*strongly suggest*

Try to memorize collocations as chunks of language, rather than as individual words.

A. Matching. Match the words to make collocations.

1. keep ___d___   **a.** attention
2. save ___b___   **b.** energy
3. pay ___a___   **c.** to an end
4. get ___f___   **d.** a secret
5. come ___c___   **e.** the law
6. break ___e___   **f.** permission

come to an end = finish

B. Identifying. The collocations in bold are from pages 63–64. Guess which of the other pairs of words do **not** collocate (a–c). Cross out the words. Use a dictionary to check your ideas.

1. **concrete purpose**
   a. ~~light purpose~~   *only*   b. sole purpose   c. clear purpose

2. **competitive advantage**   *easily seen*
   a. unfair advantage   b. distinct advantage   c. ~~sad advantage~~

3. **solve a problem**   *puzzle*
   a. solve a riddle   b. ~~solve the answer~~   c. solve a mystery

4. **draw inspiration (from)**
   a. draw attention (to)   b. ~~draw a problem (to)~~   c. draw a distinction (between)

5. **have a chance**
   a. ~~learn a chance~~   b. stand a chance   c. get a chance

6. **starting point**
   a. selling point   b. turning point   c. ~~leaving point~~

Vocabulary Practice

A. **Completion.** Complete the information with the correct form of words from the box. Five words are extra.

device	gap	gradual	insight	military
nonetheless	reproduce	riddle	vertical	vital

however — *to produce again*

The tropical boxfish, roughly the shape of a box, looks like it would have trouble moving through the water. **1.** _Nonetheless_ , the boxfish is, in fact, an excellent swimmer that cuts through the water extremely smoothly. It is such a good swimmer that engineers at Mercedes Technology Center in Sindelfingen, Germany, had a remarkable **2.** _insight_ : to use the boxfish to design the shape of a car that can cut through air as efficiently as the boxfish moves through water.

A model of the boxfish was created for them by Ronald Fricke at the Rosenstein Museum in Stuttgart, Germany. The model was placed inside a wind tunnel, a(n) **3.** _device_ that is used to study how air moves around solid objects. The boxfish shape reportedly performed over 65 percent better than today's compact cars. It should be possible to **4.** _reproduce_ that efficient shape for use in the body of a car to reduce its air resistance. Less air resistance means less fuel is required to run it.

A boxfish found in the Temae Reef, French Polynesia

Engineers set to work to try to solve the **5.** _riddle_ of how this unlikely shape could be so efficient. Their efforts were successful, and the car they created is the Mercedes Bionic concept car. However, the car is currently just for testing and not for sale.

B. **Definitions.** Match the definitions to the correct form of words from the box in **A**.

essential

1. _vital_ : necessary or very important

2. _gradual_ : occurring in small stages over a long period of time, rather than suddenly

3. _military_ : relating to soldiers or a country's armed forces

4. _vertical_ : standing or pointing straight up

5. _gap_ : a space between two things or a hole in the middle of something solid

Word Partnership
Use *vital* with: (adv.) **absolutely** vital; (n.) vital **importance**, vital **information**, vital **link**, vital **organs**, vital **part**, vital **role**.

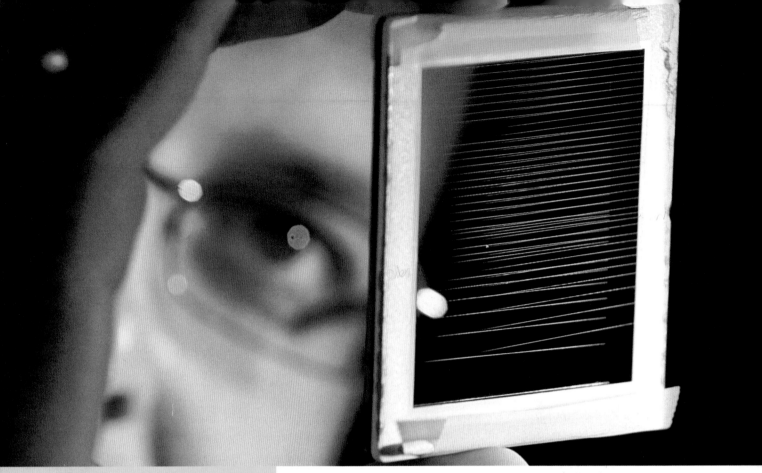

Before You Read

A. Completion. Read the information below and complete the sentences (1–4) using the words in **bold**.

Goats bred by Nexia Biotechnologies contain a spider gene that causes them to make a spider-silk protein in their milk. This protein is being used in a new **fiber** that's five times stronger than steel.

Spider silk joins a long list of fibers, both natural and **synthetic**, that have been used to create **textiles** that are then used to make, for example, clothing. Some recently created textiles are **high-tech** industrial secrets.

1. ___textiles___ are types of woven cloth.
2. ___high-tech___ activities or equipment involve an advanced level of technology.
3. ___fiber___ is a thin thread of a natural or artificial substance.
4. ___synthetic___ products are made from chemicals or artificial substances.

Biochemist Thomas Scheibel from the University of Bayreuth, holds a frame with artificial spider's thread. This synthetic substance is very strong—stronger even than real silk.

B. Predict. Look quickly at the photos, captions, and headings in the reading on pages 71–73. Check (✓) the topics you think you'll read about. Then read the passage and check your answers.

☐ high-tech protective clothing
☑ intelligent clothes
☐ extremely strong fabrics
☐ famous fashion models

THE FUTURE OF FASHION: DREAMWEAVERS

1 **ALEX SOZA IS A YOUNG AND EXTREMELY CREATIVE**
Danish fashion designer. He says his ideas come
to him in dreams. "I daydream. That's how I
get ideas." One of his inventions, a jacket that
5 stays **suspended** in the air like a balloon after
it is taken off, arose from such a daydream. He
explained, "I was on the subway, and this picture
of a floating jacket popped into my mind." Alex
Soza is one of many dreamers and pioneers who
10 are turning textile **fantasies** into **realities**.

High-Tech Textiles

Not so long ago, all fibers used to make textiles
came from natural sources: wool from the hair
of sheep, cotton from the cotton plant, silk from
15 silk worms. The first truly synthetic fiber didn't
appear until 1935, when scientists at the DuPont
Company invented nylon. Nylon is just one of
various industrially produced substances called
polymers. Polymers can be pulled into a thread,
20 which makes them well suited for use in textile
manufacturing.

Synthetic textiles have come a long way since
nylon. Kevlar, a textile that is stronger than
steel, is used in bulletproof vests and ropes used
25 by astronauts in space. Other high-tech fibers
can resist very high temperatures—perfect for
firefighters and race-car drivers. While not all
companies are **forthcoming** about their products
for fear of having their ideas stolen, Huges
30 Vinchon, an executive at Dubar-Warneton, a
manufacturer of high-tech textiles in France, is
happy to display some of the amazing synthetic
fibers his company creates. There is an oil-eating
textile that absorbs five times its weight in oil,
35 and is perfect for cleaning up oil spills. Another
absorbs vibrations.[1] ("Can you imagine a
motorboat you can't hear?" he says.) There is also
an ordinary-looking cloth bag that is "completely
water soluble,"[2] according to Vinchon. "It's
40 strong enough to carry heavy objects. But if I dip
it in boiling water, it disappears."

---

1 If something **vibrates**, it shakes with repeated small,
quick movements.
2 If something is water **soluble**, it will dissolve in water.

A model human ➤ made of copper tests protective clothing for firefighters in temperatures of over 1,350°C (2,500°F).

Some high-tech textiles draw their inspiration from nature. Spider silk is a natural fiber that is five times as strong as steel. Unfortunately, spiders cannot be farmed, as they will eat each other. A Canadian biotechnology firm, Nexia, has come up with a possible alternative to spider farming: They have inserted the spider-silk protein gene into goats, **thereby** causing them to produce spider-silk protein in their milk. Nexia's head, Jeff Turner, is already dreaming of applications for the new fiber, named BioSteel. "Why use rockets to lift objects into orbit?[3] . . . Why not have a [big] satellite and dangle a rope down to Earth and pull them up? . . . [There's] not a rope that will hold its weight at that length—but spider silk with its high strength-to-weight ratio could."

45
50
55

3 An **orbit** is the curved path in space that an object follows as it moves around a planet, moon, or star.

Wearable Electronics

Textiles have always been used in clothing, and modern, high-tech textiles may redefine what clothes are all about. "In the past, clothing protected us from the elements," says Ian Scott, head of technology for women's wear at British department store Marks & Spencer. "Then clothing became about fashion. The future is about clothing that can do something for you. It's no longer passive. It's active." One example of this active clothing that he hopes to sell in the next few years is an "intelligent bra," a sports bra that can sense stress and adjust its dimensions to give perfect support.

Other wearable electronics are being pioneered at a design laboratory in London run by the European manufacturer Philips Electronics. They are in the planning stages for various high-tech products, including an intelligent apron. This electronic apron acts as a kind of remote-control device. It has a built-in microphone that allows the wearer to operate kitchen appliances using voice commands. Another planned product is the Queen of Clubs outfit. According to a Philips spokesperson, "Here's an outfit for the girl who's really into clubbing. Sensors[4] hidden in her clothes allow her to affect the lights and beat of the music. . . . So that she can make contact with other people across the dance floor, she has . . . pants with lights that flash when someone is trying to get in touch."

While there are many interesting clothing innovations to look forward to, the only item so far sold in stores was marketed a few years ago as the first wearable electronics jacket. The jacket, called the ICD+, sold for about a thousand dollars. It had an MP3 player and cell phone. Headphones were built into the hood, and it had a microphone in the collar. Clive van Heerden, director of Intelligent Fibres, pointed out that it was an early first step and a conservative one. "We want to make the jacket that makes the coffee and picks up the kids and keeps track of the shopping list, but it's not going to happen overnight."

Future Warriors

One of the most important areas of clothing innovation is for military purposes. High-tech textiles are everywhere at the U.S. Army research center in Natick, Massachusetts. As part of their Future Warrior program, researchers are developing uniforms that will make a soldier difficult or impossible to see. Fibers in the uniform would take on the same color, brightness, and patterns of the wearer's surroundings. A soldier dressed in such a uniform would become nearly invisible to the enemy.

The researchers at Natick are also working on **portable** buildings that are made of what are essentially large, high-strength textile balloons. Called air beams, these building materials would allow a team to build a structure large enough to hold airplanes in a **fraction** of the time a conventional metal structure would take. The largest air beams, about 0.75 meters (2.5 feet) in diameter and 24 meters (78 feet) long, are so **rigid** that you can hang a heavy truck from one. Yet they can be packed into a truck. Whereas a conventional metal hangar[5] takes ten people five days to set up, one made of air beams can be set up by six people in just two days.

Today's textile innovators are creating astonishing things. From Alex Soza's artistic jacket that defies **gravity** to smart aprons to invisible military uniforms, high-tech textiles will soon be appearing in more and more parts of our lives. Who can **foresee** what these textile pioneers will dream up next? "It's about imagination!" says Alex Soza, with a bright look in his eye. "It's a beautiful dream! It's turning science fiction into scientific fact!"

---

4 A **sensor** is an instrument that reacts to certain physical conditions, such as heat or light.
5 A **hangar** is a large building in which aircraft are kept.

Reading Comprehension

Purpose

1. What is the main purpose of the passage?
   a. to provide a historical overview of innovative fashion styles
   b. to introduce the reader to developments in high-tech textiles
   c. to convince the reader to buy the latest synthetic fashions
   d. to explain how modern fashions are often inspired by nature

Inference

2. Why does Huges Vinchon mention a motorboat you can't hear?
   a. to evoke admiration for a fabric that can absorb vibrations
   b. to explain one of the properties of an oil-absorbing fabric
   c. to give an example of how quietly his textile factory runs
   d. to show that he is not afraid of having his ideas stolen

Inference

3. Which person do you think would be most likely to design a coat made of paper with six sleeves that three people can wear together?
   a. Alex Soza
   b. Huges Vinchon
   c. Jeff Turner
   d. Ian Scott

Detail

4. Which of these items has actually been sold in stores?
   a. the Queen of Clubs outfit
   b. the intelligent bra
   c. the intelligent apron
   d. the ICD+ jacket

Paraphrase

5. What does Clive van Heerden mean, when talking about the jacket, that "it's not going to happen overnight"? (lines 104–105)
   a. It's not going to happen until tomorrow.
   b. It's going to take a short time to happen.
   c. It's going to take a long time to happen.
   d. It's probably never going to happen.

Reference

6. The word *they* in line 127 refers to _____.
   a. heavy trucks
   b. air beams
   c. metal hangars
   d. airplanes

Cohesion

7. The following sentence would best be placed at the end of which paragraph? *Thanks to them, the world of high-tech textiles is an exciting place to be these days.*
   a. paragraph 1 (starting line 1)
   b. paragraph 2 (starting line 12)
   c. paragraph 8 (starting line 106)
   d. paragraph 9 (starting line 117)

Critical Thinking

Discussion: Which of the products mentioned in the reading do you think would sell well if they become available in stores? Why?

Evaluating: Jeff Turner of Nexia thinks his company's BioSteel could make it possible to lift things into orbit using spider silk. What challenges do you think he would face?

Understanding Synonyms and Antonyms

A synonym is a word that has the same meaning as, or is very similar to, another word. For example, a synonym of the word *synthetic* is *artificial*. Writers often use synonyms to avoid overusing the same words. Knowledge of a word's synonym(s) greatly increases your vocabulary. It can also help you put ideas into your own words when paraphrasing.

An antonym has the opposite meaning to another word, for example, *synthetic* and *natural*. When you learn a new word, list any synonyms and antonyms, for example, *synthetic = artificial, synthetic ≠ natural*.

A. Matching. Circle the word that is closest in meaning to the word in **bold**. Look back at the reading to check your ideas.

1. **various** (line 18)
   a. numerous b. future c. hilarious

2. **commands** (line 81)
   a. answers b. questions c. instructions

3. **invisible** (line 116)
   a. unclear b. unseen c. unprepared

4. **astonishing** (line 132)
   a. amazing b. puzzling c. frightening

B. Substitution. Read the excerpt from the reading below. Replace the words in **bold** with antonyms from the box. Then look at paragraph 5 to check your answers.

active	always	future	give	high-tech
modern	past	protected	sell	women's

Textiles have **never** (1. ___always___) been used in clothing, and **traditional** (2. ___modern___), **low-tech** (3. ___high tech___) textiles may redefine what clothes are all about. "In the **future** (4. ___past___), clothing **exposed** (5. ___protected___) us from the elements," says Ian Scott, head of technology for **men's** (6. ___women's___) wear at British department store Marks & Spencer. "Then clothing became about fashion. The **past** (7. ___future___) is about clothing that can do something for you. It's no longer passive. It's active." One example of this **passive** (8. ___active___) clothing that he hopes to **buy** (9. ___sell___) in the next few years is an "intelligent bra," a sports bra that can sense stress and adjust its dimensions to **take** (10. ___give___) perfect support.

Vocabulary Practice

A. Completion. Complete the information by circling the correct word in each pair.

Born in 1935, Christo is one of the best-known living artists. However, the art he is famous for could never fit inside a museum. He is an "environmental artist" who changes the look of a place on a very large scale, often with colorful fabric, **1. (rigidly / thereby)** allowing people to look at that place in a new way.

Christo worked closely alongside his wife, Jeanne-Claude, from their marriage in 1958 until her death in 2009. Once the couple had settled on an artistic idea, it took an incredible amount of planning, work, and money in order to turn their **2. (fantasies / realities)** into **3. (fantasies / realities).** Some examples of their large-scale works are:

Surrounded Islands (1983). Eleven islands in Miami were surrounded by 600,000 square meters (6.5 million square feet) of floating pink fabric.

The Gates (2005). In New York City's Central Park, 7,503 metal gates with orange fabric **4. (gravity / suspended)** from them were set up along the park's pathways.

Christo's **5. (portable / forthcoming)** project is called *The Mastaba*, a structure made of over 400,000 oil barrels built at Al Gharbia, 160 kilometers (100 miles) from Abu Dhabi.

Christo and Jeanne-Claude's "The Gates" in Central Park, New York City, U.S.A.

B. Words in Context. Complete each sentence with the correct answer.

1. An example of a **rigid** material is _____.
   a. cotton
   b. wood

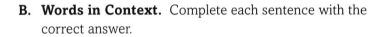
small portion

2. If you bought some clothes at a **fraction** of their original price, you _____.
   a. saved money
   b. spent too much

3. **Gravity** is particularly important when you are designing _____.
   a. a rocket
   b. clothing

4. If you **foresee** an event, you _____ it.
   a. remember
   b. predict

5. A **portable** device is easily _____.
   a. carried
   b. used

> **Word Link**
> The prefix **fore-** has the meaning of "before," e.g., *foresee, forecast, forestall, foreground.*

VIEWING Kinetic Sculpture

Before You Watch

A. Definitions. Read the information below and match each word in **bold** with its definition.

A kinetic sculpture is **literally** a piece of art on wheels. **Contestants** in the Kinetic Sculpture Race can focus on making their vehicles more kinetic (which means they are able to move on their own) or making them more eye-catching. Of course, they have to remember this is no simple race down the street, but a full **obstacle course** over a great distance!

1. _____: actually; without any exaggeration

2. _____: a path along which objects are placed making it difficult to travel

3. _____: people who take part in a competition

B. Discussion. Look at these entries in the race. Do you think they would move easily? Do you think their creators want to win the race, show their creativity, or both?

While You Watch

A. True or False. Mark the statements **T** (True) or **F** (False).

1. Entries in the race can be driven by one person or by a team of drivers.　　**T**　　**F**
2. The race goes through water, sand, mud, and ice.　　**T**　　**F**
3. The race began in the 1960s, when Hobart Brown decorated his own bike.　　**T**　　**F**
4. The race is more about having fun than actually winning.　　**T**　　**F**

B. Completion. Complete these quotes with the missing words.

Jen Ernst, Student:

"Some people really work on the **1.** _____, the scorpion sculpture, and some people have been really working on the **2.** _____ aspect."

Hobart Brown, Race Founder:

"The true artwork or the true art form is the **3.** _____ of everybody from the kid up to the adult, and the kid looks up to the adult and says I want to get **4.** _____, too."

Jeff Bartolomeo, Teacher:

"My main idea is to build a machine that can overcome all the **5.** _____ that the race organizers set out. Now, other folks could really care less, I think, about that part of the race. They just want to build something that can **6.** _____ their artwork. It's just a fun day of **7.** _____."

After You Watch

A. Discussion. Discuss these questions with a partner.

1. Imagine that you are going to enter the race. What shape will your kinetic sculpture be?

2. Look back at what student Jen Ernst says. Which would you most likely work on, the sculpture aspect or the engineering aspect?

3. Look back at what founder Hobart Brown says. What do you think he means?

4. Read about four more unusual races below. Which would you like to participate in the most? The least?

Joggling World Championships

Joggling is a combination of jogging and juggling. The rules are simple—joggers must juggle while they run. If a jogger drops something, he or she must go back and pick it up.

Knaresborough Bed Race

Contestants in the U.K. race in teams of six, with one extra person on the bed. Each team decorates their own bed. The bed runs on four wheels, but also needs to be able to float.

The Great Singapore Duck Race

In this charity event, people buy rubber ducks and put their name on them. Then all the ducks are thrown into the Singapore River. The first duck across the finish line is the winner.

The Empire State Building Run-Up

In this New York City race, contestants run up the 1,576 steps of the Empire State Building. Runners usually get to the top in about 10 minutes, slightly slower than the elevator.

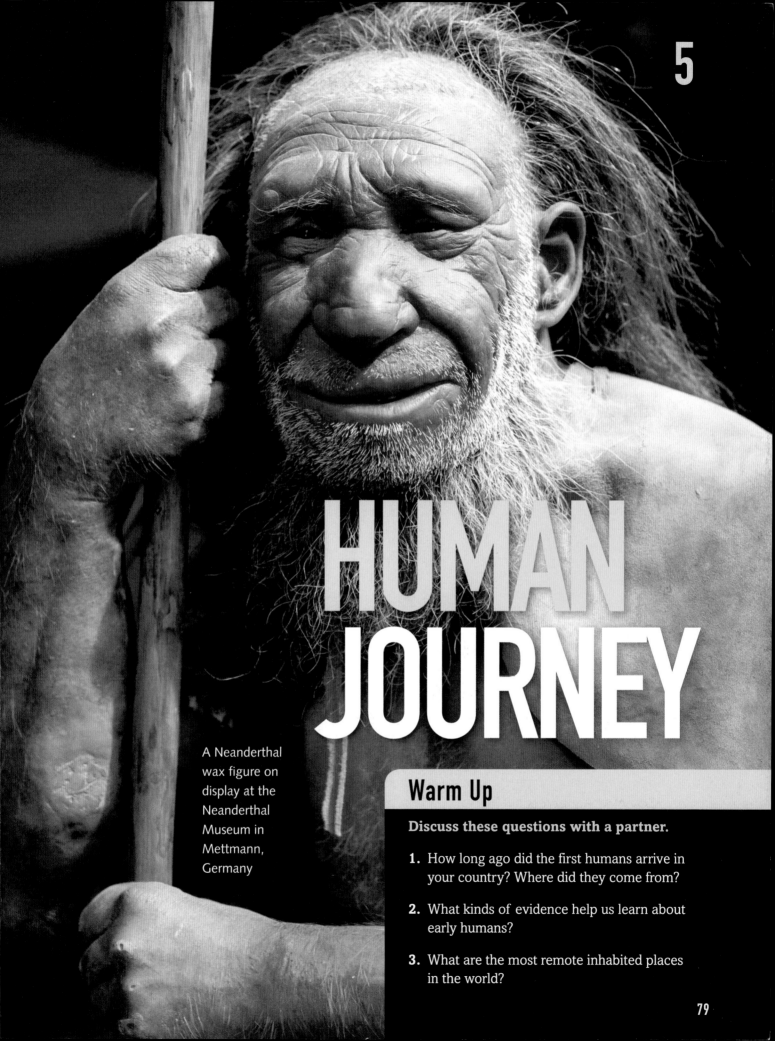

5

HUMAN JOURNEY

A Neanderthal wax figure on display at the Neanderthal Museum in Mettmann, Germany

Warm Up

Discuss these questions with a partner.

1. How long ago did the first humans arrive in your country? Where did they come from?

2. What kinds of evidence help us learn about early humans?

3. What are the most remote inhabited places in the world?

Before You Read

A. Completion. The map on page 82 shows the likely migration routes of our human ancestors as they populated the world. Study the map and complete the sentences below.

1. The first modern humans began spreading out from the continent of
   Africa.

2. The continent most recently populated by modern humans is
   South America.

3. Modern humans crossed over to North America from the continent of
   Asia.

4. Europe was populated by modern humans _40,000 – 30,000_
   years ago.

B. Skim. Skim the passage on pages 81–83. What kinds of evidence are scientists looking for to help them understand the migrations of our human ancestors?

∧ Modern genetic evidence indicates that humans left Africa about 60,000 years ago. Fanning out across the continents, they gave rise to new faces and races.

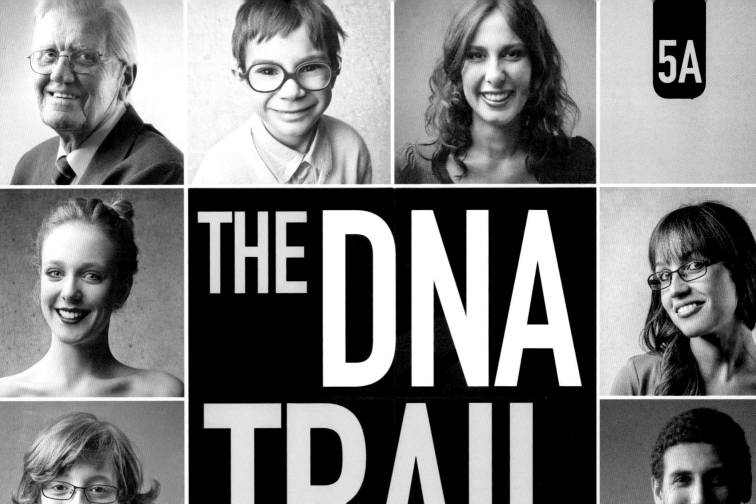

THE DNA TRAIL

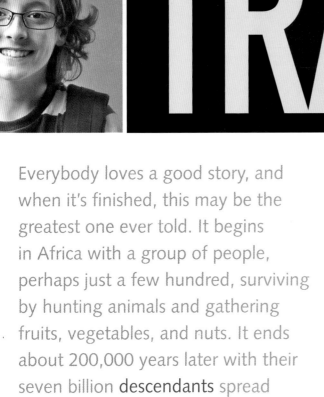

1 Everybody loves a good story, and when it's finished, this may be the greatest one ever told. It begins in Africa with a group of people,
5 perhaps just a few hundred, surviving by hunting animals and gathering fruits, vegetables, and nuts. It ends about 200,000 years later with their seven billion **descendants** spread
10 across the Earth, living in peace or at war, their faces lit by campfires[1] and computer screens.

In between is an exciting tale of survival, movement, isolation, and **conquest**, most
15 of it occurring before recorded history. Who were those first modern people in Africa? What routes did they take when they left their home continent 60,000 years ago to expand into Europe and Asia? When and how did
20 humans reach the Americas? For decades, the only **proof** was found in a small number of **scattered** bones and artifacts[2] that our ancestors left behind on their journeys. In the past 20 years, however, DNA technologies have
25 allowed scientists to find a record of ancient human migrations in the DNA of living people.

---

1 A **campfire** is a fire that is made outdoors, usually for warmth or cooking.
2 An **artifact** is a human-made ornament, tool, or other object, especially one that is historically or culturally interesting.

HUMAN MIGRATION

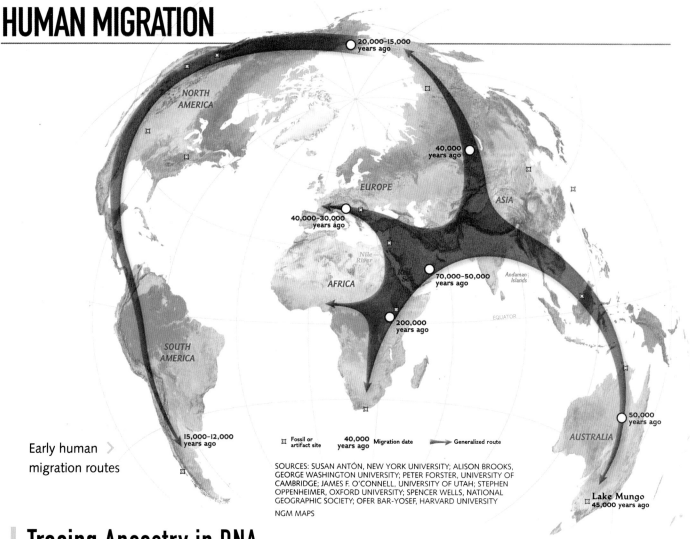

Early human migration routes

20,000–15,000 years ago

40,000 years ago

40,000–30,000 years ago

70,000–50,000 years ago

200,000 years ago

15,000–12,000 years ago

50,000 years ago

Lake Mungo 45,000 years ago

NORTH AMERICA

SOUTH AMERICA

EUROPE

ASIA

AFRICA

AUSTRALIA

Nile River

Andaman Islands

EQUATOR

⊠ Fossil or artifact site   40,000 years ago Migration date   ➤ Generalized route

SOURCES: SUSAN ANTÓN, NEW YORK UNIVERSITY; ALISON BROOKS, GEORGE WASHINGTON UNIVERSITY; PETER FORSTER, UNIVERSITY OF CAMBRIDGE; JAMES F. O'CONNELL, UNIVERSITY OF UTAH; STEPHEN OPPENHEIMER, OXFORD UNIVERSITY; SPENCER WELLS, NATIONAL GEOGRAPHIC SOCIETY; OFER BAR-YOSEF, HARVARD UNIVERSITY

NGM MAPS

Tracing Ancestry in DNA

"Every drop of human blood contains a history book written in the language of our genes," says

30   population geneticist[3] and National Geographic Explorer-in-Residence, Spencer Wells. The human genetic code, or genome, is 99.9 percent **identical** throughout the world. But while the **bulk** of our DNA is the same, what's left is

35   responsible for our individual differences—in eye color or disease risk, for example. On very rare occasions, a small change, called a mutation, can occur, which is then passed down to all of that person's descendants. Generations later, finding

40   that same mutation in two people's DNA indicates that they share the same ancestor. By comparing mutations in many different populations, scientists can **trace** their ancestral connections.

These ancient mutations are easiest to track in

45   two places: in DNA that is passed from mother to child (called mitochondrial DNA, or mtDNA for short), and in DNA that travels from father to son (known as the Y chromosome, the part of DNA that determines a child will be a boy). By comparing

50   the mtDNA and Y chromosomes of people from various populations, geneticists can get a rough idea of where and when those groups separated in the great migrations around the planet.

Out of Africa

55   In the mid-1980s, a study compared mtDNA from people around the world. It found that people of African descent had twice as many genetic differences from each other than as did others. Because mutations seem to occur at a steady rate

60   over time, scientists were able to conclude that

---

3 A **geneticist** is a scientist who studies DNA and genes.

modern humans must have lived in Africa at least twice as long as anywhere else. They now calculate that all living humans maternally descend from a single woman who lived **roughly** 150,000 years ago in Africa, a "mitochondrial Eve." If geneticists are right, all of humanity is linked to Eve through an unbroken chain of mothers. This Eve was soon joined by "Y-chromosome Adam," the putative[4] genetic father of us all, also from Africa. DNA studies have confirmed that all the people on Earth, with all their shapes and colors, can trace their ancestry to ancient Africans.

What seems virtually certain is that at a remarkably recent date—probably between 50,000 and 70,000 years ago—one small group of people, the ancestors of modern humans outside of Africa, left Africa for western Asia, either by migrating around the northern end of the Red Sea or across its narrow southern opening.

Once in Asia, genetic evidence suggests, the population split. One group stalled[5] temporarily in the Middle East, while the other commenced a journey which would last tens of thousands of years. Moving a little further with each new generation, they followed the coast around the Arabian Peninsula, India, and Southeast Asia, all the way to Australia. "The movement was probably imperceptible," says Spencer Wells. "It was less of a journey and probably more like walking a little farther down the beach to get away from the crowd."

Although archeological evidence of this 13,000-kilometer (8,000-mile) migration from Africa to Australia has almost completely vanished, genetic traces of the group that made the trip do exist. They have been found in the DNA of indigenous[6] peoples in the Andaman Islands near Myanmar, in Malaysia, and in Papua New Guinea, and in the DNA of nearly all Australian aborigines. Modern discoveries of 45,000-year-old bodies in Australia, buried at a site called Lake Mungo, provide some physical evidence for the theories as well.

People in the rest of Asia and Europe share different but equally ancient mtDNA and Y-chromosome mutations. The mutations which they possess show that most are descendants of the group that stayed in the Middle East for thousands of years before moving on. Perhaps about 40,000 years ago, modern humans first advanced into Europe.

Peopling the Americas

About the same time as modern humans pushed into Europe, some of the same group that had paused in the Middle East spread east into Central Asia, where they eventually reached as far as Siberia, the Korean peninsula, and Japan. Here begins one of the last chapters in the human story—the peopling of the Americas. Most scientists believe that today's Native Americans descend from ancient Asians who crossed from Siberia to Alaska in the last ice age, when low sea levels would have exposed a land bridge between the continents. They probably traveled along the coast—perhaps a few hundred people moving from one piece of land to the next, between a freezing ocean and a wall of ice. "A coastal route would have been the easiest way in," says Wells. "But it still would have been a hell of a trip." Once across, they followed the **immense** herds[7] of animals into the **mainland** and spread to the tip of South America in as little as a thousand years.

Genetic researchers can only tell us the basic outlines of a story of human migration that is richer and more complex than any ever written. Most of the details of the movements of our ancestors and their countless[8] individual lives in different times and places can only be imagined. But thanks to genetic researchers, themselves descendants of mtDNA Eve and Y-chromosome Adam, we have begun to unlock important secrets about the origins and movements of our ancient ancestors.

---

4 If something is **putative**, it is a commonly accepted thing.
5 If a process **stalls**, or if someone or something stalls it, the process stops but may continue at a later time.
6 **Indigenous** people or things belong to the country in which they are found, rather than coming there or being brought there from another country.
7 A **herd** is a large group of animals of one kind that live together.
8 If something is **countless** there are too many of it to be counted.

Reading Comprehension

Multiple Choice. Choose the best answer for each question.

Gist

1. Another title for this reading could be _____.
   a. Finding Y-Chromosome Adam
   b. Who Were the First Humans?
   c. What DNA Teaches Us About Our History
   d. The Discovery of DNA in Africa

Paraphrase

2. Which of the following is closest in meaning to *Every drop of human blood contains a history book written in the language of our genes* in lines 28–29?
   a. A drop of blood contains genetic information that can reveal a person's ancestral history.
   b. The organization of information in a history book is similar to the organization of DNA within a gene.
   c. Every drop of blood contains enough DNA information to fill many history books.
   d. Although people speak different languages, all human blood contains the same language.

Detail

3. What happened to the first group of humans that moved from Africa into Asia?
   a. Most of the migrants turned back into Africa.
   b. They divided into two groups.
   c. Most of the migrants moved directly into Europe.
   d. They stayed in the Middle East for tens of thousands of years.

Sequence

4. Which area was first to be populated by human migrants?
   a. Europe   b. Australia
   c. western Asia d. South America

Vocabulary

5. In line 88, the word *imperceptible* could be replaced with _____.
   a. unnoticeable   b. unpredictable
   c. illogical   d. unbelievable *given*

Detail

6. Which of the following is NOT cited as evidence for the great migration to Australia?
   a. several archeological discoveries in Asia
   b. DNA of people in Southeast Asia
   c. DNA of native people in Australia
   d. discovery of human remains in Australia

Fact or Theory

7. Which statement is theory, not a fact?
   a. Mutations are easiest to find in mtDNA and in the Y chromosome.
   b. Almost no archeological evidence of the human journey from Africa to Australia has been found.
   c. Bodies discovered at Lake Mungo are about 45,000 years old.
   d. Humans traveled along the coast of a land bridge between Siberia and Alaska.

Critical Thinking

Analyzing: What evidence does the author use to show that humans began in Africa? Is it possible that this theory is wrong? Why or why not?

Discussion: Why do you think the population in Asia split into two?

Reading Skill

Understanding Relative Clauses (I)

or object

Writers use relative clauses to give additional information about people or things without starting another sentence. Relative pronouns introduce relative clauses. We use *who* and *whom* for people, *which* for things, and *that* for either.

*I spoke with a man **who / that** knew a lot about early human populations.*

*He talked about a theory **which / that** explains how humans migrated.*

When the relative pronoun acts as a subject of the clause (see above), we must keep the pronoun. Otherwise, it is optional.

*The man (**who / whom / that**) I spoke to was a professor.*

*The theory (**which / that**) he talked about made a lot of sense.*

Be careful: *that* can also follow certain verbs (e.g., *show, suggest, indicate*) to introduce a clause, so it is not always a relative pronoun.

*Genetic evidence indicates **that** humans left Africa as long as 70,000 years ago.*

complex sentences

A. Analyzing. Underline the relative clauses in each sentence.

1. For decades, the only proof was found in a small number of scattered bones and artifacts that our ancestors left behind on their journeys.

2. They now calculate that all living humans are related to a single woman who lived roughly 150,000 years ago in Africa.

3. One group stalled temporarily in the Middle East, while the other commenced a journey which would last tens of thousands of years.

4. The mutations which they possess show that they are descendants of the group that stayed in the Middle East for thousands of years before moving on.

5. About the same time as modern humans pushed into Europe, some of the same group that had paused in the Middle East spread east into Central Asia.

6. Most scientists believe that today's Native Americans descend from ancient Asians who crossed from Siberia to Alaska in the last ice age.

7. Genetic researchers can only tell us the basic outlines of a story of human migration that is richer and more complex than any ever written.

B. Analyzing. Now cross out the relative pronoun in each sentence above if it's optional.

Vocabulary Practice

A. Completion. Complete the information using the correct form of words from the box. Three words are extra.

bulk	conquer	descendants	identical	immense
mainland	proof	roughly	scatter	trace

overcome ?

the greater part

Before modern humans, or *Homo sapiens*, migrated out of Africa perhaps 60,000 years ago, scientists tell us that another group, Neanderthals, had occupied Europe and Asia for **1.** ___roughly___ *to live* ? 200,000 years. Although there were probably no more than 15,000 of them at their population's peak, groups of Neanderthals were **2.** ___scattered___ over a(n) **3.** ___immense___ area throughout Europe, into the Middle East, and even as far east as Mongolia.

In 1856, the first Neanderthal bones were found in Germany's Neander Valley by workers digging for stones. These thick bones indicated that Neanderthals were shorter than modern humans, but physically stronger. Their tools were rough and simple, and not as refined as those of later *Homo sapiens*. Additionally, their food was not as varied; the *like* ? **4.** ___Bulk___ of their diet was the meat of large and medium-sized animals. At some point after modern humans entered Europe and Asia, the Neanderthals vanished from Earth. The reason for their disappearance remains a mystery. There are, however, a number of theories. As modern *Homo sapiens* **5.** ___conquered___ their lands, they may have killed the Neanderthals off. Other possible causes include diseases introduced by the newcomers, or climate change.

Another theory was that the Neanderthals had children with *Homo sapiens*, and gradually became part of their group. However, 1997 DNA analysis by geneticist Svante Pääbo and his colleagues at the University of Munich determined that Neanderthal DNA is not included in the DNA of modern humans. This is rather convincing **6.** ___proof___ that the majority of Neanderthals probably died out, and people alive today are not their **7.** ___descendants___.

Neanderthals used simple tools to hunt for food.

B. Definitions. Match words from the box in **A** with their definitions below.

1. ___mainland___ : the largest part of a country or continent, contrasted to the islands around it

2. ___identical___ : similar in every detail; exactly alike

Trace (n) small amount
3. ___trace (v)___ : to find or discover something by investigation

4. ___proof___ : a piece of evidence showing that something is true or exists

5. ___descendants___ : related people in later generations

6. ___conquer___ : to take complete control of another group's land by force

> **Word Partnership**
> Use **proof** with: (*adj.*) **convincing** proof, **final** proof, **living** proof; (*v.*) **have** proof, **need** proof, **offer** proof, **provide** proof, **require** proof, **show** proof.

FANTASTIC VOYAGE

Before You Read

A. Matching. Read the information in the caption and match each word in **bold** with its definition.

1. _____expanded_____ : became larger
2. _Anthropologist_ : scientists who study people and/or cultures
3. _____canoes_____ : wooden boats of a traditional style
4. _____horizon_____ : the line where the sky seems to meet the land or sea
5. _____Colonize_____ : to settle a new place and establish control over it

B. Scan. Scan the captions on pages 87–91 to find the answers to these questions.

1. What was uncovered in Vanuatu?

   a. a pot   b. a canoe   c. bones

2. The Lapita were _____.

   a. ocean explorers   b. anthropologists   c. traders

3. How long ago did the Lapita people travel east from New Guinea?

   a. 1,000 years ago   b. 3,000 years ago   c. 5,000 years ago

Anthropologists believe the Polynesians are descendants of an earlier group of Pacific Ocean explorers called the Lapita. Together, they **expanded** their world to include nearly every island in the Pacific Ocean. Why did these brave adventurers sail their **canoes** over the **horizon**? How did they locate and **colonize** hundreds of distant islands scattered across nearly a third of the Earth?

1   **IT IS MID-AFTERNOON ON THE ISLAND OF BORA BORA** in French Polynesia, and it feels like a carnival.[1] The air smells of barbecue, and thousands of cheering spectators crowd the
5   shore to see the end of the Hawaiki Nui Va'a, a challenging 130-kilometer (80-mile) Polynesian canoe race that virtually stops the nation.

  "This is our heritage," says Manutea Owen, a former canoe champion and a **revered** hero on
10   his home island of Huahine. "Our people came from over the sea by canoe. Sometimes when I'm out there competing, I try to imagine what they must have endured and the adventures they had crossing those huge distances."

revere = to feel or show great respect

The Hokule'a, a ＞ modern Hawaiian voyaging canoe built on ancient designs, arrives in Hawaii after a 6,100-kilometer (3,800-mile) voyage.

Pioneers of the Pacific

15 Manutea Owen's ancestors colonized nearly every island in the South Pacific Ocean in what was perhaps the most remarkable feat[2] of
20 human **navigation** before humans went to the moon. Only recently have scientists begun to understand where these amazing voyagers came from, and how, with simple canoes and no navigation equipment, they could manage to find and colonize hundreds of distant islands
25 scattered across an ocean that covers nearly a third of the globe. This expansion into the Pacific was accomplished by two extraordinary civilizations: the Lapita and the Polynesians.

---

1 A **carnival** is a public festival with music, processions, and dancing.
2 If you refer to something as a **feat**, you admire it because it is an impressive and difficult achievement.

From about 1300 to 800 B.C., the Lapita people colonized islands that **stretch** over millions of square kilometers, including the Solomon Islands, the Santa Cruz Islands, Vanuatu, Fiji, New Caledonia, and Samoa. Then, for unknown reasons, they stopped. There was an **interval** of around 1,000 years before the civilization of the Polynesians, descendants of the Lapita, launched a new period of exploration. Then they **outdid** the Lapita with unbelievable feats of navigation, expanding the boundaries of their oceanic world until it was many times the size of that explored by their ancestors. Their colonies included the Cook Islands, French Polynesia, Easter Island, and Hawaii, eventually reaching South America around 1000 A.D.

How Did They Do It?

There is one **stubborn** question for which archeology has yet to provide any answers: How did the Lapita and early Polynesian pioneers accomplish, many times over, a feat that is **analogous** to a moon landing? Very little evidence remains to help scientists understand their remarkable sailing skills. Unfortunately, no one has found an **intact** Lapita or early Polynesian canoe that might reveal how they were sailed. Nor do the oral histories[3] and traditions of later Polynesians offer any insights as to how they were able to navigate areas of open ocean hundreds or even thousands of kilometers wide without becoming lost. "All we can say for certain is that the Lapita had canoes that were capable of ocean voyages, and they had the ability to sail them," says Geoff Irwin, a professor of archeology at the University of Auckland, in New Zealand. Nonetheless, with little evidence, scientists have been able to develop some theories about the secrets of these explorers' success.

Sailors have always relied upon the so-called trade winds, winds that blow steadily and in predictable directions over the ocean's surface. Geoff Irwin notes that the Lapita's expansion into the Pacific was eastward, against steady trade winds. Sailing against the wind, he argues, may have been the key to their success. "They could sail out for days into the unknown . . . , secure in the knowledge that if they didn't find anything, they could turn around and catch a swift ride home on the trade winds." For returning explorers, successful or not, the geography of their own archipelagos[4] provided a safety net, ensuring that sailors wouldn't sail past and be lost again in the open ocean. Vanuatu, for example, is a chain of islands 800 kilometers (500 miles) long with many islands within sight of each other. Once sailors hit that string of islands, they could find their way home.

Irwin hypothesizes that once out in the open ocean, the explorers would detect a variety of clues to follow to land: seabirds and turtles that need islands on which to build their nests, coconuts and twigs[5] carried out to sea, and the clouds that tend to form over some islands in the afternoon. It is also **conceivable** that Lapita sailors followed the smoke from distant volcanoes to new islands.

---

3 **Oral history** is the study of spoken memories, stories, and songs.
4 An **archipelago** is a group of islands, especially small islands.
5 A **twig** is a very small, thin branch that grows out from a main branch of a tree or bush.

This pot was recently uncovered in a 3,000-year-old burial site on Éfaté Island, Vanuatu.

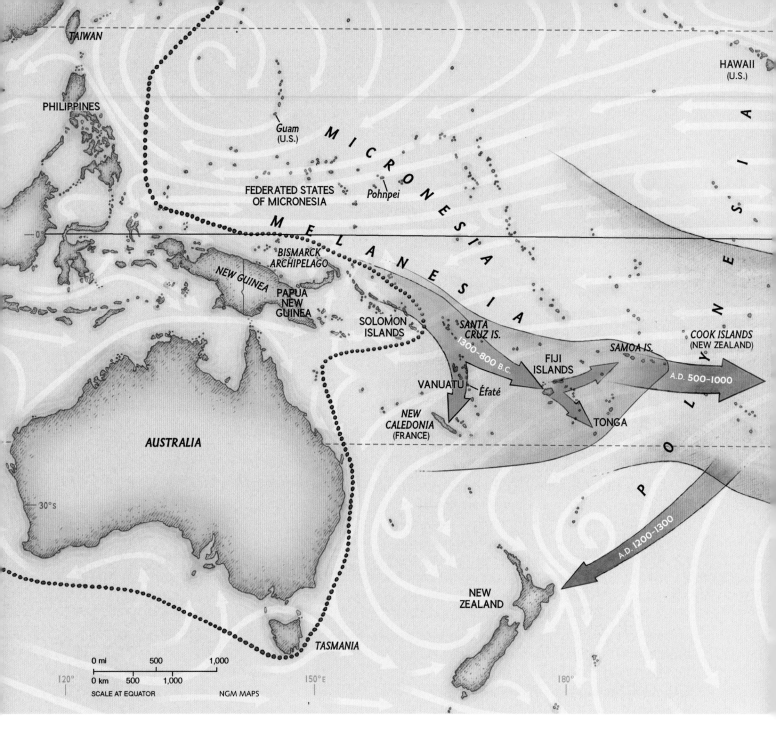

Helped by El Niño?

95

These theories rely on one unproven point—that the Lapita and early Polynesians had mastered the skill of sailing against the wind using a sailing technique called "tacking." Rather than

100 give all the credit to their bravery and ability to tack, Athol Anderson of the Australian National University believes that they may also have been lucky—helped by a weather phenomenon known as El Niño.

105 El Niño occurs in the Pacific Ocean when the surface water temperature is unusually high. It **disrupts** world weather in a variety of ways, but one of its effects is to cause trade winds in the South Pacific to weaken or to reverse direction

110 and blow to the east. Scientists believe that El Niño phenomena were unusually frequent around the time of the Lapita expansion, and again between 1,200 and 1,600 years ago, when the early Polynesians began their even more distant

115 voyages. Anderson believes that the Lapita may have been able to take advantage of trade winds

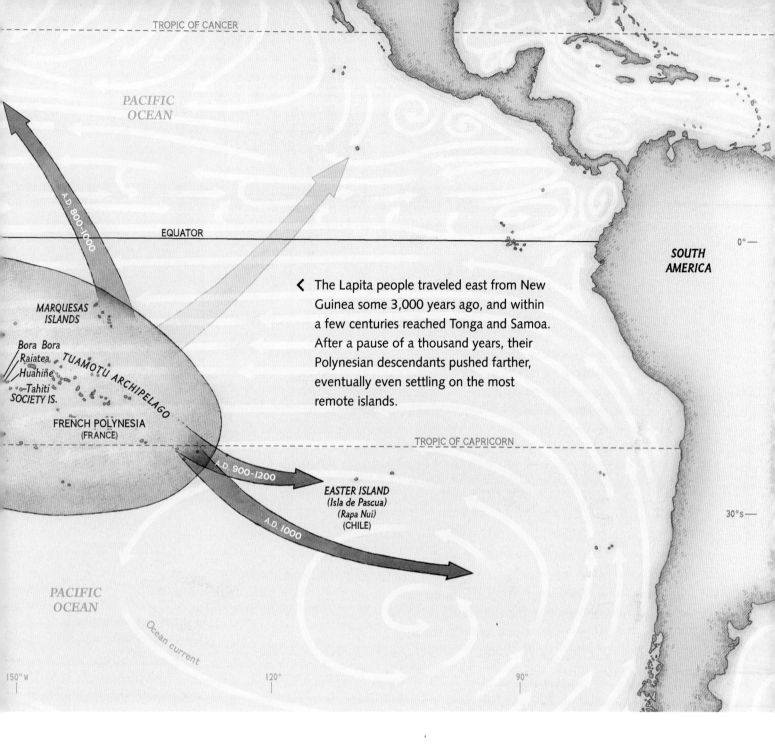

The Lapita people traveled east from New Guinea some 3,000 years ago, and within a few centuries reached Tonga and Samoa. After a pause of a thousand years, their Polynesian descendants pushed farther, eventually even settling on the most remote islands.

blowing east instead of west, and thereby voyage far to the east without any knowledge of tacking techniques.

120   The success of the Lapita and their descendants may have been due to their own sailing skill, to reverse trade winds, to a mixture of both, or even to facts still unknown. But it is certain that by the time Europeans came to the Pacific, nearly every

125   piece of land, hundreds of islands and atolls[6] in all, had already been discovered by the Lapita and Polynesians. Exactly why these ancient peoples set out on such giant migrations remains a mystery.

130   However, as Professor Irwin puts it, "Whatever you believe, the really fascinating part of this story isn't the methods they used, but their motives. The Lapita, for example, didn't need to pick up and go; there was nothing forcing them, no overcrowded homeland. They went because

135   they wanted to go and see what was over the horizon."

---

6 An **atoll** is a small coral island or group of islands.

Reading Comprehension

Multiple Choice. Choose the best answer for each question.

Gist

1. Another title for this reading could be _____.
- a. How Ancient Peoples Explored the Pacific
- b. How El Niño Helped the Lapita
- c. The Race Between the Lapita and the Polynesians
- d. The Myth That the Lapita Explored the Pacific

Reference

2. The phrase *these amazing voyagers* on line 21 refers to _____.   *trips*
- a. men who went to the moon
- b. the Lapita and early Polynesians
- c. today's Polynesians
- d. Manutea Owen and the people of Bora Bora

Fact or Theory

3. Which of the following statements is a fact, not a theory?
- a. The Lapita followed smoke from volcanoes to find new islands.
- b. Lapita sailors knew how to sail against the wind.
- c. The Lapita stopped exploring when the weather changed.
- d. No one has found an intact Lapita canoe.

Detail

4. How might El Niño have assisted early Pacific sailors?
- a. by making the water temperature more comfortable
- b. by reversing the direction of the trade winds
- c. by making tacking easier
- d. by providing more wood to build canoes

Detail

5. What is true for both the Lapita and the early Polynesians?
- a. They reached South America.
- b. They may have been helped by El Niño.
- c. They colonized New Caledonia and Samoa.
- d. Their navigational techniques are well understood.

Paraphrase

6. What does Irwin mean by *they wanted to go and see what was over the horizon* in lines 135–136?
- a. They were motivated by a curiosity about new places.
- b. They hoped for greater security in faraway places.
- c. They desired better living conditions on other islands.
- d. They needed to find food and fresh water overseas.

Main Idea

7. What would be a good heading for the final paragraph?
- a. A Mystery Solved
- b. Descendants of the Lapita
- c. But Why Did They Go?
- d. An Uncertain Future

^ The Lapita had canoes that were able to withstand long ocean voyages.

Critical Thinking

Evaluating: Was the success of ancient sailors due to sailing skill, reverse trade winds, a mixture of both, or even to facts still unknown? Which do you think is most likely? Why?

_____

Discussion: Why do you think the Lapita and the Polynesians set out on such giant migrations?

— This is a photograph of my grandmother with all her descendants

-Their plans of conquest never became reality

Papers are scattered everywhere

Synthesizing Information

When you read a passage, it's important to read all the information related to the text. This can include footnotes, photo captions, charts, graphs, timelines, and maps. They can contain important information that you may need to combine with information from the text to fully comprehend the passage.

to understand — to include

A. Multiple Choice. Choose the best answer for each question.

1. In the photo on page 88, where might the Hokule'a be returning from, based on the Polynesian migration route?
   a. Australia
   b. the Marquesas Islands
   c. New Guinea
   d. South America

2. Which people probably created the pot in the photo on page 89?
   a. the Lapita
   b. Polynesians
   c. Hawaiian
   d. Cook Islanders

3. Which of these is NOT an archipelago?

   a large group of islands

   a. Tuamotu
   b. the Solomon Islands
   c. Easter Island
   d. the Philippines

4. If the usual trade winds were reversed due to El Niño, where might someone sailing from French Polynesia end up?
   a. Easter Island
   b. the Cook Islands
   c. Hawaii
   d. New Zealand

A restored *moai* at Rapa Nui National Park, Easter Island. These moai were symbols of authority and power for ancient Polynesians.

A. Completion. Complete the information by circling the correct word in each pair.

Fifteen years ago, most experts would have agreed that the first people in the Americas arrived by walking across a land bridge that crossed the Bering Strait between Siberia and Alaska. They then traveled south through an open area of ground between great sheets of ice that **1. (navigated / stretched)** across North America at that time. Today, however, this theory is being challenged.

An alternative theory suggests that instead of a single first migration, various groups of people came to the Americas at **2. (intervals /** ~gap~ **analogies)** spaced well apart in time. Another theory proposes that ancient people might have **3. (outdone / navigated)** their way along the shoreline using kayaks, just as adventurous tourists do today.

Looking at ancient tools found in America, archeologist Dennis Stanford noticed that their shape was similar to tools used by the Solutrean culture of southwestern Europe. He thinks it is _possible_ **4. (conceivable / intact)** that people of that culture may have kayaked across the Atlantic from Europe to America.

The science of archeology often produces theories that are based on very small bits of evidence. Today's archeologists know that being **5. (stubborn / intact)** and holding on to one theory while shutting out the others isn't good science. As new evidence is discovered that **6. (reveres / disrupts)** existing theories, they adjust those theories to explain the new facts.

^ Archeologists discovered a digging stick in Chile. They estimate it to be about 12,500 years old.

B. Words in Context. Complete each sentence with the correct answer.

1. A person who is **revered** is highly _____.
   a. respected   b. feared

2. Two things that are **analogous** are _____.
   a. similar   b. different

3. If an ancient tool is found **intact**, it is _____.
   a. broken   b. complete

   overcome - best

4. Someone who wants to **outdo** others is _____.
   a. caring   b. competitive

5. Someone who is **stubborn** usually _____ their opinion.
   a. sticks to   b. changes

> **Thesaurus**
> **stubborn** Also look up: (*adj.*) *determined, adamant, persistent, headstrong, steadfast, relentless*

Cellphone has disrupted communication - people have

VIEWING Journey of Discovery

Before You Watch

A. Discussion. Look at the pictures below of the *Mata Rangi III*, a boat built entirely of grasslike plants called reeds. Then discuss these questions with a partner.

1. Why do you think the boat was built?
2. Do you think a boat like this could travel across an ocean? Why, or why not?
3. What do you think happened to the *Mata Rangi I* and *II*?

While You Watch

A. Sequencing. Number these events from 1 to 4 in the order they happened.

a. The crew of the *Mata Rangi III* goes to Cape Verde.

b: The crew has to deal with boredom and depression.

c. The *Mata Rangi III* hits rough weather.

d. Muñoz has to act quickly because of flooding.

heis descendant of

B. Summary Completion. Complete the summary of the video using words from the box.
Two words are extra.

built	boredom	drowning	flexible	flooding	hunger
modern	ocean	rough	small	south	strong

The Boat

- Based on those in pre-European
  1. ___south___ America
- **2.** ___built___ in Spain by Aymara
  Indians from Bolivia
- Made of reeds with no
  3. ___modern___ materials
- Named the *Mata Rangi III*

The Route

- Began in Barcelona, Spain
- Continued to Morocco
- Will go to Cape Verde and across
  4. ___ocean___ to Colombia

Journey of Discovery

On the Open Sea

- Heavy winds and **5.** ___flooding___ seas
- **6.** _____ of the main cabin
- Worries of falling and **7.** ___drowning___
- Clouds eventually cleared and boat survived

Lessons Learned

- Reeds are **8.** ___strong___ enough to
  survive difficult conditions for long periods
  of time
- **9.** ___small___ boat not for
  everyone
- Had to fight **10.** ___boredom___ and
  depression

After You Watch

A. Discussion. Discuss these questions with a partner.

1. Do you think the *Mata Rangi III* was capable of crossing the Atlantic Ocean?
   Do an Internet search on Kitín Muñoz to find out if his journey was successful.

2. Do you think that the *Mata Rangi III* project was worth the time and effort?
   Explain why or why not.

3. Muñoz says he uses expeditions like that of the *Mata Rangi III* to draw attention
   to the threats that face indigenous people and their way of life. Do you think he
   was successful in doing this?

CONSERVATION CHALLENGES

An adult and a juvenile gorilla at the
Bwindi Impenetrable Park, Uganda

Warm Up

Discuss these questions with a partner.

1. What places on Earth are the least affected by the modern world?

2. What kinds of pressures is the natural world facing today?

3. What can we do to protect endangered forests and animals?

Before You Read

A. Quiz. Look at the caption on the right and information below.
Then read the sentences and circle **T** (True) or **F** (False).

Though often called koala "bears," koalas are not bears at all. They are
marsupials, a type of mammal that carries its young in a pouch. A baby
koala emerges from its mother's pouch after about six months. It then
rides on its mother's back or stomach until it's about a year old.

> Koalas live in eastern
> Australia, where there
> are large numbers of
> eucalyptus trees. They
> sleep in tree branches
> for up to 18 hours a
> day. When not asleep,
> they eat mainly the
> leaves of eucalyptus
> trees—about a
> kilogram (2.2 pounds)
> a day.

1. Koalas live in eastern Australia.	**T**	**F**
2. Koalas eat eucalyptus leaves up to 18 hours a day.	**T**	**F**
3. Koalas are actually a type of bear.	**T**	**F**
4. Baby koalas stay in their mother's pouch for about six months.	**T**	**F**

B. Predict. Which of these dangers to koalas do you think the
article will mention? Check (✓) your answers. Then read the
passage to see if you were right.

- ☐ getting caught in fences
- ☐ the loss of eucalyptus trees
- ☐ koalas killing other koalas
- ☐ being captured for zoos
- ☐ dog attacks
- ☐ falling out of trees
- ☐ getting hit by vehicles
- ☐ disease

RACING TO RESCUE KOALAS

> Megan Aitken carefully carries a male koala that was hit by a car.

1 **IT'S TWO IN THE MORNING**, and a koala is caught in barbed wire[1] on a fence, like a prisoner trying to escape. A phone rings in the home of Megan Aitken in a **suburb** of Brisbane, a city on the east
5 coast of Australia. Aitken, 42, runs a volunteer organization devoted to rescuing wild koalas. Before she is even told the location, she has thrown her clothes on over her pajamas.

When Aitken arrives on the scene, Jane Davies
10 and Sandra Peachey, two other volunteers, are already there. The koala is holding on tightly to a chain-link fence. Its fur is caught in barbed wire. There are tall eucalyptus trees not far beyond the fence." He was obviously trying to get to the
15 trees on the other side," Aitken says. Standing in the bright light of car headlights, Aitken puts on heavy leather gloves. Despite their cute appearance, koalas can be ferocious[2] when **resisting** capture. If they feel threatened, they
20 will fight and bite, and Aitken has the scars to prove it. Next, she places a cage on the ground near the animal and opens up a thick blanket. Then the three rescuers rapidly get to work.

Davies throws the blanket over the animal.
25 Peachey opens the lid of the cage, while Aitken firmly **grasps** the koala through the blanket, frees it from the fence, and drops it into the cage. "Well done, ladies!" Aitken shouts.

Looking down at the koala they have just
30 captured, Aitken checks the animal's physical condition. In the event that the koala is sick or injured, it must be taken to the Australia Zoo Wildlife Hospital 40 minutes away. Provided it's healthy, like this one is, it will be released
35 somewhere near the place it was found. This is because koalas live within such a small area and feed in the same trees over and over. However, this is Deception Bay, a dense suburb with few areas with trees, so finding a **suitable** area is
40 not easy. The women study a street map with flashlights.

---

1 **Barbed wire** is wire that has sharp pieces of metal attached to it. It is used to make fences.

2 A **ferocious** animal is violent, and dangerous when it attacks.

A koala's natural behavior is to hug its mother or human caregiver.

"This is the whole problem," Aitken says. "There are so few places left for the koala." In the end, they take the animal to a small park
45 nearby and set the cage below a eucalyptus tree. Standing back, they open the lid of the cage, and the koala dashes up the trunk. "Good luck, little one," says Aitken.

Koalas at Risk

50 "Koalas are getting caught in fences and dying, being killed by dogs, struck by vehicles, even dying simply because a homeowner cut down several eucalyptus trees in his backyard," says Deidré de Villiers, one of the **chief** koala
55 researchers at the Queensland Department of Environment and Resource Management. For 15 years, de Villiers, 38, has been studying koalas and the reasons for their decline. She is working on ideas to make development more
60 koala-friendly.

De Villiers insists that koalas and humans can live together "if developers **get on board**

with koala-sensitive designs," such as lower speed limits for streets, green corridors for koala
65 movement, and—most especially—preserving every precious eucalyptus tree. Unfortunately, koalas have another problem.

"Disease is another huge issue," says veterinarian Jon Hanger from the Royal Society
70 for the Prevention of Cruelty to Animals in Queensland. Hanger has discovered that as many as half of Queensland's koalas are affected by a **devastating**, often fatal disease called chlamydiosis. Unless it's treated, it can make
75 reproduction impossible for females. "Koala populations that used to be **vibrant** are becoming extinct," says Hanger. "The more koalas we lose, the more valuable each rescued koala becomes."

A True Friend to Koalas

80 At her home south of Brisbane, de Villiers' brings out Ruby, one of the five koalas she is currently taking care of. "Ruby still sleeps in the basket hugging her teddy bear," she says. "She was

LOSING THEIR EUCALYPTUS

Before the arrival of the Europeans more than two centuries ago, about ten million koalas lived in forests along the east coast of Australia. Here eucalyptus leaves—their primary food source—were plentiful. Since then, koalas have been killed in great numbers, and nearly two-thirds of their forest habitat has been cleared. Today, there may be fewer than 100,000 wild koalas.

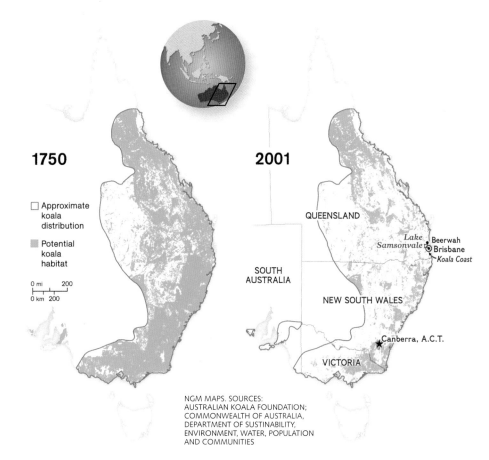

1750

☐ Approximate koala distribution

▓ Potential koala habitat

0 mi   200
0 km   200

2001

QUEENSLAND

Lake Samsonvale / Beerwah / Brisbane / Koala Coast

SOUTH AUSTRALIA

NEW SOUTH WALES

★ Canberra, A.C.T.

VICTORIA

NGM MAPS. SOURCES:
AUSTRALIAN KOALA FOUNDATION;
COMMONWEALTH OF AUSTRALIA,
DEPARTMENT OF SUSTINABILITY,
ENVIRONMENT, WATER, POPULATION
AND COMMUNITIES

85 rescued from the jaws of a dog." Every other day, de Villiers cuts and collects eucalyptus leaves, the koala's primary food, from a nearby plantation.[3] Over the past 12 years, she has cared for more than 60 koalas.

90 On a morning not long after the visit to her home, de Villiers sets out into the forest northwest of Brisbane to catch Tee Vee, a wild koala she has been monitoring for more than a year. Using a receiver that looks like an old-fashioned rooftop TV antenna, she walks along,
95 listening for a signal from the koala's radio collar. She eventually picks up a faint signal and follows it as it grows louder and louder. "I see her!" she says finally. The koala is holding on to a tree branch 15 meters (50 feet) or so
100 directly above.

Capturing a koala high in the trees is **complicated**. First, a device shoots a ball of string over a tree branch close to the koala. The string is attached to a climbing rope, which is
105 then pulled up over the branch and tied firmly to something on the ground. A ladder is set

against the tree. Then de Villiers climbs up the ladder and moves toward the koala. Tee Vee gets annoyed and starts moving backward down the
110 trunk. Then, suddenly, the koala jumps into the air and lands on the ground, where she is quickly captured in a blanket.

Tee Vee is given medicine to calm her down, and de Villiers gets to work. She measures the length
115 of the koala's body and head, and checks the teeth and the condition of the fur. "I think she has a baby," de Villiers says suddenly.

She carefully opens the koala's pouch and pulls out a 10-centimeter- (four-inch-) long baby
120 koala. Just then, everyone in the group says "ahhh" all **at once**. De Villiers examines the baby for any problems, and then gently replaces it in the mother's pouch. "As long as there are still healthy babies, there's still hope,"
125 she whispers.

---

3 A **plantation** is a large piece of land on which crops such as rubber, coffee, tea, or sugar are grown.

Reading Comprehension

Multiple Choice. Choose the best answer for each question.

Gist

1. What is this reading mainly about?
   a. how one woman is saving koalas from extinction
   b. threats to koalas and what is being done to protect them
   c. ways that humans and koalas can learn to live together
   d. new methods for studying koalas in the wild

Detail

2. What does Megan Aitken use the blanket for?
   a. to catch the koala after it falls from a tree
   b. to cover the koala so it doesn't harm her
   c. to cover the cage so the koala inside stays calm
   d. to keep the koala warm after it's placed in a cage

Detail

3. Why is the koala that Aitken caught released near where they found it?
   a. because koalas are not allowed to be in public parks
   b. because koalas feed in the same trees again and again
   c. because it's the only place nearby that has eucalyptus trees
   d. because that's where the koala probably has its baby

Detail

4. According to Deidré de Villiers, what is the main thing that developers must do to protect koalas?
   a. lower speed limits in areas with koalas
   b. build green corridors for koala movement
   c. preserve koalas' existing eucalyptus trees
   d. create special koala-only habitat zones

Inference

5. What can we infer about the 60 koalas de Villiers has cared for?
   a. Most of them died.
   b. Most were rescued from the wild.
   c. Most later became pets.
   d. Most were later taken to Queensland.

Inference

6. Why does de Villiers capture Tee Vee?
   a. to attach a signaling device to her
   b. to see if she had her baby
   c. to check on her condition
   d. to take her to an animal hospital

Reading Maps

7. According to the map on page 101, which of these statements is true?
   a. South Australia no longer has any koalas.
   b. Queensland had about the same number of koalas in 1750 as in 2001.
   c. There are about 100,000 koalas in New South Wales.
   d. The area with the highest potential for koala habitat is northern Queensland.

Critical Thinking

Analyzing: Which do you think is the bigger threat to koalas—disease or habitat loss? Is one threat easier to deal with than the other?

Discussion: If healthy koalas get captured, they are released near where they were found. Do you think this is a good idea? Are there other alternatives you can think of?

Recognizing Conditional Relationships

There are several structures that express conditional relationships. The most common way is with *if*.

Even if is used to emphasize that the action will happen regardless of the condition.

*You probably won't see koalas **even if** they're in the area.*

As long as and *provided (that)* are also used to express a condition.

*You can get a photo with a koala at a zoo **as long as** / **provided that** you pay for it.*

Unless is followed by an affirmative verb to mean "if . . . not."

*The koala might die **unless** it gets treatment. = The koala might die if it doesn't get treatment.*

In case and *in the event (that)* are used when talking about precautions.

*Have your camera ready **in case** / **in the event that** you see a koala.*

A. Scanning. Look back at the reading on pages 99–101 and answer the questions.

1. When will koalas fight and bite?

   _____

2. If a sick or an injured koala is captured, what will happen to it?

   _____

3. What will happen if a healthy koala is captured?

   _____

4. According to Deidré de Villiers, what can happen if developers get on board with koala-sensitive designs?

   _____

5. If chlamydiosis is not treated in koalas, what can become impossible for females?

   _____

6. If there are still healthy koala babies, what does de Villiers believe?

   _____

Vocabulary Practice

A. Completion. Complete the information by circling the correct word or phrase in each pair.

Large and flightless, with shiny black feathers and a colorful head, the cassowary lives in the rain forests of northern Australia. It is a shy bird, but is seen more and more in **1. (vibrant / suburban)** areas. Sadly, cassowaries are being found dead on highways and in pig traps. There are perhaps only between 1,500 and 2,000 left in the wild, but no one knows for sure.

What is clear is the cassowary has problems. They are a target of dogs and wild pigs. Traffic is also a problem. Roads carve up the forest, so their habitat is no longer a single area. This makes it hard for young cassowaries to find their own territories. It takes a certain amount of **2. (suitable / complicated)** habitat to sustain a population.

But the biggest threat is development. Large areas of forest in northern Queensland have been cut down, which has had a **3. (devastating / chief)** effect on cassowary numbers. Locals are trying to slow or even stop the development. Some have begun replanting open fields. Others are encouraging more farmers to **4. (at once / get on board)** and **5. (grasp / resist)** clearing their land in the first place. They are also trying to create protected areas. The hope is to link forest sections so cassowaries don't have to cross highways. Like koalas further south, cassowaries are under threat.

B. Words in Context. Complete each sentence with the correct answer.

1. When you **grasp** something with your hand, you hold it _____.
   a. loosely   b. tightly

2. If two things happen **at once**, they happen at _____.
   a. the same time   b. different times

3. Something that is **complicated** is usually _____ to understand.
   a. easy   b. difficult

4. The **chief** researcher would have a _____ ranking.
   a. low   b. high

5. A **vibrant** city has _____.
   a. great energy and life   b. sadness and despair

6. The **suburbs** of a city are _____ the city center.
   a. inside   b. outside

There may be fewer than 3,000 cassowaries left in the wild.

Word Partnership
Use **vibrant** with: (n.) vibrant **city**, vibrant **populations**, vibrant **nightlife**, vibrant **culture**, vibrant **atmosphere**, vibrant **color**.

FOR THE
LOVE
OF
ELEPHANTS

Before You Read

A. Discussion. Look at the map on page 107 and answer the questions below.

1. Which area of Africa had a larger range of elephants in 2007?

   a. Senegal   b. South Sudan

2. Which country that used to have elephants no longer does?

   a. Mauritania   b. Mozambique

3. Why do you think elephant populations have declined so much since 1979?

   _____

An elephant matriarch leads her herd in Samburu National Reserve, Kenya.

B. Matching. The passage on pages 106–109 is in two parts. Skim and match each part to a description. Check your ideas as you read the whole passage.

An Encounter •   • a description of Samburu National Reserve, Kenya
at Sunset   • a short biography of Douglas-Hamilton

Saving the •   • an elephant attack on Douglas-Hamilton and others
Elephants   • conflict between Douglas-Hamilton and African authorities

1 Author David Quammen writes about an extraordinary experience among the elephants of Samburu National Reserve, Kenya.

An Encounter at Sunset

Late one afternoon, biologist Iain Douglas-Hamilton stopped by my tent and asked if I wanted to drive out and see some elephants before sunset. I asked him if he would like to take a walk instead.
10 I knew that walking around the reserve could be risky, but surely we could at least climb the little hill just behind camp. He agreed, and we did. The view of the river from the top was magnificent. Just north of us was a larger hill known as Sleeping
15 Elephant. I asked him if he had ever climbed that one. He told me he hadn't, but, with a mischievous[1] look in his eye, said that we could.

We walked toward Sleeping Elephant: two middle-aged white men and a young Samburu man
20 named Mwaniki. We walked only five minutes before we saw a female elephant with two babies ahead of us. We paused, admiring these noble creatures from a safe distance until they seemed to **withdraw**, and then we went on, unable to
25 foresee that our lives were in danger. Seconds later, we looked up to see the female staring angrily at us from 70 meters (230 feet) away. Her ears were spread wide, showing us her **agitation**.

Mwaniki and I turned and ran, and we managed to
30 put a safe distance between us and the elephant. Mwaniki continued to run all the way back to camp to get help. At first, Douglas-Hamilton also turned and ran—then thought better of it, turned back, threw his arms out, and yelled to stop the
35 elephant. Sometimes this works, but the female kept coming. Douglas-Hamilton turned again and ran, but the elephant caught him as he tried to **evade** her. She lifted him and then threw him as he yelled for help. She stepped forward and stabbed[2]
40 her sharp, rigid tusks[3] downward at him. Then she backed off about ten steps and paused. This was the moment, he told me later, when he had time to wonder whether he would die.

45 I ran back to Douglas-Hamilton, and to my surprise, he wasn't dead. After stabbing at him once and missing, the elephant had turned away. She went off to find her babies. Douglas-Hamilton was scratched, but not badly hurt; his shoes, glasses, and watch were gone, but he was OK.
50 He stood up. Then a dozen people arrived from camp, and helped retrieve his things.

Afterwards, Douglas-Hamilton and I hypothesized about what had triggered the attack. It was possible that we surprised her. Perhaps it was
55 her mother's **instinct** to defend her calves. It was also conceivable that she had recently been frightened by a lion and was in an agitated state. The more difficult question, however, was why, at the last minute, did she decide not to kill him?
60 I suppose we will never know, but I like to think that, after confusing him with an enemy, she finally recognized in Douglas-Hamilton a **genuine** friend of elephants.

Saving the Elephants

65 "If you had asked me when I was ten years old what I wanted to do," Douglas-Hamilton says, "I'd have said: I want to have an airplane; I want to fly around Africa and save the animals." Later, while studying zoology[4] at Oxford University, he
70 found his goals hadn't changed. "Science for me was a passport to the bush,"[5] he says, "not the other way around. I became a scientist so I could live a life in Africa and be in the bush."

Early in his career in Africa, he went to Tanzania
75 as a research volunteer in Lake Manyara National Park. He bought himself a small airplane, which he could use for tracking elephants. There at Manyara, Douglas-Hamilton did the first serious study of elephant social structure and spatial

---

1 A **mischievous** person likes to have fun by playing harmless tricks on people or doing things they are not supposed to do.
2 If you **stab** someone, you push a sharp object into their body.
3 **Tusks** are the two very long, curved, pointed teeth of an elephant, wild boar, or walrus.
4 **Zoology** is the scientific study of animals.
5 The wild, uncultivated parts of some hot countries are referred to as the **bush**.

VANISHING ELEPHANTS

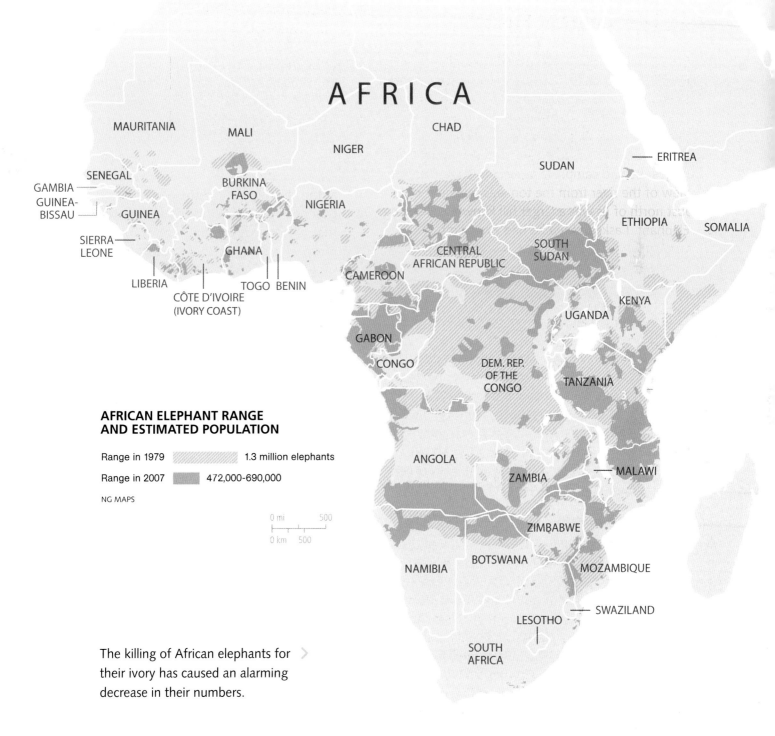

AFRICA

MAURITANIA
MALI
NIGER
CHAD
SENEGAL
GAMBIA
GUINEA-BISSAU
GUINEA
BURKINA FASO
NIGERIA
SUDAN
ERITREA
SIERRA LEONE
GHANA
ETHIOPIA
SOMALIA
LIBERIA
CÔTE D'IVOIRE (IVORY COAST)
TOGO
BENIN
CENTRAL AFRICAN REPUBLIC
SOUTH SUDAN
CAMEROON
GABON
CONGO
DEM. REP. OF THE CONGO
UGANDA
KENYA
TANZANIA
ANGOLA
MALAWI
ZAMBIA
ZIMBABWE
NAMIBIA
BOTSWANA
MOZAMBIQUE
SWAZILAND
LESOTHO
SOUTH AFRICA

AFRICAN ELEPHANT RANGE AND ESTIMATED POPULATION

Range in 1979 — 1.3 million elephants

Range in 2007 — 472,000–690,000

NG MAPS

0 mi 500
0 km 500

The killing of African elephants for their ivory has caused an alarming decrease in their numbers.

Biologist Iain Douglas-Hamilton conducts an aerial survey of Samburu National Reserve, Kenya

80 behavior (which includes where they go and
how long they stay there) using a radio tracking
system. He also became the first elephant
researcher to focus closely on living individual
animals, not just trends within populations or
85 the analysis of dead animals. He got to know
individual elephants and their personalities, gave
them names, and watched their social interactions.

Then came the difficult years of the late 1970s
and '80s, when Douglas-Hamilton sounded the
90 alarm against the widespread killing of African
elephants. The killing was driven by a sudden
sharp rise in the price of ivory⁶ and made easy by
the widespread availability of automatic **weapons**.
Douglas-Hamilton calculated elephant losses
95 throughout Africa at somewhere above 100,000
animals annually. He decided to do something.

With funding from several conservation NGOs,⁷
Douglas-Hamilton organized an immensely
ambitious survey of elephant populations
100 throughout the continent. From the results,

compiled in 1979, he figured that Africa then
contained about 1.3 million elephants, but that
the number was declining at too fast a rate. Some
experts in the field disagreed, and struggle between
105 the two sides over elephant conservation policy in
the 1980s became known as the Ivory Wars.

Douglas-Hamilton spent years investigating the
status of elephant populations in Zaire, South
Africa, Gabon, and elsewhere, both up in his
110 airplane and on the ground. He flew into Uganda
during the **chaos** that followed the **collapse** of
the government of the time and saw the bodies of
slaughtered⁸ elephants all over the national parks.
"It was a dreadful time. I really spent a terrible 20
115 years doing that," he says now. However, his work
helped greatly to support the 1989 decision under
the Convention on International Trade in Endangered
Species to **abolish** the international sale of ivory.

---

6 **Ivory** is a hard, cream-colored substance that forms the
tusks of elephants.
7 An **NGO** (non-governmental organization) is an organization
that is not run by the government.
8 If large numbers of people or animals are **slaughtered**, they
are killed in a way that is cruel or unnecessary.

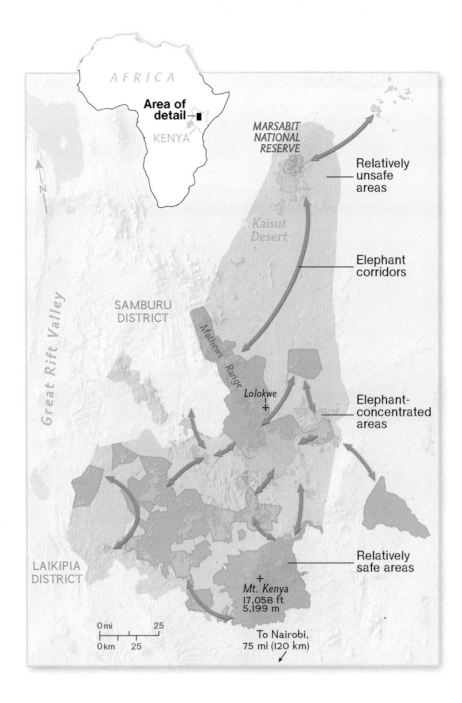

The orange arrows show the movement of elephant herds in Samburu National Reserve, Kenya.

In 1997, Douglas-Hamilton came to Samburu
120 National Reserve in Kenya. By that time, he had established his own research and conservation organization, Save the Elephants. Today, he divides his time between teaching a new generation of elephantologists and studying the
125 movement of elephants using global positioning system (GPS) technology. The data he acquires from elephants wearing GPS collars[9] is used by the Kenya Wildlife Service to provide better wildlife-management and land-protection advice
130 to the government. Save the Elephants now has GPS tracking projects not just in Kenya but also in Mali, South Africa, and the Democratic Republic of the Congo.

Following the attack outside his camp, Douglas-
135 Hamilton was able, using his equipment, to identify the elephant that threatened him as Diana, one of the females from a herd he had been tracking for some time. Diana was just like any other elephant—sensitive, unpredictable,
140 and complex. Although her behavior on that afternoon had been violent, at the last moment she had made a choice. And not even Iain Douglas-Hamilton, with all his modern equipment and years of experience, can know exactly why
145 she attacked him—or why she let him live.

9 A **collar** is a band of leather or plastic that is put around the neck of an animal.

Reading Comprehension

Multiple Choice. Choose the best answer for each question.

Inference

1. Why did Douglas-Hamilton have *a mischievous look in his eye* when he agreed to go walking with the author (lines 16–17)?
   a. He knew that it must be a dangerous thing to do.
   b. He was really supposed to be finishing his work.
   c. He had a surprise planned for the author.
   d. He thought the author was afraid of elephants.

Cohesion

2. The following sentence would best be placed at the end of which paragraph? *Trumpeting loudly, she charged.*
   a. paragraph 1 (starting line 6)
   b. paragraph 2 (starting line 18)
   c. paragraph 3 (starting line 29)
   d. paragraph 4 (starting line 44)

Vocabulary

3. In line 33, what does *thought better of it* mean?
   a. decided not to do what he had intended
   b. decided it was better to do what he had intended
   c. decided not to change other people's intentions
   d. decided that he should think more about it before doing it

Paraphrase

4. Which of the following is closest to Douglas-Hamilton's meaning when he said, "Science for me was a passport to the bush" in lines 70–71?
   a. My scientific education took place mostly in the bush.
   b. I took a trip to the bush to study science.
   c. The reason I studied science was to be able to work in the bush.
   d. In my opinion, science can be good preparation for the bush.

Detail

5. Douglas-Hamilton was the first elephantologist to _____.
   a. track elephants with an airplane
   b. study trends in elephant populations
   c. get to know individual elephants
   d. analyze the bodies of dead elephants

Cause and Effect

6. What cause of elephant population decline does the writer mention?
   a. the lifting of the ban on ivory sales
   b. the widespread availability of automatic weapons
   c. a decrease in the amount of funding for conservation NGOs
   d. the spread of disease among elephant populations

Detail

7. What is the name of Douglas-Hamilton's own research and conservation organization?
   a. Ivory Wars
   b. Kenya Wildlife Service
   c. Samburu National Reserve
   d. Save the Elephants

Critical Thinking

Analyzing: Why do you think Douglas-Hamilton's work is funded by conservation NGOs and not by local governments in Africa?

Discussion: Do you think, if elephant populations continue to rise, that people should be allowed to buy ivory again? Why or why not?

Reading Skill

Sequencing Information

When you sequence information, you put things in the order in which they occur. Knowing the order of key events will help you clearly see what happens first, second, third, etc., and any cause/effect relationships. Sequencing information is especially useful for stories or biographical texts. As you read, you can list events, note events on a timeline, or write a short summary.

A. Sequencing. Two events in this summary are not in the correct order. Look back at the section "An Encounter at Sunset" to check. Then underline the two sentences here and draw arrows to the correct places.

Biologist Iain Douglas-Hamilton, author David Quammen, and local guide Mwaniki decided to go for a walk late one afternoon. They walked toward Sleeping Elephant, a large hill. After about five minutes, they saw a female elephant with two babies. They stopped to look and then continued to walk. Soon after, they looked up to see the elephant staring at them angrily. Quammen and Mwaniki turned and ran. Douglas-Hamilton ran as well, but then turned back and threw his arms in the air, yelling. Mwaniki continued to run to camp to get help. The elephant didn't stop. Douglas-Hamilton turned around and ran. The elephant tried to stab him with her tusks, but missed. The elephant lifted him up and threw him to the ground. The elephant backed off and went to look for her babies. Douglas-Hamilton thought he might die. Quammen went to check to see if he was alive. People then arrived from the camp.

B. Sequencing. Scan for years and other time references in the section "Saving the Elephants." Then number the events (**1–6**) in the order in which they happened.

_____ **a.** The international sale of ivory was abolished.

_____ **b.** Douglas-Hamilton did the first serious study of elephant social structure.

_____ **c.** Douglas-Hamilton went to Samburu National Reserve in Kenya where he began studying elephant movements using GPS technology.

_____ **d.** The results of Douglas-Hamilton's elephant population survey were compiled, leading to the so-called Ivory Wars.

_____ **e.** Douglas-Hamilton went to Lake Manyara National Park in Tanzania as a research volunteer.

_____ **f.** Douglas-Hamilton organized a survey of elephant populations throughout Africa.

Vocabulary Practice

A. Completion. Complete the information using the correct form of words from the box. Five words are extra.

abolish	agitated	chaos	collapse	compile
evade	genuine	instinct	weapon	withdraw

Hunting and habitat destruction have forced the roughly 900 remaining mountain gorillas in the Democratic Republic of the Congo to **1.** _____ to just a few protected areas. Virunga National Park is one such area. Unfortunately, even there they aren't safe. On July 22, 2007, several people armed with automatic **2.** _____ killed a mountain gorilla family in Virunga. The largest male of the family, a 230-kilogram (500-pound) gorilla named Senkwekwe, probably smelled the killers coming near. As he was used to seeing many park visitors, he is unlikely to have been very **3.** _____. However, this was the last time he would see a human.

The gorillas weren't killed for their meat; their bodies were simply left on the ground. Finding the killers was difficult, as men with guns are a common sight in the country. Fortunately, the person who may have ordered the killings was not able to **4.** _____ the police. The chief warden of Virunga National Park at the time of the killings was arrested. The warden was reportedly connected to illegal charcoal production in the park. In Virunga, trees are illegally cut down to produce charcoal, an important and valuable fuel. Park rangers are frequently killed in their efforts to **5.** _____ this illegal trade. It is thought that the warden had the gorillas killed to damage the reputation of a ranger who was challenging the charcoal producers.

A mountain gorilla at the Virunga National Park, Congo

B. Definitions. Match the words from the box in **A** with their definitions.

1. _____ : very worried or upset
2. _____ : not false, real
3. _____ : complete disorder and confusion
4. _____ : to pull back, move back, or remove
5. _____ : to put an end to
6. _____ : to avoid or escape
7. _____ : to fall down or stop working
8. _____ : natural behavior or reaction
9. _____ : to collect and put together many pieces of information

> **Word Partnership**
> Use **chaos** with: (v.) **bring** chaos, **cause** chaos; (adj.) **complete** chaos, **total** chaos.

VIEWING A Match Made in Africa

Before You Watch

A. Words in Context. These words are from the video. Complete each sentence with the correct answer.

1. If you are an **orphan**, your parents are _____.

   a. rich   b. dead

2. **Formula** is something a _____ would drink.

   a. baby   b. teenager

3. A **dart** is a small object with a _____ on one end.

   a. sharp point   b. dull blade

4. A **dehydrated** person needs _____.

   a. food   b. water

5. When you **adopt** an animal, you _____.

   a. care for it   b. give it away

B. Discussion. Look at the picture of an elephant and a sheep. Why do you think they became friends? Discuss with a partner.

∧ An elephant and a sheep form an unlikely bond at a game reserve.

While You Watch

A. Sequencing. As you watch the video, number the events **1–10** in the order they happened.

- ☐ The rescue team shot a dart at the elephant.
- ☐ The elephant met a sheep.
- ☐ The elephant drank water, but not formula.
- ☑ 7 The baby elephant was orphaned.
- ☐ The rescue team took the elephant to a game reserve.
- ☐ The elephant and the sheep took walks together.
- ☐ The staff named the elephant.
- ☐ The elephant became calm and comfortable with the sheep.
- ☐ The elephant began to drink milk.
- ☑ 6 The elephant charged, causing the sheep to hide.

B. Completion. Circle the correct word to complete each caption.

1. When a baby is darted, other elephants become (**sad** / **protective** / **frightened**).

2. At the reserve, the baby elephant refuses to (**eat food** / **drink milk** / **sleep**).

3. When they first meet, the elephant and sheep (**become fast friends** / **hurt each other** / **don't get along**).

4. The staff names the elephant Themba, which means (**"inseparable"** / **"survivor"** / **"hope"**).

After You Watch

A. Discussion. Discuss these questions with a partner.

1. Why do you think Themba and Albert became friends?

2. Here are some other animals that have become friends. Which pairing is the most unusual to you? Why?

a giraffe and an ostrich	**a hippo and a tortoise**	**a dog and an owl**
a bear and a lion	**a dog and a cheetah**	**a cat and a fox**
a rabbit and a deer	**a tiger and a chimp**	**a dog and an elephant**

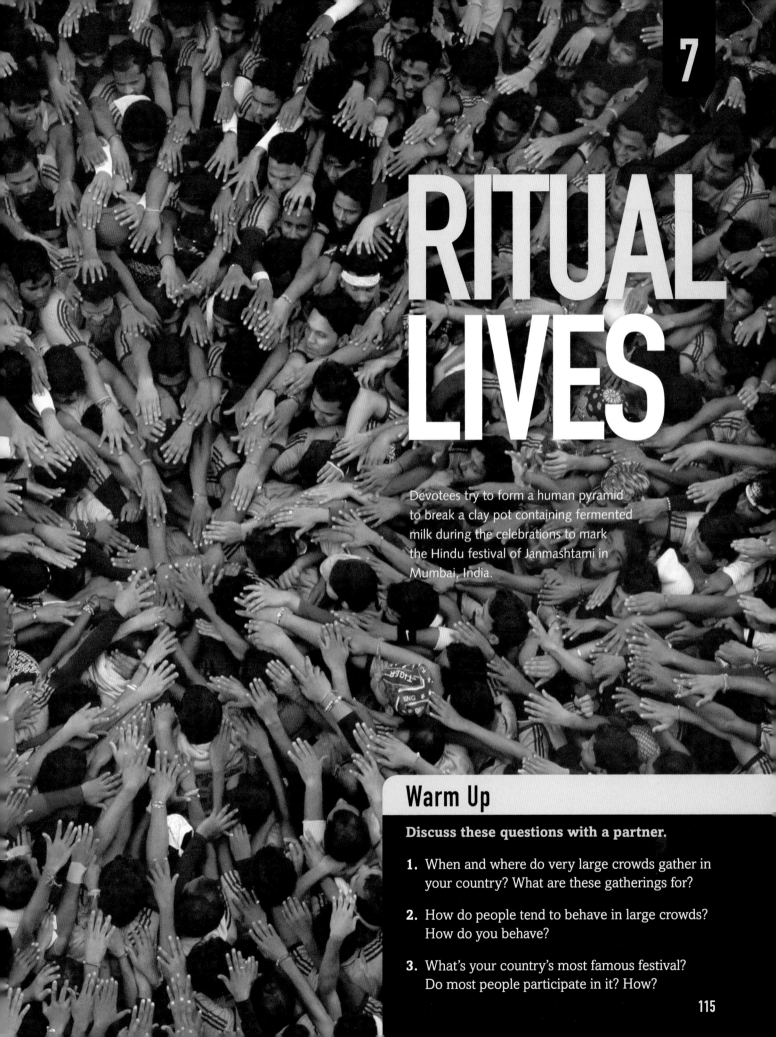

7

RITUAL LIVES

Devotees try to form a human pyramid to break a clay pot containing fermented milk during the celebrations to mark the Hindu festival of Janmashtami in Mumbai, India.

Warm Up

Discuss these questions with a partner.

1. When and where do very large crowds gather in your country? What are these gatherings for?

2. How do people tend to behave in large crowds? How do you behave?

3. What's your country's most famous festival? Do most people participate in it? How?

Before You Read

A. Completion. Look at the photo and read the caption. Then complete the sentences below using the words in **bold**.

1. When a large group of people or animals run together in a wild and uncontrolled way to escape from something, it is called a(n) _____.

2. _____ are people who make a journey to a holy place for religious reasons.

3. If you _____ in a sea, river, or lake, you swim, play, or wash yourself in it.

4. A(n) _____ place has too many things or people in it.

B. Scan. Quickly scan the reading on pages 117–118 to match each person with a description (**a–c**). Then read the whole passage.

1. _____ Rahul Mehrotra   **a.** a psychologist from the University of St. Andrews

2. _____ Stephen Reicher   **b.** a professor of urban design and planning

3. _____ Nick Hopkins   **c.** a psychologist from the University of Dundee

During the Kumbh Mela festival, tens of millions of **pilgrims** gather at the Ganges River to **bathe** in its waters. The crowds are carefully managed to avoid a **stampede**. In spite of polluted water and cold, **overcrowded** conditions, pilgrims report returning home healthier than they came.

A CROWD IN HARMONY

1   **IT IS BEFORE DAWN** on the second major bathing day of the festival, and fog covers the river. Tens of millions of people will bathe in the River Ganges here in Allahabad, India, in a single
5   day. In the moonlight, the crowd grows on the riverbank. There are thousands here already, but this crowd is calm and united. There is no pushing or panic, only a sense of purpose as they enter the icy water to bathe and come out
10   again. People cooperate and help one another. Afterward, they are joyful.

As the day **progresses**, the number of people wading into the river increases. Some splash in the water, some drop flowers into it, and
15   others light oil lamps and set them floating on the river. There are men who splash into the water theatrically with swords[1] in hand. There are unwilling children whose parents drag them into the water fully clothed. There are holy men
20   dressed in bright orange robes with skin covered in **sacred** white ash. There are other holy men wearing the ash but little or no clothing, as their religion requires. There are people everywhere, but somehow, incredibly, no one is
25   stepped on, no one is drowned, and no one is heard screaming for help. All is **harmony**.

It is the Kumbh Mela, the largest and most sacred gathering of all Hindu pilgrimages. It is also considered to be the largest peaceful
30   gathering of people anywhere in the world. Each year, several million Hindus bathe here in the sacred River Ganges. Every 12 years, the gathering becomes much larger, and a giant tent city is set up to house participants
35   during the festival. In 2013, the Kumbh lasted 55 days, and it is estimated that 70 million pilgrims participated in activities such as ritual bathing, praying, singing, feeding the poor, and religious discussion.

---

1 A **sword** is a weapon with a long blade.

The Kumbh tent city covered more than 25 square kilometers (10 square miles). It was divided into 14 areas, each with its own hospital, police station, roads, grocery store, and supplies of electricity and drinking water—an extraordinary achievement. The basic crowd-control strategy was to avoid dangerous overcrowding at "hot spots" such as bridges and train stations. "Incredibly well **organized**, incredibly clean, very efficiently run," said Rahul Mehrotra, a professor of urban design and planning at Harvard University, who observed the festival.

The Scientific Approach

Psychologists like Stephen Reicher from the University of St. Andrews in the U.K. **suspect** that crowds have a positive impact on the health of the individuals within them. "What our research shows is that, actually, crowds are critical to **society**," he says. "They help form our sense of who we are, they help form our relations to others—they even help determine our physical well-being."

Reicher and his colleagues came to this, the largest Hindu festival, to test the idea that crowds are beneficial and to confirm the healthful effects of the Kumbh on its participants. Before the start of the 2011 festival, his researchers went out into the Indian countryside to question a group of **prospective** pilgrims about their mental and physical health. They also questioned people who didn't plan to attend. The researchers returned to question both groups a month after the Kumbh had ended. Those who stayed in their villages reported no real change over the period of the study. The pilgrims, on the other hand, reported a 10 percent improvement in their health, including less pain, less anxiety, and higher energy levels. What's more, the good effects lasted long afterward.

Why should belonging to a crowd improve your health? The psychologists think shared identity is the cause. "You think in terms of 'we' rather than 'I,'" explains Nick Hopkins, a colleague of Reicher's from the University of Dundee in the U.K. This way of thinking alters human relationships. Members of the crowd support one another, competition becomes cooperation, and people are able to achieve their goals in a way they wouldn't be able to alone.

The Power of Crowds

Unfortunately, in spite of the mutual support so **evident** elsewhere at the Kumbh, on February 10, 2013, 36 people died in a stampede at the train station. Somehow the crowd had lost its harmony. Reicher wrote that one possible cause was that the pilgrims no longer formed a psychological crowd. They no longer saw those around them as fellow pilgrims, but rather as competitors for seats on a train.

Strangely, before this unfortunate incident, Reicher had interviewed a pilgrim who was asked to describe the feeling in the crowd at the station. "People think they are more powerful than you, they can push you around," she said. She was then asked to describe the feeling in the Kumbh: "People are concerned about you. They treat you in a polite manner." The stampede was an example of what can happen when the psychological cooperation of a crowd breaks down.

Incidents such as the stampede are rare at the Kumbh, and this one is unlikely to **dissuade** pilgrims from attending the event in the future. The police will undoubtedly learn from this experience and make the station safer. But in crowds as large as those at the Kumbh, individuals must put their **faith** in the power of "psychological cooperation," as Stephen Reicher calls it. In other words, "Love thy[2] neighbor." One day, it could even save your life.

---

2 **Thy** is an old-fashioned word meaning *your*.

A man immerses himself in the waters of the Ganges River.

SOME OF THE LARGEST PEACEFUL GATHERINGS IN HISTORY

Estimated Number of People	Gathering	Location	Year
30 million*	Kumbh Mela	Allahabad, India	2013
20 million	Imam Husayn Shrine	Karbala, Iraq	2013
15 million	Funeral of Annadurai	Tamil Nadu, India	1969
5–9 million	Funeral of Ayatollah Khomeini	Tehran, Iran	1989
5 million	World Youth Day	Manila, the Philippines	1995
5 million	Funeral of President Nasser	Cairo, Egypt	1970
4.2 million	Rod Stewart concert	Rio de Janeiro, Brazil	1996
4 million	Funeral of Umm Kulthum	Cairo, Egypt	1975
3.16 million	Hajj pilgrimage	Mecca, Saudi Arabia	2012
3 million	Coronation of Queen Elizabeth II	London, United Kingdom	1953

* 30 million gathered on a single day. A total of 70 million people gathered at the Kumbh Mela over a period of 55 days.

Reading Comprehension

Multiple Choice. Choose the best answer for each question.

Purpose
1. What is the purpose of the first two paragraphs?
   a. to explain why Hindus are religious
   b. to describe a typical day in Allahabad, India
   c. to describe the calm atmosphere of a religious gathering
   d. to explain how people travel to a major festival

Detail
2. Which of these statements does NOT describe the Kumbh Mela?
   a. the most sacred of all the Hindu pilgrimages
   b. the largest peaceful gathering of people in the world
   c. a festival that involves people bathing together in a river
   d. an event that happens only once every 12 years

Paraphrase
3. What's another way of saying *crowds are critical to society* (lines 58–59)?
   a. It's good for crowds to criticize societies.
   b. Society determines the safety of crowds.
   c. Crowds are an important part of society.
   d. Crowds can be a disadvantage in any society.

Vocabulary
4. What does *What's more* mean in line 78?
   a. In addition
   b. Likewise
   c. To illustrate
   d. In any event

Detail
5. Why did Stephen Reicher and his colleagues attend the Kumbh Mela?
   a. to test their theory that crowds are beneficial to society
   b. in the hopes of gaining a sense of peace and harmony
   c. to see how long their own positive mental attitude would last
   d. to confirm their idea that people in the countryside live happier lives

Cause and Effect
6. According to Nick Hopkins, how does "shared identity" affect human relationships?
   a. It turns cooperation into competition.
   b. Individuals in a crowd no longer think about the crowd.
   c. People become much more religious than they were before.
   d. People achieve more together than they could alone.

Cause and Effect
7. What does Reicher think might be the reason there was a stampede?
   a. There weren't enough seats on the train.
   b. The people didn't form a psychological crowd.
   c. There were too many people on the train.
   d. Some pilgrims couldn't get into the Kumbh Mela.

Critical Thinking

Interpreting: Some sporting events with large crowds have become violent. How do you think the researchers would account for this?

Discussion: How do you feel when you are in a large crowd? Do you think being in a large crowd could improve your health?

Understanding Words from Context

It's important to keep reading even when you come across unfamiliar words. You can sometimes guess the meaning of a word you don't know by looking at the words around it—the word's context. First, determine the word's part of speech, and then look to see if there are synonyms, antonyms, or examples that can help you determine its meaning.

In the sentence below, we may not know the adjective *sacred* and the noun *pilgrims*. However, we can guess that *sacred* means special in some way, and that a *pilgrim* is someone who does something for religious reasons.

The water of the Ganges is **sacred** *to members of the Hindu religion, and tens of millions of* **pilgrims** *come to bathe here during the festival.*

A. Scan. Scan the first two paragraphs of the reading on page 117. Find the **bold** words below and underline them.

B. Multiple Choice. Use the context in the reading to decide the word or phrase that is closest in meaning to each word.

1. **united**
   a. working separately
   b. together as one
   c. unafraid of others

2. **panic**
   a. extreme fear
   b. extreme tiredness
   c. extreme calmness

3. **cooperate**
   a. talk a lot
   b. work together
   c. stay away from others

4. **joyful**
   a. very clean
   b. very happy
   c. very helpful

5. **wading**
   a. walking through water
   b. drinking water
   c. removing water

6. **splash**
   a. shout loudly
   b. drink happily
   c. cause water to move messily

7. **drag**
   a. move quietly
   b. push easily
   c. pull with difficulty

8. **holy**
   a. angry
   b. ordinary
   c. religious

9. **robes**
   a. short, dark hair
   b. long, loose clothing
   c. large, colorful flowers

Vocabulary Practice

A. Completion. Complete the information using the correct form of words from the box. Two words are extra.

faith	harmony	organized
prospective	sacred	suspect

More and more, people are flocking to religious sites on and off the beaten path. Religious tourism, also known as
1. "_____ tourism," is a fast-growing industry that produces an estimated 18 billion dollars in revenue a year. People go on faith-based trips for a variety of reasons, whether as individuals, small groups, or larger **2.** _____ tours. Some go on pilgrimages. Others go as leisure travelers to view the customs and rituals of a faith and culture that aren't their own. Some of the most famous places to visit include the **3.** _____ cities of Mecca, Jerusalem, Varanasi, and Karbala. Other popular sites include Fatima, Portugal; Shikoku, Japan; and Lourdes, France.

Countries that receive large numbers of faith tourists expect the numbers will continue to rise. In India and Saudi Arabia, for example, hotel chains are building for the expected increase in visitors. North American tour companies now directly target
4. _____ religious travelers. Rising incomes, lower travel costs, and a desire to find journeys with a purpose are fueling an increase across different faiths—both in traditional sites and lesser-known spots.

⌃ The Basilica of Fatima is an important pilgrimage site in Portugal.

B. Words in Context. Complete each sentence with the correct answer.

1. When a group of people **progress**, they _____.
   a. stop completely   b. move forward

2. If someone's intentions are **evident**, they are _____.
   a. clear   b. unknown

3. **Society** refers to _____ who share common laws, traditions and values.
   a. a community   b. a tribe

4. If you're trying to **dissuade** someone, you're trying to convince the person _____ something.
   a. to do   b. not to do

5. Things that are in **harmony** _____ with one another.
   a. go well   b. don't go well

6. If you **suspect** something, you _____ it is probably true.
   a. don't believe   b. believe

> **Word Link**
> The word root **gress** means "to step," or "to move from one level to another," e.g., *progress, digress, transgress, regress, aggressive.*

WHY WE CELEBRATE

Before You Read

A. Scanning. Scan the text and photos on pages 123–127 and match the photographers (**1–5**) to the image descriptions (**a–e**).

1. _____ Reza   **a.** music festival to raise funds
2. _____ Joel Sartore   **b.** a traditional dance ritual
3. _____ Chris Johns   **c.** people in fancy costumes and masks
4. _____ Sam Abell   **d.** a religious pilgrimage
5. _____ Jason Edwards **e.** carnival rides and booths

Reza's photograph of Muslim pilgrims surrounding the Ka'aba in the Al-Haram mosque in Mecca, Saudi Arabia

B. Predict. Historically, what reasons do you think first caused humans to gather in public and celebrate? With a partner, discuss your ideas. Then read the passage and check your ideas.

Chris Johns' photograph of Makishi dancers performing before a group of boys in a ritual that celebrates their progression into adulthood

Celebrating Humanity

Celebrations, after the pattern of Thomas Alva Edison's famous quote,[1] often appear to be one percent inspiration and 99 percent preparation. People around the world take celebrating seriously, and many of them are willing to go to great effort and expense to plan and participate in public celebrations.

Exactly when and where human beings began coming together in public to celebrate as a group is unknown and unknowable. **Logic** suggests that the first public celebrations were related to the patterns of existence and probably **spiritual**. Chris Johns' photograph of Makishi dancers in Zambia (above) is a **glimpse** of a celebration little changed since prehistoric times. In hunter-gatherer societies,[2] success in the never-ending search for food, clothing, and **shelter** must have triggered the need to celebrate together.

A hunt producing plenty of meat and skins, a good **harvest**, or the discovery of an easily-defended place to live were all events that ensured a group's survival and well-being. The earliest parades may have been processions[3] of successful hunters returning to a joyful welcome by their thankful families. As civilizations developed, with agriculture, cities and towns, trade, social and political structures, organized religions, calendars, and record-keeping, such celebrations became more regular and formal and served a broader social purpose.

There are records of religious parades and processions dating back to 3000 B.C. Parades were also used to demonstrate military power and celebrate military victories; to attract customers

---

1 Edison said, "Genius is one percent inspiration and 99 percent perspiration."
2 **Hunter-gatherer** societies obtain their food from wild plants and animals.
3 A **procession** is a group of people walking, riding, or driving in a line as part of a public event.

Joel Sartore's photograph of carnival rides at the Kansas State Fair

to events such as the circus[4] by giving the public a sample of the entertainment; or to celebrate ethnic affiliation[5] and holidays. The *New York Times* of October 28, 1917, summed it up by
40 saying, "If you take the parades out of history, you have precious little history left."

Parades and other public celebrations have also become important economic events in many places around the world. At the Kansas
45 State Fair in Hutchinson, where Joel Sartore's photograph (above) makes the carnival rides spin like neon tornadoes, or at the month-long Kumbh Mela festival in India, money is being made.

50 In some places, the **commercial** aspect has made us forget the original reason for the celebration. Carnival celebrations in Venice, Italy, date back to the late 13th century, when the Senate of the Venetian Republic declared a new
55 public holiday. It was a festival on the day before the **solemn** six-week religious period known as Lent. The official celebrations were held in large, public spaces. The unofficial celebrations, which involved people in masks partying all
60 over the city, grew in popularity over the next five centuries until the republic was conquered in 1797. After that, Carnival nearly disappeared for over a century.

In the current version of Carnival, hundreds of
65 thousands of visitors attend the celebrations in Venice. Most of the city's **inhabitants** avoid the official celebrations, as well as the unofficial ones in the city squares, canals, sidewalks, and bridges. They leave these areas to the crowds
70 of tourists whose purchases of meals, lodgings, and Carnival masks bring great sums of money into the economy of the city and the region.

---

4 A **circus** is a traveling company of entertainers who often give performances under a large tent.
5 **Ethnic affiliation** means belonging to a group related by race or culture.

One cannot blame the tourists. They are attracted by Venice's unique and **undeniable** magic. Sam
75 Abell's photograph (above) captures both the commercial and traditional sides of Carnival. In it, two Carnival participants in costumes float like beautiful white ghosts in front of the Doge's Palace, just ahead of a woman in a pink winter
80 jacket, wearing a camera around her neck, who seems not at all impressed by the Carnival couple.

Religious celebrations take place year-round in mosques, synagogues, temples, cathedrals, churches, and homes all over the world. There are
85 pilgrimages each year in Asia, Europe, the Middle East, and South America. The Hajj, the pilgrimage to the city of Mecca made by Muslims, is the world's largest annual pilgrimage, made by three

million people each year. Reza's photograph of
90 thousands of people filling Mecca's Al-Haram mosque (page 123) gives a powerful sense of the extreme size and the constant motion of the Hajj.

Of course, many modern celebrations are not
95 connected to any religion. In the Internet era, electronic communication makes it possible to organize celebrations almost instantly. "Flash mobs," are a new way of gathering and celebrating. Planned online, they bring together
100 tens, hundreds, or thousands of individuals to perform some unusual or funny act in a public place. Flash mobs not only reflect the increased speed of communication but also a lighter attitude to celebration. No longer is public

^ Jason Edwards' photograph of a crowd gathering despite the rain to raise funds for wildfire relief in Melbourne, Australia

105 celebrating something necessarily linked to human survival, religion, or deep traditions.

This does not mean, however, that modern celebrations are not socially conscious.[6] Photographers such as Szilard Koszticsak and
110 Jason Edwards have managed to capture the commitment and passion of a celebration's organizers and participants. One **striking** image evoking community spirit is Edwards' photograph of crowds in Melbourne, Australia,
115 (above) gathering despite the rain for a music festival to raise funds for wildfire relief.

The level of civic engagement[7] caught by Koszticsak and Edwards with their cameras is a reminder of the time and effort people around
120 the world devote to celebrating, whether it is with family and friends at home or with tens of thousands of people crowded into a square or stadium. Throughout history, across countries and cultures, the experience of a heartfelt
125 celebration is always worth the often significant amount of time and money spent planning, preparing, organizing, and carrying out an event. The priority given to celebrating seems to put it alongside food, shelter, love, and freedom
130 as a fundamental need of humanity.

---

6 To be **socially conscious** means to feel a sense of responsibility regarding problems and injustice in society.

7 **Civic engagement** means working to make a positive change in one's community.

Reading Comprehension

Multiple Choice. Choose the best answer for each question.

<table>
<tr><td>Purpose</td><td>

1. What is the purpose of the first sentence in the first paragraph?
a. to show that Thomas Alva Edison was right
b. to illustrate how we continue to be inspired to celebrate
c. to emphasize that a great deal of preparation goes into celebrations
d. to imply that even with the best preparations, we don't know how to truly celebrate
</td></tr>
<tr><td>Fact or Theory</td><td>

2. Which of these statements about parades is a theory, but not a fact?
a. The earliest parades were hunter-gatherers returning from a successful hunt.
b. There are records of religious parades dating back to 3000 B.C.
c. Parades became more regular and formal as civilizations developed.
d. Parades have become an important way to make money for people around the world.
</td></tr>
<tr><td>Detail</td><td>

3. Why did Venice's Carnival nearly disappear for a hundred years?
a. The Venetian Republic was conquered.
b. It became too commercial for the people of Venice.
c. The Senate didn't approve of the partying that was taking place.
d. The religious period on which the festival was founded was no longer practiced.
</td></tr>
<tr><td>Main Idea</td><td>

4. What is the main idea of paragraph 9 (starting line 82)?
a. Three million people make the Hajj each year.
b. The most important type of celebration is the religious celebration.
c. Religious celebrations take place year-round and can be found all over the world.
d. It is important for Muslims to try and make the Hajj as part of their religion.
</td></tr>
<tr><td>Inference</td><td>

5. Which of these would describe a flash mob?
a. Four strangers meet at a concert and then decide to perform together in a public square.
b. Someone announces on social media a series of performances at their school.
c. An online group secretly plans and performs a dance in a crowded train station.
d. The number of people watching a street performer grows to several hundred.
</td></tr>
<tr><td>Inference</td><td>

6. Which of these statements would the author probably agree with?
a. We will soon learn who, where, and why humans first began to celebrate.
b. Celebrations are as important to humans as food, shelter, love, and freedom.
c. Celebrations, though important, are often not worth the time and money.
d. Modern celebrations are now just for fun, and sadly lack any social impact.
</td></tr>
<tr><td>Detail</td><td>

7. Which photographer's photo shows a modern, socially conscious gathering?
a. Joel Sartore
b. Chris Johns
c. Sam Abell
d. Jason Edwards
</td></tr>
</table>

Critical Thinking

Interpreting: In the fourth paragraph, the author sums up with the quote, "If you take the parades out of history, you have precious little history left." What is meant by this?

Discussion: Think of several celebrations and gatherings in your country. Using ideas from the reading, explain their purpose. What do you know about their origins?

Understanding Word Roots and Affixes

An English word can consist of a **root**, which contains the basic meaning of the word, and one or more **affixes**. Affixes are prefixes or suffixes that can be added to change a word's part of speech or its meaning. A word may have no affixes (*idea*), a prefix (*oversleep*) or a suffix (*powerful*), or both (*multicultural*). Building up your knowledge of affixes and the meanings of common word roots can greatly increase your vocabulary.

A. Classification. Work with a partner. Look at the words from the reading below. Write them in the correct column.

disappear	ensure	harvest	holiday
inhabitant	Internet	joyful	music
people	popularity	prehistoric	religious
spiritual	undeniable	unknowable	unknown

Prefix only	Suffix only	Both prefix and suffix	Neither prefix nor suffix

B. Matching. Look at these words that share a common word root. Underline the roots and match them to their meanings.

1. _____	century	centimeter	cents	**a.** carry
2. _____	bicycle	cyclone	cycle	**b.** new
3. _____	terminal	terminate	determine	**c.** hundred
4. _____	novice	renovate	novelty	**d.** write
5. _____	microphone	telephone	phonetics	**e.** circle
6. _____	export	portable	porter	**f.** sound
7. _____	inscribe	describe	scribble	**g.** end

Vocabulary Practice

A. Completion. Use the correct words to complete the information below.

Every fall, the **1. (inhabitants / shelters)** of Santa Fe, New Mexico, build Zozobra, a 15-meter (50-foot) ghostlike cloth and wooden puppet. Anyone with anxiety, worry, or sadness can write down their thoughts on pieces of paper and leave them in a box. These will be left at the feet of Zozobra, to be burned along with the puppet.

The Zozobra festival started in 1924 when local artist William Shuster came up with the idea. His puppet was inspired by the Holy Week celebrations of the Yaqui Indians in Mexico, who burned paper figures to rid their community of evil. Shuster came up with the name *Zozobra*, which means "anxiety" or "gloom" in Spanish.

Before Zozobra is lit on fire, people dance at his feet and his "death sentence" is **2. (solemnly / strikingly)** given. As he burns, firecrackers inside him explode. It is said that with him go all the anxiety and worries people had from the past year. It is **3. (logically / undeniably)** a very **4. (striking / glimpsing)** image—seeing Zozobra burn against the dark desert sky.

For some, the celebration is **5. (sheltering / spiritual)**. For others, it's a chance to socialize. For many, it's simply for fun. In any event, the celebration has become more **6. (commercial / harvested)** in recent years. More than 50,000 buy tickets to attend every year.

⌃ The burning of Old Man Gloom, also known as Zozobra, in Santa Fe, New Mexico, U.S.A.

B. Words in Context. Complete each sentence with the correct answer.

1. If you **glimpse** something, you _____ it for a very short time.
   a. hear   b. see

2. Someone would probably want to find **shelter** if _____.
   a. it were a beautiful day   b. it were raining hard

3. The **harvest** is the time of year when crops are _____.
   a. planted   b. gathered

4. If someone uses **logic** in their argument, they are being _____.
   a. reasonable   b. unreasonable

5. If something is **undeniable**, it is _____.
   a. certain   b. uncertain

> **Thesaurus striking**
> Also look up: (*adj.*)
> *impressive, distinct, stunning, eye-catching, breathtaking*

VIEWING Festival of Lights

Before You Watch

A. Matching. Here are some words you will hear in the video. Match the words with their definitions.

1. _____ adorn
2. _____ commemorate
3. _____ display
4. _____ garland
5. _____ lotus

    a. an arrangement of objects meant to decorate or advertise

    b. a type of flower that grows on the surface of water

    c. a ring that is made of flowers or leaves

    d. to make something attractive by adding something beautiful

    e. to do something in order to remember an important event

∧ The five-day Indian celebration of Diwali, or "festival of lights," is enjoyed by millions.

While You Watch

A. Noticing. Check (✓) the things that people do to celebrate Diwali, according to the video.

- ☐ create garlands of flowers
- ☐ visit temples with their families
- ☐ pick lotus flowers from their gardens
- ☐ dress up in nice outfits
- ☐ watch parades
- ☐ bathe in the river
- ☐ create pictures made of sand
- ☐ share food with neighbors
- ☐ go shopping
- ☐ watch fireworks

B. Correction. The captions below are not accurate. Use the information in the video to correct each caption.

1. Diwali has sometimes been compared to the holiday of New Year's Eve.

_____

_____

2. Diwali commemorates the forces of good over the forces of darkness.

_____

_____

3. Garlands of flowers are made to adorn people's bodies.

_____

_____

4. The lotus flower that people create on their doorways is a symbol of happiness.

_____

_____

After You Watch

A. Discussion. Discuss these questions with a partner.

1. What would you like about Diwali? Is there anything you wouldn't like?

2. What celebration in your culture is Diwali most similar to? In what ways?

3. Think of a holiday or festival that you celebrate. Has the way people celebrate it changed over the years? Has the way you celebrate changed? If so, in what way?

8

INVESTIGATIONS

A forensic officer dusts a door for fingerprints

Warm Up

Discuss these questions with a partner.

1. What kinds of technology do police use to solve or prevent crimes?

2. Should the police be able to put surveillance cameras in any public space?

3. Do you know of any mysterious deaths or unsolved crimes? What do you think happened?

Before You Read

A. Definitions. Read the caption. Use the correct forms of the words in **bold** to complete the sentences below.

1. If something, such as a chemical or disease, is
   _____ in something else, it exists within that thing.

2. _____ is a serious disease caused by the spread of abnormal body cells.

3. A _____ is someone who is kept in a
   _____ as a punishment or because they have
   been captured.

B. Predict. Scan the reading to find the five headings. Each heading suggests a possible reason for Napoleon's death. With a partner, discuss what kind of information might be contained in each section. Then read the passage and check your ideas.

⌃ After the Battle of Waterloo in 1815, the French Emperor Napoleon Bonaparte was sent as a **prisoner** to the island of St. Helena. In 1821, he died there and the cause of death was reported as stomach **cancer**. However, in 1961, an analysis of Napoleon's hair revealed the **presence** of arsenic—raising suspicions that he may have been poisoned.

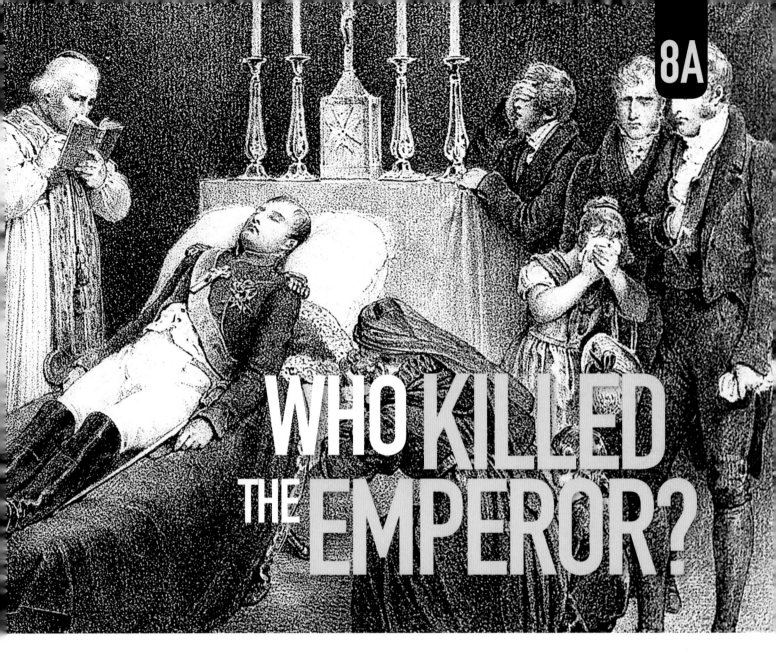

WHO KILLED THE EMPEROR?

1 **IT'S A STORY AS compelling** as any murder mystery. It begins
in 1821 on the remote British island of St. Helena in the South
Atlantic Ocean. This is where Napoleon Bonaparte—one-time
Emperor of France—is confined as a prisoner after losing his
5 final battle at Waterloo in 1815. In February 1821, Napoleon's
health reportedly begins to fail, and he dies three months later
at the age of 52. An autopsy[1] performed the next morning
reveals a stomach ulcer,[2] possibly cancerous.

The real cause of death, however, has been in **dispute**
10 ever since. Many are convinced that, in fact, Napoleon was
murdered. Historians, toxicologists,[3] doctors, and other experts,
as well as amateur investigators, have considered the question
of how and why he died, but so far they have not been able to
reach an agreement.

1 An **autopsy** is an
examination of a dead
body by a doctor who cuts
it open in order to try to
discover the cause of death.
2 An **ulcer** is a sore area on
the outside or inside of your
body that is very painful
and may bleed.
3 **Toxicologists** are scientists
who study poisons and
their effects.

Political Murder?

Ben Weider, founder of the International Napoleonic Society and head of a large body-building business based in Canada, is a **proponent** of the theory that Napoleon was poisoned with arsenic, a deadly chemical. Weider has **relentlessly** sought the cause of Napoleon's death for more than four decades and has put considerable resources into solving the mystery. In his view, Napoleon was poisoned by the British and by French royalists,[4] who wanted him out of the way once and for all.[5] Weider offers as the central point of his hypothesis the hair analysis done by Pascal Kintz, a French toxicologist at the Legal Medicine Institute of Strasbourg. Kintz subjected samples of Napoleon's hair to analysis and confirmed that it contained arsenic. While Kintz can't say exactly how or why the arsenic was there, Weider is convinced that "the poisoning of Napoleon was planned and deliberate."

Poisoned by His Wallpaper?

David Jones, an immunologist[6] at the University of Newcastle in England, has studied the walls at Longwood House, the building on St. Helena where Napoleon lived his last years. He found that the wallpaper was painted with a substance containing the deadly poison arsenic. According to Jones, conditions on the hot and humid island caused arsenic to be released into the air.

Then again, paint may not have been the only source of arsenic on St. Helena. Some toxicologists say that it is not uncommon for people who eat large amounts of seafood to have an unusually high level of arsenic in the blood. Because St. Helena is a small island 2,000 kilometers (1,200 miles) from the nearest mainland, it is likely that a large part of Napoleon's diet was comprised of seafood. Additionally, the doctors who examined Napoleon's body after his death didn't find any of the usual **symptoms** associated with arsenic poisoning, such as bleeding inside the heart.

Doctors' Mistake?

Steven Karch, an American heart disease expert, believes that Napoleon was killed by his own doctors. They gave him large doses of dangerous chemicals commonly used as medicine at the time. According to Karch's theory, the day before Napoleon's death, they gave him a massive amount of mercurous chloride, a chemical which was once given to patients with heart disease. That and other medications, Karch believes, **disrupted** Napoleon's heartbeat and resulted in his heart **ceasing** to beat. While Karch admits that arsenic exposure was a partial cause, he believes it was the doctors' errors that actually brought on the heart attack.

Disease?

Cancer and ulcers, as reported by doctors who examined the body, were the cause of Napoleon's death, believes Jean Tulard, the preeminent[7] Napoleon historian in France.

---

4 A **royalist** is someone who supports their country's royal family or who believes that their country should have a king or queen.

5 If something happens **once and for all**, it happens completely or finally.

6 An **immunologist** is a scientist who studies the body's immune system.

7 If someone is **preeminent** in a group, they are more important, or capable, than other people in the group.

< A piece of wallpaper from Napoleon's house

Napoleon Crossing the Alps, painted by French artist Jacques-Louis David

The house Napoleon lived in on St. Helena

Tulard remains unconvinced by Kintz's hair analysis. In his estimation, the hair that was
80 tested may not even have been Napoleon's. Tulard also discounts the poisoning theory on the grounds that no one has yet found anything linking the British or the French royalists—or anyone else for that matter—to any plot against
85 Napoleon's life. Still, doubts remain that cancer was one of the main causes. One cancer specialist believes that Napoleon probably didn't have advanced stomach cancer, because people with that disease always lose a lot of weight.
90 Napoleon, according to reports, had never lost any weight during his stay on St. Helena. In fact, he had gained a fair amount.

A Case of Revenge?

"One of my ancestors did it," says François
95 de Candé-Montholon. "I'm an aristocrat.[8] Aristocrats don't like revolution, and Napoleon made revolutions." Candé-Montholon's great-great-great-great grandfather, the Count of Montholon, was stationed with Napoleon on St.
100 Helena. Napoleon had a love affair—and fathered a child—with the count's wife. The count, it is observed, had control of Napoleon's wine cellar and food. Could he, motivated by revenge, have poisoned the wine?

105 "Everyone is right, and no one is right," says Paul Fornes of the Georges Pompidou Hospital in Paris. Fornes has reviewed the 1821 autopsy report and other historical records and concludes: "Napoleon may have died with cancer, but he didn't die of
110 cancer." Likewise, he says that although the hair analysis indicates the presence of arsenic, no one can say if he was intentionally given the arsenic, or if it killed him. In Fornes's opinion, evidence for murder by poisoning is **inconclusive** and
115 wouldn't hold up[9] in a court of law.

Napoleon Bonaparte's body was returned to France in 1840, and it has rested in a truly **grand** tomb in Paris ever since. Some think it is time to open the tomb and to examine the remains
120 using modern methods. French historian and doctor Jean-François Lemaire, however, believes that serious science and history have little to do with it anymore: "We are now in the world of entertainment," he says. It seems unlikely that
125 new facts will settle the issue—people just enjoy the mystery too much.

---

8 An **aristocrat** is someone whose family has a high social rank, especially someone who has a title.

9 If an argument or a theory **holds up**, it is true, even after close examination.

Reading Comprehension

Multiple Choice. Choose the best answer for each question.

Main Idea

1. What is the main idea of the reading?
   a. Napoleon was probably murdered by the British or the French.
   b. Napoleon died of either stomach ulcers or cancer.
   c. Depressed and in failing health, Napoleon killed himself.
   d. The cause of Napoleon's death is the center of a debate.

Detail

2. Which person strongly believes that Napoleon was murdered?
   a. Ben Weider
   b. Pascal Kintz
   c. Jean Tulard
   d. Paul Fornes

Cause and Effect

3. What caused the wallpaper at Napoleon's house to release arsenic into the air?
   a. a doctor spilling arsenic
   b. a new paint for the ceiling
   c. the hot and humid weather
   d. the removal of old wallpaper

Detail

4. Which of the following do both David Jones and Steven Karch believe?
   a. Napoleon's death was due to a medical mistake.
   b. Arsenic played a part in Napoleon's death.
   c. Napoleon's diet contributed to his death.
   d. The reasons for Napoleon's death cannot be explained.

Vocabulary

5. In line 72, what does *brought on* mean?
   a. led to
   b. prevented
   c. revealed
   d. cured

Inference

6. Why does François de Candé-Montholon seem proud that his ancestor murdered Napoleon?
   a. Because he has a personal dislike of Napoleon.
   b. Because by murdering Napoleon, his ancestor became an aristocrat.
   c. Because his ancestor had control of Napoleon's wine cellar and food.
   d. Because Napoleon caused revolutions and had wronged his family.

Detail

7. Which theory does Paul Fornes think is the least likely?
   a. Napoleon was accidentally poisoned by arsenic.
   b. Napoleon was accidentally killed by his doctors.
   c. Napoleon's death was due to cancer and ulcers.
   d. Napoleon was murdered.

Critical Thinking

Evaluating: Which of the theories do you think is the most likely? Why?

_____

Discussion: Some people want to open the tomb and examine Napoleon's remains using modern methods. Do you think this is a good idea?

Evaluating Theories

When a text presents one or more theories on a topic, it's important to evaluate them carefully. The reader needs to weigh any evidence to determine how well the evidence supports the theory. Questions to ask while reading include:
- What evidence supports the theory (facts, examples, expert opinions, etc.)?
- How well does the evidence support the theory?
- How credible are the sources of information?

A. **Multiple Choice.** Check (✓) all the evidence that supports each theory. You can have more than one answer.

1. Napoleon was poisoned with arsenic as an act of political murder.

   a. ☐ Literary sources describe how the British and French wanted Napoleon dead.

   b. ☐ Samples of Napoleon's hair showed it contained arsenic.

   c. ☐ A letter was found saying the poisoning of Napoleon was planned and deliberate.

2. Napoleon was accidentally poisoned by arsenic.

   a. ☐ The wallpaper of the building Napoleon lived in contained arsenic.

   b. ☐ Napoleon's diet probably consisted of large amounts of seafood, which contains arsenic.

   c. ☐ Doctors who examined Napoleon's body after his death didn't find the usual symptoms associated with arsenic poisoning.

3. Napoleon was accidentally killed by his doctors.

   a. ☐ Doctors gave Napoleon mercurous chloride the day before his death.

   b. ☐ Mercurous chloride and other chemicals caused Napoleon's heart to stop.

   c. ☐ Doctors admitted that they gave Napoleon too much arsenic.

4. Napoleon's death was due to cancer and ulcers.

   a. ☐ Doctors who examined Napoleon's body after his death found cancer and ulcers.

   b. ☐ Napoleon probably didn't have advanced cancer when he died.

   c. ☐ Napoleon had gained some weight on St. Helena.

5. Napoleon was poisoned as an act of revenge.

   a. ☐ An unfriendly aristocrat had control over Napoleon's wine.

   b. ☐ Napoleon was planning a new revolution while on St. Helena.

   c. ☐ Napoleon had a love affair with a count's wife.

B. **Discussion.** Work with a partner. How well does the evidence you checked in **A** support each theory?

Vocabulary Practice

A. Completion. Complete the information using the correct form of words from the box. One word is extra.

cease	compelling	dispute
inconclusive	proponent	symptom

Fugu, or puffer fish, is a delicacy in Japan, but it can also be deadly. The skin, liver, and other internal parts of the fish contain tetrodotoxin, a powerful toxin that causes nerves to **1.** _____ functioning properly. **2.** _____ of fugu poisoning include difficulty moving and breathing—eventually leading to death. There is no cure for *fugu* poisoning. You might think that this is a(n) **3.** _____ reason to stay away from this dangerous food, but *fugu* is in fact quite popular. *Fugu* chefs are strictly trained and must be licensed. Japan has also forbidden the public sale of *fugu* liver since 1983.

The source of the *fugu's* poison is a subject of **4.** _____. Some believe that *fugu* produce their own poison. However, Tamao Noguchi, a researcher at Nagasaki University, believes that the poison comes from the small animals that the fish eat. Noguchi has raised *fugu* in a laboratory, controlled their diet, and produced toxin-free fish. Noguchi is a(n) **5.** _____ of lifting the ban on *fugu* liver, and hopes his research will help. "A great delicacy; once you eat, you cannot stop," he says.

Fugu chef Kaneharu Koshima proudly poses with a masterfully created dish.

B. Words in Context. Complete each sentence with the correct answer.

1. A building described as **grand** is probably _____.
   a. large and impressive
   b. in need of repair

2. If a test for a poison is **inconclusive**, the poison _____ been found.
   a. has
   b. hasn't

3. You would probably feel _____ if someone **disrupted** your presentation.
   a. thrilled
   b. annoyed

4. An attack that is **relentless** _____.
   a. ends quickly
   b. goes on for a long time

5. A crime of **revenge** is carried out by someone who _____.
   a. has been wronged in some way
   b. is in great need of money

Usage In informal American English, one thousand dollars is sometimes referred to as a **grand**. The plural form doesn't require an *s*, e.g., **three grand**, **ten grand**.

IN THE LAB

Before You Read

A. Definitions. Read the information below and match the words in **bold** to their definitions.

> Alphonse Poklis (left) and Marcella Fierro (right)

The little poison dart frog (shown on page 143) is small enough to sit on your fingertip, but one frog has enough toxin to kill around two **dozen** people or a couple of elephants. The toxin works by attacking the nerves, causing **paralysis**. There is no known **antidote**, and death comes very quickly.

1. A(n) _____ is a group of 12 people or things.

2. A medicine or substance taken to stop the harmful effects of a poison is a(n) _____.

3. _____ is the condition where a person is unable to move or feel anything in parts (or all) of his or her body.

> Red amanita mushrooms are mildly poisonous to humans. >

B. Match. Scan the first paragraph of the reading on page 143. Match the people below to the descriptions.

1. _____ Patricia Cornwell   **a.** medical examiner in Richmond, Virginia

2. _____ Alphonse Poklis   **b.** writer of crime novels

3. _____ Marcella Fierro   **c.** director of toxicology at VCU

WITH MARCELLA AND ALPHONSE

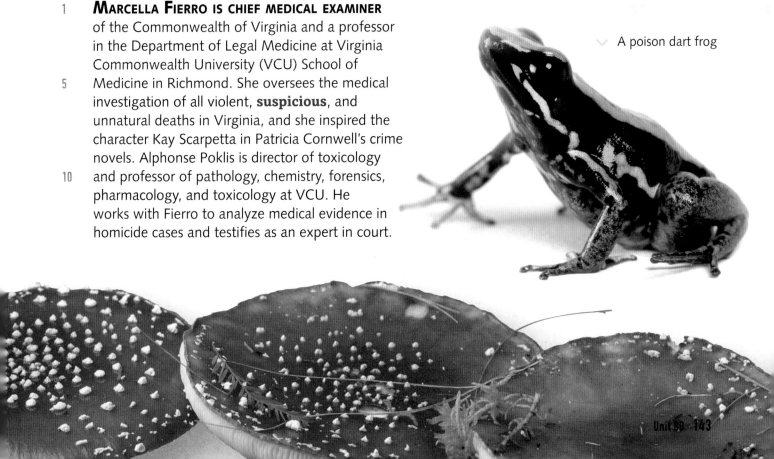

1   **MARCELLA FIERRO IS CHIEF MEDICAL EXAMINER** of the Commonwealth of Virginia and a professor in the Department of Legal Medicine at Virginia Commonwealth University (VCU) School of
5   Medicine in Richmond. She oversees the medical investigation of all violent, **suspicious**, and unnatural deaths in Virginia, and she inspired the character Kay Scarpetta in Patricia Cornwell's crime novels. Alphonse Poklis is director of toxicology
10 and professor of pathology, chemistry, forensics, pharmacology, and toxicology at VCU. He works with Fierro to analyze medical evidence in homicide cases and testifies as an expert in court.

A poison dart frog

National Geographic: At what point do you get called in?

Marcella Fierro: We see any death that is sudden, unexpected, violent, or where there is **allegation** of foul play. If we have the body before it's in the ground, we deal with it. But often it takes time for an allegation to be made or for someone to believe it. Perhaps a family member has a **motive**: There's dissension[1] about property, inheritance, a new wife, a child not getting a fair share. Those things set a chain of events into motion. The body has to be exhumed.

NG: Then what? How do you proceed?

MF: I take umpteen tissue samples at autopsy: heart, liver, lungs, brain, spleen, hair, nails. Blood tells you what was going on in the body at the time of death. Vitreous humor[2] from the eye is great. It's clean. No fermentation[3] or contamination from bacteria. Al and I work together. What poisons are **candidates**? What's best to collect? You have to have a strategy.

---

1 A difference of opinion can be the cause of **dissension** between people.
2 The **vitreous humor** is the transparent, jellylike tissue that fills the eyeball, behind the lens.
3 Bacteria and yeast break down complex molecules through a process called **fermentation**.

We'd want to know what poison the defendant would have access to. If it's a farmer, we look for agricultural things like pesticides[4] or herbicides. We need to have an idea of where we are going. We can easily run out of tissue and blood samples before we run out of tests to do.

NG: So the technology you use to detect poisons in a corpse must be pretty sophisticated?

Alphonse Poklis: Very. I call it the vanishing zero. In the 1960s, it took 25 milliliters of blood to detect morphine. Today, we can use one milliliter to do the same work. **In terms of** sensitivity, we've gone from micrograms to nanograms,[5] which is parts per billion, to parts per trillion with mass spectrometry. You can find anything if you do the research. Of course some substances are more apparent. You can smell cyanide the minute you open a body at autopsy. Cyanide works fast—like in movies where the captured spy bites on the capsule[6] and dies. It's a chemical **suffocation**; cyanide hits the mitochondria[7] in the cells, and every cell is **deprived of** oxygen. You die quickly, dramatically, violently.

---

4 **Pesticides** are chemicals that are used to kill insects.
5 A **nanogram** is one billionth of a gram.
6 A **capsule** is a small case that contains a substance.
7 **Mitochondria** produce energy that is needed by cells in the body to function.

TERMINOLOGY

Pathology: the study of organs, tissues, and bodily fluids to diagnose diseases

Forensics: scientific tests or techniques that are used to investigate crimes

Exhume: to dig out (something buried, usually a corpse) from the ground.

Corpse: a dead body, usually of a human being rather than an animal (called a carcass)

Mass spectrometry: an instrument to measure the mass and concentration of atoms and molecules

Morphine: a drug that is obtained from the opium poppy plant and is used medicinally to relieve pain

Cyanide: a poisonous white powder that smells like almonds

Homicide: the killing of one person by another

Pharmacology: the study of how drugs work, including their uses, and effects

Toxicity: the degree to which a substance can affect an organism

NG: Is there a personality profile specific to poisoners?

60 **AP:** The poisoner tries to cover up what he or she does. Poison is the weapon of controlling, sneaky people with no conscience, no sorrow, no **remorse**. They are scary, **manipulative**; if you weren't convinced by the evidence, you wouldn't
65 believe they could do such a thing.

NG: A case that sticks in your mind?

MF: There was this fellow at the University of Virginia Hospital. Kept getting admitted for weird gastrointestinal[8] complaints. The doctors
70 were twisting themselves inside out to figure it out. He'd get better; his wife would come in to see him in the hospital and bring him banana pudding. Someone finally ordered a heavy metals [toxicity test] on him, but he was discharged[9]
75 before the results came back—off the charts for arsenic. By the time someone saw the labs, it was too late. We called the wife Banana Pudding Lily.

NG: How many cases of suspected homicidal poisonings do you evaluate in the course
80 of a year?

AP: Frankly, relatively few. It's not in the American character. If you are going to kill someone and you are a true American, you shoot them. A real man doesn't sneak
85 around. In our culture everything is solved in 30 minutes, so you aren't going to plan, go someplace to get poison, and figure out "How am I going to give it?" In our culture, we act directly.

90 **NG:** You're the expert. If you had to design the perfect poison for murder, what would it be made of?

AP: I could think of a few things, but I'm not going to share them.

---

8 **Gastrointestinal** refers to anything related to the stomach or intestines.
9 If you are **discharged** from the hospital, you are sent home by the hospital.

Fierro's most memorable > case was a woman who poisoned her husband by putting arsenic in banana pudding.

Reading Comprehension

Multiple Choice. Choose the best answer for each question.

Detail **1.** What is the relationship between Marcella Fierro and Alphonse Poklis?
  a. They work together to analyze medical evidence in homicide cases.
  b. They are both law professors at Virginia Commonwealth University.
  c. They had worked with Kay Scarpetta in the past, but now work as a team.
  d. They are both people that author Patricia Cornwell based characters on in her books.

Vocabulary **2.** In line 18, what does *foul play* mean?
  a. death by an unknown reason
  b. poor training for lab workers
  c. a sudden change in what one thought was true
  d. criminal behavior, often resulting in death

Cause and Effect **3.** According to the article, what might cause a body to be exhumed?
  a. an autopsy performed before burial was not conducted properly
  b. new forensics techniques that didn't exist when the body was buried
  c. mother and child want to say good-bye one last time
  d. an allegation that a family member had a motive for murder

Detail **4.** What is NOT true about cyanide?
  a. It works quickly.
  b. It has no smell.
  c. It works violently.
  d. A small amount can kill.

Inference **5.** What is probably true about Banana Pudding Lily?
  a. She brought food to several patients at the hospital.
  b. Doctors quickly suspected her of trying to kill her husband.
  c. She wanted lab tests done on her husband.
  d. She poisoned her husband with arsenic.

Detail **6.** According to Poklis, why don't Americans use poison to kill others?
  a. It's not easy to find poison in the U.S.
  b. Americans don't know the effects of poison.
  c. Shooting someone is more like what they see in movies.
  d. Using a gun to kill is faster and more direct.

Vocabulary **7.** Look at the terminologies on page 144. Which sentence is closest in meaning to: *She exhumed the corpse to see if the man had been a victim of homicide?*
  a. She dug up the dead body and performed an autopsy to see how the man was killed.
  b. She dug up the dead body to see if the man had been murdered.
  c. She dug up the dead body and checked for toxins to find out how the man died.
  d. She dug up the dead body and used forensics to see what killed the man.

Critical Thinking

Interpreting:
Look back at how Alphonse Poklis describes people who murder using poison. In your own words, what does he think of these people?

Evaluating:
What do you think of what Poklis says about the character of Americans? How serious do you think he is? How accurate do you think he is?

Understanding Idiomatic Expressions

Spoken language in particular, such as that found in interviews, often contains idiomatic expressions. Like with other vocabulary, context may help you understand their meaning. To gain a richer understanding of idioms, expose yourself to them as much as possible—through reading, watching movies, and listening to native speakers. If you have no idea what an idiom means, consult a dictionary.

A. Matching. Match the idioms in **bold** with their meanings.

1. _____ You want me to quit my job? **Over my dead body!**
2. _____ I was completely wrong about the cause of death. That's **a bitter pill to swallow**.
3. _____ You're new, so it will take time to **learn the ropes**.
4. _____ I'm **on the fence** whether or not to take the job.
5. _____ The autopsy results can't be right. Something is **fishy**.
6. _____ This isn't the right answer. Let's **start from scratch**.
7. _____ I know you disagree with your supervisor, but in this case it's best to **bite your tongue**.
8. _____ I can't go to work today. I'm a little **under the weather**.

a. undecided
b. suspicious
c. under no circumstances
d. an unpleasant truth
e. not feeling well
f. say nothing
g. begin from the beginning
h. become experienced

B. Multiple Choice. The idioms in **bold** are from the reading. Choose the correct meaning.

1. If we have the body **before it's in the ground**, we deal with it.
   a. before it gets buried
   b. before it starts to smell

2. There's dissension about property, inheritance, a new wife, a child not **getting a fair share**.
   a. receiving a reasonable amount
   b. being wanted by both parents

3. I take **umpteen** tissue samples at autopsy: heart, liver, lungs, brain, spleen, hair, nails.
   a. a messy mix of
   b. an extremely large number of

4. A case that **sticks in your mind**?
   a. caused a headache
   b. is remembered clearly

5. The doctors were **twisting themselves inside out** to figure it out.
   a. trying extremely hard
   b. arguing with one another

6. Someone finally ordered a heavy metals [toxicity test] on him, but he was discharged before the results came back—**off the charts** for arsenic.
   a. extremely high
   b. not written down

Vocabulary Practice

A. Completion. Complete the information with the correct form of words from the box. Four words are extra.

allegation	candidate	deprived of	frankly	in terms of
manipulative	motive	remorse	suffocation	suspicious

Poison is a killer, effective in small amounts, and often undetectable. **1.** _____, we would be **2.** _____ much entertainment value without poison. Comic book superheroes and villains in movies and plays would be much duller. Spiderman exists because of a spider bite. The Teenage Mutant Ninja Turtles fell into a sewer along with a container of toxic materials. Hamlet was killed by a poison-dipped sword. The fatal attraction: Snow White's poison apple, the art of the snake handler, the risk of eating *fugu*.

Consider arsenic, the poison of kings and king of poisons. It does not discriminate **3.** _____ age, gender, or background. It is colorless, tasteless, odorless, and deadly. When a royal died suddenly, **4.** _____ family members often pointed to arsenic and raised **5.** _____ of murder. It was the poison of choice for Hieronyma Spara, a 17th-century Roman entrepreneur who ran a school that taught wealthy young wives how to kill their husbands without being caught. Their **6.** _____ for murder was simply to become wealthy young widows.

∧ Arsenate lead is used in pesticides and herbicides

B. Definitions. Match words from **A** with their definitions.

1. _____ : killing by depriving of oxygen

2. _____ : a reason for doing something

3. _____ : to have something taken away

4. _____ : a statement saying someone has done something wrong or illegal

5. _____ : using or controlling others in a clever, selfish, or unfair way

6. _____ : having a feeling that something is wrong or someone is behaving wrongly

7. _____ : a person or thing that meets the requirements for something

8. _____ : a feeling of being sorry for doing something bad or wrong

> **Word Link**
> The word root **leg** means "law," e.g., *allege, legal, legislature, legitimate.*

VIEWING Frog Licker

Before You Watch

A. Definitions. Read the information below. Match the correct form of each word in **bold** with its definition.

Off the southeastern coast of Africa lies the island of Madagascar. You may know Madagascar for its **exotic** lemurs, but it's also home to one of the world's most colorful **amphibians**: The Mantella poison frog.

Poison frogs aren't born poisonous, but rather they are proof of the old saying, "You are what you eat." Their **toxins** come from something in their diet, which is mainly ants, millipedes, and mites. But which of these small creatures is it exactly? And will a collapse in insect **diversity** threaten the frogs' ability to survive?

1. _____: a range of different things

2. _____: a harmful or deadly substance

3. _____: very different, strange, or unusual

4. _____: an animal such as a frog or toad that can live both on land and in water

B. Predict. Look at the title above and the picture on this page of Valerie C. Clark. Her job is to study amphibians and reptiles like frogs, snakes, and lizards. Discuss these ideas with a partner.

1. What is she doing?
2. Why do you think she is doing it?

Valerie C. Clark >

While You Watch

A. Noticing. Read the statements below. As you watch the video, mark each sentence **T** (True) or **F** (False).

1. Clark knows the frog she finds is female because of its color.   **T**   **F**

2. The only way to sample the toxins in a frog's skin is to lick it.   **T**   **F**

3. One reason that frogs are important to Clark is that they're gorgeous.   **T**   **F**

4. Clark thinks we need to save the rain forest to find the source of the frogs' toxins.   **T**   **F**

B. Completion. Complete the descriptions below with the correct words in the box. One word is extra.

chemicals	**helpful**	**medicines**	**poison**
samples	**small creatures**	**toxic**	**variety**

To understand insect diversity, Clark and her team collect samples by putting leaves and soil into different bags. As the soil dries out, the **1.** _____ leave the bag searching for wetter soil. They fall and are collected as **2.** _____.

The bitter-tasting **3.** _____ in the frogs is only mildly toxic to humans. The chemicals in the frogs' skin may be harmful to other animals, but **4.** _____ to humans. They may hold the key to new **5.** _____.

Frogs need a **6.** _____ of small creatures to eat in order for their toxins to work. This means they need a large rain forest with a diversity of life. If the rain forest continues to be destroyed, there will be fewer toxic **7.** _____ with the potential to be used for making medicines.

After You Watch

A. Discussion. Work in a group. Discuss the following questions.

1. What other animals use poison as a defense?

2. What do you understand by the saying, "You are what you eat"? How does it apply to humans?

3. Clark feels that saving the rain forest is important because it can help us find new drugs. What other reasons for saving the rain forest can you think of?

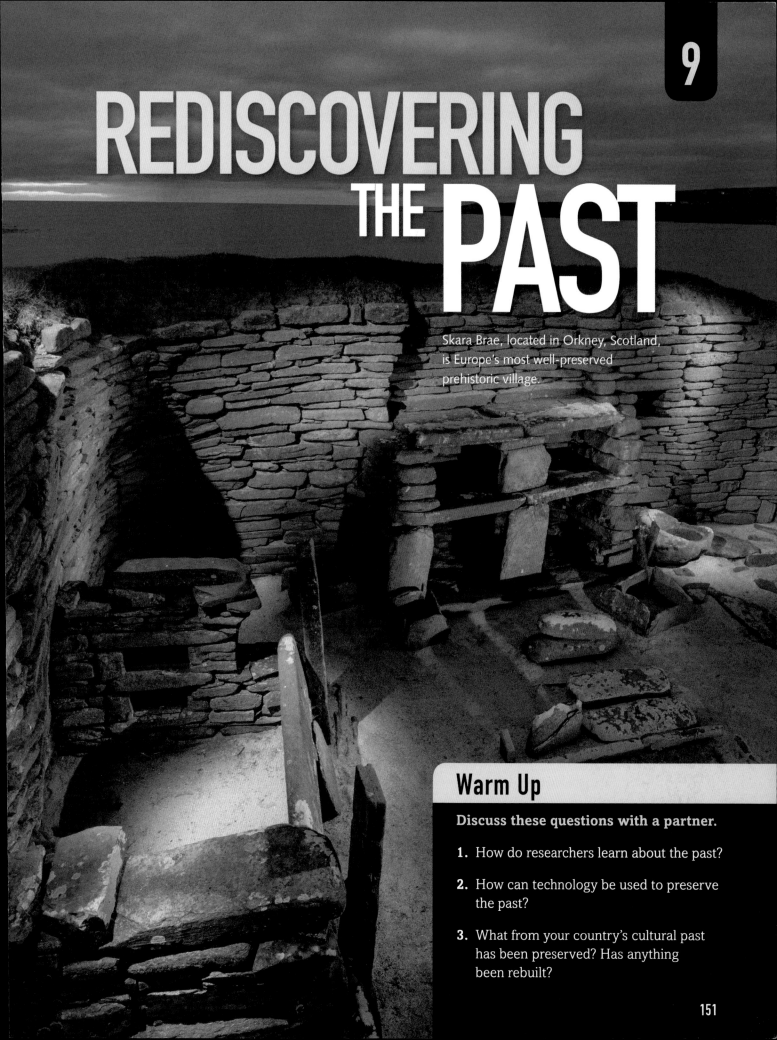

REDISCOVERING THE PAST

9

Skara Brae, located in Orkney, Scotland, is Europe's most well-preserved prehistoric village.

Warm Up

Discuss these questions with a partner.

1. How do researchers learn about the past?

2. How can technology be used to preserve the past?

3. What from your country's cultural past has been preserved? Has anything been rebuilt?

Before You Read

A. Completion. Read the caption. Then complete
the sentences with the correct form of the words in **bold**.

1. Our _____ includes important things that
   previous generations have left to us.

2. A _____ is a ray of high-energy light produced
   by a special machine.

3. A _____ image or movie appears to have
   height, width, and depth.

4. To make a digital copy of an object or a document, you
   must _____ it.

B. Predict. You are going to read about an architectural treasure
called Rani ki Vav. Look at the photograph on page 154 and try
to guess what the purpose of Rani ki Vav was. Then read the
passage to check if you are correct.

Laser beams are bounced
off the surface of Mount
Rushmore, U.S.A.
Scanning the mountain
in this way enables
researchers to create a
detailed **3-D** digital model
of the monument. Such
models are a new way of
preserving our endangered
architectural **heritage**.

VIRTUALLY IMMORTAL

1 **AFTER THE LONG, DUSTY DRIVE** from the city, the first surprises that visitors **encounter** are the shade trees and the beautiful green lawn. Then they notice the birds and monkeys swooping[1]
5 in and out of the trees. After passing through the entrance gate, a long stone pathway leads to a place where the ground begins to open up. There, on the far side of the grass, is what seems to be a magnificent temple built in a huge hole
10 in the ground. However, it is not a temple, but a well.[2] This is Rani ki Vav—the Queen's Step Well.

The weather is dry most of the year in northwestern India. Then, during the summer,
15 rain arrives suddenly and seeps[3] down through the sandy soil. Centuries ago, people dug holes to get at the water and then built stone stairways down where the water collected. These step wells were simple at first, but some
20 later became architectural works of art. Rani ki Vav is among the most magnificent.

Located near the Saraswati River in Gujarat, Rani ki Vav was built late in the 11th century by Queen Udayamati as a **memorial** to her
25 dead king. It was rarely used, and by 1300, seasonal floods had filled it with sand. Not until the 1960s did Indian archeologists begin digging it out. Witnesses were **stunned** by what was hidden beneath all that sand.

---

1 When a bird **swoops**, it suddenly moves down through the air in a smooth, curving motion.
2 A **well** is a hole in the ground from which a supply of water is extracted.
3 If water **seeps** down through the earth, it moves slowly through it.

Rani ki Vav (the Queen's Step Well) in Gujarat, India

30 Preserving the Past

"We've seen photographs, but nothing compares with seeing it **firsthand**," says Lyn Wilson, an archeological scientist from Glasgow. With the latest in digital scanning technology, she
35 and her colleagues from the Centre for Digital Documentation and Visualisation aim to reduce the chances that Rani ki Vav, or at least the data describing it, will ever be lost again.

Of all the projects they have undertaken—
40 from the standing stones of Orkney to Mount Rushmore—this is among the most difficult. By 12:30 P.M., their equipment arrives. As team members open the crates,[4] they meet their first challenge: two buses full of Indian schoolboys

---

4 A **crate** is a large box used for transporting or storing things.

45 on a class trip. They crowd around Wilson as though she's a Bollywood star. A uniformed guard gently directs them to move back with a long, swinging stick.

50 For the next two weeks, the team will have to fight the heat and cope with curious crowds while they aim laser beams at every surface of the step well in order to record the entire structure digitally. Should Rani ki Vav be lost again—through floods, war, earthquakes, or just the passage of time—
55 there will be a precise 3-D copy available on the Internet.

Tour of Rani ki Vav

A tour of the well reveals some of the extremely complex **carvings** the team must record. On a
60 lower level, seven sculptures of the four-armed god Vishnu decorate the walls. Lord Kalki sits tall on a horse, one foot about to crush an enemy's head. Then there's Varaha, a god with the head of a boar.[5] A tiny goddess standing on his shoulder
65 lovingly rubs his nose. "It reminds me of the wonderful Hollywood movie *King Kong*," remarks K. C. Nauriyal, an Indian archeologist working at the site.

Also **immortalized** in stone are the three greatest
70 Hindu gods: Brahma, Shiva, and Vishnu. Scattered among the gods slither[6] snakes and creatures called *Naga Kanya* that are half snake, half woman. There are also *apsaras*—female spirits of the clouds and water—putting on lipstick or
75 earrings, **gazing** at mirrors, or drying their hair. One of them playfully strikes a monkey as it pulls down her **garment**. Another pulls on the beard of an admiring beggar. "The spice of life," Nauriyal calls them. But one blow with a hammer
80 by a **vandal**, and their beauty would be destroyed forever.

A stairway leads to the lowest levels, and a dark passage into the well itself. Near the bottom of the well are two statues of the god Vishnu. One
85 is sleeping on the back of a large snake, and the other is sitting straight up. There was a belief that if there were two statues of Lord Vishnu in this form, the water would never dry up—but it

90 dried up anyway. Agricultural development and a warmer climate are two likely causes. And like the water, the sculptures, too, may one day disappear, surviving perhaps only as a **virtual** model online.

A Digital Copy

95 Inside a tent at the edge of the step well, archeologist Justin Barton assembles the first pieces of the 3-D digital image of Rani ki Vav. Weirdly colored columns and lintels[7] appear on the screen. The colors—greenish in the brightest areas, grading to oranges and yellows—indicate
100 reflectivity, or how readily the laser comes bouncing back. Barton grabs the images with the cursor, swinging them around like a child's building blocks, fitting each into the larger model of Rani ki Vav.

105 Back in Glasgow, the digital copy will be completed, ultimately joining more than a hundred others already in the database. But that's barely the beginning. "So much heritage is being lost on a daily basis," says Barton, "through war
110 and human aggression, environmental changes, and the wear and tear of time." Barton and his colleagues are in a race to digitally preserve for future generations as many of the world's threatened archeological treasures as they can—
115 before they disappear forever.

---

5 A **boar** is a wild pig.
6 If an animal **slithers**, it moves by twisting or sliding on the ground.
7 A **lintel** is a piece of stone or wood over a door or window.

The Scottish Ten

The expedition to Rani ki Vav is part of the Scottish Ten, a digital preservation project that aims to produce 3-D digital copies of ten world-class cultural sites. Essential to the effort is CyArk, a California-based organization founded by Ben Kacyra, the inventor of the laser scanner. CyArk has been working with various groups to scan historical sites around the world including Pompeii, Chichén Itzá, and ancient Thebes.

Reading Comprehension

Multiple Choice. Choose the best answer for each question.

Detail

1. Which of these does NOT describe Rani ki Vav?
   a. a magnificent temple
   b. a well with steps
   c. a memorial to a dead king
   d. an 11th-century structure

Detail

2. What happened to Rani ki Vav?
   a. It disappeared underwater.
   b. People took the stones away.
   c. It became filled with sand.
   d. Records of its existence were destroyed.

Reference

3. What does *this* refer to in line 41?
   a. the standing stones of Orkney
   b. recording Rani ki Vav digitally
   c. setting up scanning equipment
   d. the Mount Rushmore project

Purpose

4. The purpose of paragraphs 7–9 (lines 58–92) is to _____.
   a. compare Rani ki Vav with other monuments in India
   b. describe the most recent discoveries at Rani ki Vav
   c. explain the techniques scientists are using to scan Rani ki Vav
   d. allow the reader to visualize what the inside of Rani ki Vav looks like

Inference

5. Which statement would Justin Barton probably agree with the most?
   a. We must act quickly to digitally preserve the world's archeological treasures.
   b. We must discourage people from visiting archeological treasures until they are preserved.
   c. We must make more copies of the hundreds of digital copies currently in the database.
   d. We should wait until there are advances in digital copying before mapping more archeological treasures.

Cohesion

6. The following sentence would best be placed at the beginning of which paragraph? *The next morning at the step well, the first full day of work begins.*
   a. 2   b. 6   c. 9   d. 11

Detail

7. According to the sidebar on page 155, what is the Scottish Ten?
   a. the top ten most visited cultural sites
   b. a project that promotes digital preservation
   c. a team of ten people in Scotland working to preserve cultural sites
   d. the former name of the California-based organization CyArk

Critical Thinking

Inferring: Why do you think K. C. Nauriyal describes the carvings as "the spice of life"?

Evaluating: The Scottish Ten project aims to preserve 3-D digital copies of ten world-class cultural sites. Which cultural sites do you think are most worthy of preservation? Why?

Recognizing the Use of Ellipsis

An effective writer will not give a reader more information than necessary. A writer will omit information that a reader's common sense can easily supply. This omitted information is known as ellipsis. In these examples, the words in parentheses are not needed for the sentences to be understood.

You can be Sam's lab partner, and I'll be Dana's (lab partner).

Mark can speak Arabic, and Delia (can speak) *Hindi.*

She asked if he'd like to co-present, and he said he would (like to co-present).

Identifying what is missing is usually not a problem in short sentences, but with longer texts it can be more challenging.

A. **Analyzing.** These sentences from the reading contain ellipsis. Draw an arrow from the **bold** words to where they could go in the sentence.

1. However, it is not a temple, but a well. **it is** (paragraph 1)

2. Then, during the summer, rain arrives suddenly and seeps down through the sandy soil. **the water** (paragraph 2)

3. These step wells were simple at first, but some later became architectural works of art. Rani ki Vav is among the most magnificent. **works of art** (paragraph 2)

4. There are also *apsaras*—female spirits of the clouds and water—putting on lipstick or earrings, gazing at mirrors, or drying their hair. **putting on** (paragraph 8)

5. A stairway leads to the lowest levels, and a dark passage into the well itself. **leads** (paragraph 9)

B. **Completion.** These famous quotes contain ellipsis. Add any missing words.

1. "Wise men talk because they have something to say; fools, because they have to say something." – Plato

2. "To err is human, to forgive divine." – Alexander Pope

3. "If you don't love something, you're not going to go the extra mile, work the extra weekend, challenge the status quo as much." – Steve Jobs

Vocabulary Practice

A. Matching. Read the information below and match each word in **red** with its definition.

It's 1922. After working five years in Egypt's Valley of the Kings and finding almost nothing, Howard Carter made a remarkable discovery—the tomb of King Tutankhamun. When he first entered and **gazed** upon the tomb, he was **stunned** to find it nearly intact. Unlike other tombs in the area, no **vandals** had damaged this one. Over the next several years, Carter studied the tomb. He found chests filled with ceremonial **garments** and footwear, a series of gold coffins, and the mummy of King Tut.

For years, visitors could have a personal **encounter** with the boy king by viewing objects from his tomb in museums or taking **virtual** tours of the tomb online. Others have been able to see the tomb **firsthand**. But the huge numbers of tourists had also damaged the tomb. So in 2014 archeologists opened to the public an exact copy of the tomb. Laser scanners and high-definition printers were used to recreate the textures and colors of walls depicting Tut's afterlife.

A coffin of solid gold held King Tut's mummified remains.

1. _____ : directly; by actually seeing or experiencing something

2. _____ : a brief experience with another person

3. _____ : extremely surprised

4. _____ : items of clothing

5. _____ : looked at something in a steady way, often for a long time

6. _____ : people who deliberately harm or destroy property

7. _____ : existing or occuring on computers or on the Internet

B. Words in Context. Complete each sentence with the correct answer.

1. If someone is **immortalized**, you hope the person will be _____.

   a. forgotten by history   b. remembered forever.

2. Someone might create a **memorial** _____.

   a. before the birth of a baby   b. after the death of a family member

3. A **carving** is made by _____ material, such as stone, to create a shape.

   a. putting together   b. cutting away

> **Word Partnership**
> Use *virtual* with:
> (*n.*) virtual **reality**,
> virtual **tour**, virtual
> **environment**,
> virtual **classroom**.

IN SEARCH OF GENGHIS KHAN

Before You Read

A. Discussion. Look at the picture and read the caption and the information below. Then answer the questions (**1–2**).

The StarCAVE is a five-sided room where scientific models and animations are projected onto screens surrounding the viewer and floor. This virtual-reality environment allows scientists to go into worlds as small as atoms or as big as the universe, permitting new points of view that may help them make discoveries in their fields. Early users of the StarCAVE include researchers in medicine, engineering, archeology, earth science, and art history.

1. What kinds of discoveries do you think researchers are hoping to make using the StarCAVE?

2. What would you like to view from inside the StarCAVE? Why?

B. Predict. Albert Lin and his team visited a place in Mongolia called the Forbidden Zone. Why do you think people were forbidden from entering this area for centuries? Check (✓) your answer. Then read the passage to find out.

☐ There was a terrible volcanic eruption there.
☐ Extremely dangerous weapons were stored there.
☐ Family members of a great leader were buried there.

◄ In the photograph above, explorer Albert Lin examines digital projections of northern Mongolia from inside the StarCAVE.

MONGOLS AT WAR

Dressed > for attack, a Mongol warrior had no equal in battle.

An arsenal of varied arrowheads gave the Mongol warrior his advantage. Some were designed just for killing (far left) while others made sounds to terrify the enemy.

˅ Mongols attacked cities with fiery bombs.

˅ Borrowing technology from Arabs, Persians, and Chinese, Mongols mastered the art of ambush warfare and the use of catapults.

˄ With its thick neck, short legs, and large head, the Mongol pony seems clumsy. But, what it lacks in beauty, it makes up for in stamina and agility.

1   **GENGHIS KHAN REMAINS** to this day one of the most accomplished men to have walked the Earth. Rising from an outcast[1] to be the ruler of the largest land **empire** to have ever existed, he
5   introduced an alphabet and an official form of money, united a kingdom of tribes at war with each other, and conquered most of the known world. His empire stretched from Poland to Japan. It is estimated that one in every 200 men on the
10   planet today is related to Genghis Khan. But there are no **accounts** of the events that surrounded his death and burial—only a mystery focused around an area known as the Forbidden Zone.

From the time of the Khan's death in 1227 up
15   until 1991, the Forbidden Zone was as off-limits[2] as any place in the world. Shortly after he died, the surviving Mongol leaders ordered a group of 50 fierce families—known as the Uryangqai of the Woods—to occupy this land and kill anyone who
20   entered without permission.

---

1 An **outcast** is someone who is not accepted by a group of people or by society.
2 If a place is **off-limits** to someone, they are not allowed to go there.

△ Mongol horsemen were especially skilled at shooting targets behind them.

∨ The annual *gorugen*, or great Mongol hunt, became basic training for Genghis Khan's warriors. Encircling all the game (animals) in a given area, horsemen closed in. Each was allotted one arrow to kill, and failure was ridiculed.

They made **exceptions** only for the funeral processions of the Khan's direct descendants, who were also allowed to be buried there. This extreme degree of secrecy has led many to the conclusion
25 that the body of Genghis Khan himself lies in a tomb somewhere in this zone, along with some of the treasures of an empire vaster than those of Napoleon and Alexander the Great combined. When the U.S.S.R. **took over** Mongolia in 1924,
30 they eliminated the Uryangqai of the Woods just as they tried to erase the memory of the great Khan. The Forbidden Zone still remained off-limits, however. It wasn't until the fall of the U.S.S.R. in

1991 that entering the Forbidden Zone became
35 possible for scientists and **historians**. Even today, eight centuries after it was closed off, the Forbidden Zone has been visited by very few.

Scientist Albert Lin has been obsessed by the story of Genghis Khan ever since he took a
40 backpacking trip to Mongolia. After receiving his doctorate from the University of California at San Diego (UCSD), he decided to use the resources of UCSD to organize a tomb hunt. Some of his best friends at the university were experts in
45 various fields—UAV[3] design, remote sensing, and geographic information systems—that could, if applied in combination, provide an old-fashioned archeological expedition with **cutting-edge** advantages. Not only that, but almost all of
50 these friends were enthusiastic rock climbers, used to camping in the wilderness, ready for any adventure.

In July 2008, Lin and his team—funded by a National Geographic Waitt grant—found
55 themselves driving north from Ulaanbaatar in their rented Russian trucks. On maps, it looked like their **initial** destination—the Forbidden Zone—was about six hours away. But then came the mechanical breakdowns and deep mud pits,
60 the injured goats and stuck vehicles, and the stubborn guards at the entrance to the Forbidden Zone. After two days, they established their first base camp—two circular Mongolian tents called *yurts*—and began exploring.

65 For the next three weeks, they explored the entire Forbidden Zone and beyond, spreading out across the wilderness on foot and on horseback. They faced challenges such as wolves, exploding UAVs, and unexploded bombs buried in the earth. They
70 ate goat steak, goat stew, and something called goat bread, and they drank fermented[4] horse milk.

---

3 A **UAV** is an unmanned aerial vehicle, commonly known as a drone.

4 If a drink is **fermented**, a chemical change takes place in it so that alcohol is produced.

Albert Lin riding a horse in the open plains of Mongolia.

Once afternoon, Lin **spotted** a small, evenly shaped grassy hill in the middle of a flat field. It
75 looked like an ancient Mongolian tomb, perhaps even big enough to be that of Genghis Khan. The team risked running into a wild boar as they pushed their way through the thick bushes surrounding the hill. Unfortunately, their tests
80 showed that the hill was just a hill.

Their disappointment didn't last long. Two days later, high on a mountainside, they arrived at the location of an ancient temple that had never previously been studied. Although they didn't
85 do any digging, by simply scanning the earth near recently fallen trees, they found plenty of impressive artifacts, among them a clay medallion[5] with the face of a lion on it dating from the Khan's time.

90 The team identified dozens of potential burial sites. Rather than digging, however, Lin's approach is to scan the earth below using imaging technology. This is because of Genghis Khan's importance for the Mongolian people.
95 Not only considered by many to have been the greatest military leader of all time, Genghis

---

5 A **medallion** is a round disk usually worn on a chain around the neck.

Dr. Albert Yu-Min Lin

As a National Geographic Society Emerging Explorer in the field of technology-enabled exploration, Albert Lin uses noninvasive computer-based technologies to gather and examine archeological data without disturbing a single blade of grass. Since his return to the U.S. from Mongolia, he has continued his discoveries, transforming real-world data into the virtual world of the StarCAVE and searching areas of the Forbidden Zone he couldn't reach in the field. To date, he and his team have taken the data collected and made 3-D models to put into the StarCAVE. They've also found a temple at a site that they believe could be related to the tomb.

Khan also has great religious significance for many Mongolians. Some believers even worry that digging up his tomb could cause the end of 100 the world.

"Using traditional archeological methods would be **disrespectful** to believers," Lin says. "The ability to explore in a noninvasive[6] way lets us try to solve this ancient secret without overstepping[7] 105 cultural barriers. It also allows us to empower Mongolian researchers with tools they might not have access to otherwise."

110 Lin also believes the search for Genghis Khan's tomb has importance that goes beyond Mongolia's borders. "Today's world still benefits from Genghis Khan's ability to connect East with West," says Lin. "He **forged** international relations that have never been broken. By locating his tomb, we hope to emphasize how 115 important it is for the world to protect such cultural heritage treasures."

---

6 **Noninvasive** archeological techniques do not involve digging and do not cause damage.
7 If someone **oversteps** limits or boundaries, they do something that is not acceptable or permitted.

Reading Comprehension

Multiple Choice. Choose the best answer for each question.

Main Idea

1. What is the main idea of the first paragraph?
   a. Genghis Khan united a kingdom of tribes that had been at war with each other.
   b. Genghis Khan was a great leader, but little is known about his private life.
   c. Genghis Khan accomplished a lot in his life, but his death is still a mystery.
   d. Genghis Khan's death and burial have been a mystery until very recently.

Detail

2. Why do many people believe that Genghis Khan is buried in the Forbidden Zone?
   a. There has been secrecy about the area for many years.
   b. Because the Uryangqai of the Woods were eliminated.
   c. Because the U.S.S.R. forbade anyone from entering the area.
   d. Because scientists have found artifacts they believe belonged to Genghis Khan.

Detail

3. What advantage did Albert Lin's expedition to Mongolia have?
   a. It consisted of experts from a variety of fields.
   b. It was the first expedition in Mongolia to use technology.
   c. It was the first scientific team allowed into the Forbidden Zone.
   d. The team all had previous experience working in Mongolia.

Inference

4. In lines 69–72, why does the author probably include the sentence: *They ate goat steak, goat stew, and something called goat bread, and they drank fermented horse milk.*?
   a. to show how the expedition conditions were unfamiliar and challenging for the scientists
   b. to emphasize that life at the camp was similar to how Genghis Khan probably lived
   c. to say that no matter how challenging the work was, they had plenty to eat and drink
   d. to explain that the scientists had made contact with local people

Paraphrase

5. What's another way of saying *The team risked running into a wild boar* (lines 77)?
   a. The team ran into a wild boar.
   b. The team was prepared in case they ran into a wild boar.
   c. The team was hoping for a chance to run into a wild boar.
   d. The team was in danger of running into a wild boar.

Detail

6. Why didn't Albert Lin dig up any artifacts in Mongolia?
   a. It would have been disrespectful to do so.
   b. Digging them up probably would have destroyed them.
   c. Because they were located in burial sites.
   d. The team did not find any artifacts in the area

Purpose

7. What is the purpose of the last paragraph?
   a. to illustrate what Albert Lin had learned from earlier archeological digs in Mongolia
   b. to explain the advantages of image technology over traditional archeological methods
   c. to show how the StarCAVE can teach young Mongolians about their cultural heritage
   d. to discuss how the world benefited from Genghis Khan's ability to connect East with West

Critical Thinking

Discussion: Do you think artifacts that are found by scanning the earth should be left there, or should they be removed? Why?

Evaluating: Besides archeological research, what else could the StarCAVE imaging technology be used for?

Understanding Relative Clauses (II)

Relative clauses are very common in English. Writers often reduce these clauses, meaning they delete unnecessary words. Readers need to recognize sentences with reduced relative clauses to be sure they have a full understanding of the writer's meaning. Look at these rules for when you can and cannot delete relative pronouns and verbs.

You can delete the relative pronoun if a new subject and verb follows it.
This is the tomb (that) they found.

You can delete the relative pronoun and *be* if they're followed by a prepositional phrase.
The artifacts (which were) in the tomb are priceless.

You can delete the relative pronoun and *be* if the verb is in a progressive tense.
The man (who is) scanning the tomb is Albert Lin.

You cannot delete the relative pronoun and *be* if they're followed by an adjective, a noun, or a verb other than *be*.

The man who is angry / who is a scientist / who works in Mongolia is Albert Lin.

A. **Analyzing.** Each sentence (1–6) contains a relative clause. Check (✓) the ones that can be reduced. Then reduce them by crossing out the unnecessary words.

1. ☐ Genghis Khan united a kingdom of tribes that were at war with each other.
2. ☐ There are no accounts of the events that surrounded his death and burial.
3. ☐ Mongol leaders killed anyone who entered the land without permission.
4. ☐ This has led many to the conclusion that his body lies in a tomb in this zone.
5. ☐ One in every 200 men who are on the planet today is related to Genghis Khan.
6. ☐ It allows us to empower researchers with tools that they might not have access to.

B. **Completion.** Each sentence contains a reduced relative clause. Add any necessary pronouns and verbs to make the sentences non-reduced.

1. Genghis Khan is a hero to the people living in Mongolia today.
2. The men scanning the earth found plenty of artifacts.
3. They scanned the earth near some recently fallen trees.
4. The research methods he used were noninvasive.

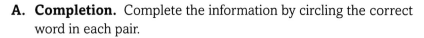

Vocabulary Practice

A. Completion. Complete the information by circling the correct word in each pair.

The wooded hills of New England hide a secret—they weren't always forested. Instead, many were once covered with roads and farms.

This "lost" New England of the colonial era has started to emerge, thanks to archeologists piercing the forests with the latest in high-tech scanners. **1. (Historian / Initial)** scan results have shown huge areas that were once settled. Scientists have **2. (forged / spotted)** farm walls, roads, and homes hidden within Connecticut's Pachaug State Forest. Many of these individual farms don't appear in the historical **3. (accounts / empires)** from the colonial era.

The **4. (exception / cutting-edge)** technology bounces lasers off the ground to generate precise pictures of surface features. Scientists using the same kind of technology have made new discoveries while looking at Mayan cities, the plain of Stonehenge, and European palaces.

How did these farms become lost in the first place? There had once been extensive farming across New England, but with industrialization people started to head west, abandoning their farms. The forests eventually **5. (forged / took over)**, covering the walls, roads, and homes until their recent discovery.

∧ Green Fall Pond Loop, in Pachaug State Forest, Connecticut, U.S.A.

B. Words in Context. Complete each sentence with the correct answer.

1. An **empire** (e.g., the Roman empire) is a group of countries controlled by _____.
   a. one ruler   b. many rulers

2. If you **forged** an agreement between two sides, it probably took _____ effort.
   a. very little   b. a great deal of

3. An **exception** is something that _____ a rule.
   a. does not follow   b. follows

4. If a student is **disrespectful** to a teacher, the teacher will feel very _____.
   a. pleased   b. annoyed

5. A **historian** is a person who studies _____.
   a. the future   b. the past

> **Word Partnership**
> Use **exception**
> with: (*adj.*) **notable**
> exception, **obvious**
> exception; (*v.*)
> **make an** exception;
> (*prepositional phrase*)
> **with the** exception
> **of**; (*phrase*) **the**
> exception **to the rule**.

VIEWING | Secrets of Stonehenge

Before You Watch

A. Definitions. Read the information below and match each word in **bold** with its definition.

Stonehenge is one of the most famous ancient monuments in the world. This mysterious circle of standing stones on the Salisbury **Plain** in southern England has stood for more than 4,000 years. Researchers have long believed that it was a lone, **solitary** monument. However, some researchers now think that Stonehenge may have been part of a much larger **complex**, that included houses made of **timber**.

1. _____: large pieces of wood that are part of a building

2. _____: without anyone or anything else

3. _____: a group of related buildings or structures

4. _____: a large area of flat land without trees

B. Discussion. There have been many theories about the purpose of Stonehenge. Which of the following do you think are most likely? Discuss with a partner.

1. It was a temple to the sun or moon. ☐
2. It was a cemetery—a place to bury the dead. ☐
3. It was an astronomical calendar. ☐
4. It was a place where sick people became cured. ☐
5. It was a place from which to observe the stars. ☐
6. It's a natural site that was created by moving glaciers. ☐
7. It's a site that was built by aliens from space. ☐

While You Watch

A. Multiple Choice. You will hear from a researcher who is an expert in what is called "the archeology of death." Circle his theory about Stonehenge.

   a. Stonehenge was built on the exact site of an earlier community after its people died.

   b. People were killed at the site, and later a monument was built to satisfy the gods.

   c. Stonehenge is a small part of a larger community where people buried their dead.

B. Multiple Choice. Choose the correct answer for each question.

   1. Who is Michael Parker Pearson?

   a. a historian

   b. a writer

   c. an archeologist

   2. What did Pearson discover in 2006?

   a. houses of people who built Stonehenge

   b. stone monuments similar to Stonehenge

   c. burial places under Stonehenge

   3. According to Pearson, what is true about Durrington Walls?

   a. It was a small community for its time.

   b. People lived in wood homes there.

   c. The stones of Stonehenge came from there.

   4. What does Pearson think happened to people who died at Durrington Walls?

   a. They were cremated at Durrington Walls.

   b. They were buried at Durrington Walls.

   c. They were taken to Stonehenge for burial.

After You Watch

A. Discussion. Discuss these questions with a partner.

   1. What do you think of Pearson's theory? Does it make sense to you?

   2. Why do you think Stonehenge continues to fascinate so many people?

   3. Is there a mysterious structure, monument, carving, or place in your country? What makes it mysterious?

10

EARTH AND BEYOND

An artist's illustration
of a huge meteor
striking the Earth

Warm Up

Discuss these questions with a partner.

1. What do astronomers use to
study and explore our solar system?

2. What can we learn about Earth from
studying our solar system?

3. What in our solar system could be
dangerous to life on Earth?

169

Before You Read

A. True or False. Read the information below. Then circle **T** (True), **F** (False), or **NG** (Not Given).

Scientists believe that at the center of our galaxy—the enormous group of stars that includes our sun—is an object called a black hole. Black holes are the heaviest objects in the universe, and their powerful gravity can pull in and destroy planets or even stars.

1. There is a black hole at the center of our galaxy.   **T   F   NG**
2. Black holes are the lightest objects in the universe.   **T   F   NG**
3. Their powerful gravity can pull in planets and stars.   **T   F   NG**
4. They are created by the collapse of a star.   **T   F   NG**

B. Scan. The reading contains several terms related to astronomy. Quickly scan the reading for the terms below (**1–5**). Then match them with their meanings.

1. _____: white dwarf   **a.** an extremely bright explosion of a star
2. _____: supernova   **b.** a dead star about the size of the Earth
3. _____: neutron star   **c.** a vast collection of separate universes
4. _____: event horizon   **d.** the boundary surrounding a black hole
5. _____: multiverse   **e.** a dense, spinning ball several kilometers wide

An artist's illustration of a black hole. The force of gravity within a black hole is so great that nothing in the universe can withstand its pull.

BLACK HOLES

1   A black hole is certainly among the
    most amazing things in the universe.
    Born when a star collapses, it is so
    dense that even light cannot escape the
5   pull of its gravity. That such a thing can
    even exist challenges our imagination.
    It is a notion that Albert Einstein himself
    thought too **preposterous** to be real.
    But Einstein was wrong.

10 ## The Death of a Star

    Our sun is only an average-size star. After it
    burns up the last of its fuel, the outer **layers**
    will float away and the center will become much
    smaller, pulled in by the force of gravity. What will
15 remain is a dead star known as a white dwarf.
    This dead star will be a million[1] times smaller than
    the current size of the sun—about the size of
    the Earth.

    For a star ten times as heavy as our sun, death
20 is much more dramatic. The outer layers are
    thrown far into space in an explosion that creates
    a supernova, one of the brightest objects in the
    universe. The center, meanwhile, is **squashed** by
    gravity into a **spinning** ball several kilometers wide
25 called a neutron star. A neutron star is so dense
    that a sugar-cube-size piece of a neutron star
    would weigh a billion[2] tons on Earth.

    But this is nothing compared to the death of a star
    20 times the weight of our sun. The star's center
30 collapses. Temperatures reach 100 billion degrees.
    Nothing can resist the force of its gravity. Pieces of
    iron bigger than Mount Everest are easily **squeezed**
    into little bits of sand. Even atoms are destroyed.
    Everything is squashed with overwhelming force,
35 becoming tinier and tinier, denser and denser, until
    the star becomes a black hole.

    ---

    1 One **million** is a one followed by six zeros: 1,000,000.
    2 One **billion** is a one followed by nine zeros: 1,000,000,000.

The Power of Gravity

The force of gravity inside black holes is stronger than anything in the universe. Not
40 even light can escape their gravity—and this causes the blackness. At the same time, it's impossible to see inside one. A black hole is a place completely cut off from the rest of the universe by a boundary called an event horizon.
45 Nothing inside can be observed from the outside and **vice versa**. Anything entering a black hole—a star, a planet, a person— is lost forever.

Although it was his own theory of relativity
50 that first predicted their existence, Albert Einstein never believed black holes were real. He felt nature would not permit such objects. It seemed impossible to him that the force of gravity could become powerful enough
55 to cause the center of an enormous star to disappear from the universe.

Later, in the 1960s, there was a radical shift in the way science thought about black holes. This was largely due to the fact that powerful
60 new telescopes began to be widely used. These allowed astronomers to see more than ever before.

What astronomers found was that at the center of most galaxies—and there are more
65 than 100 billion galaxies in the universe—is a large collection of stars and gas and dust. At the very center of this collection is an object so heavy and so dense, with a force of gravity so strong, that there is only one possible
70 explanation: It's a black hole.

These holes are truly immense. The one at the center of our galaxy, the Milky Way, is 4.3 million times heavier than the sun. A nearby galaxy, Andromeda, has one that weighs as
75 much as 100 million suns. Other galaxies are thought to contain billion-sun black holes, while some are as heavy as ten billion suns.

The holes didn't begin life this large. They gained weight by consuming entire stars,

Swallowed by a Black Hole

What would happen to you if you fell into a black hole? Some physicists believe there is what's called a fire wall around black holes, and that you would burn up the moment you entered one. Einstein's general theory of relativity, however, predicts that you would pass through, unaware that you were lost to the rest of the universe.

It's often said that black holes are infinitely deep, but this is not true. There is a bottom, but you wouldn't live to see it. Gravity, as you fell, would grow stronger. The pull on your feet, if you were falling feet first, would be so much greater than the pull on your head that you would be stretched until you were ripped apart. Physicists call this being "spaghettified." But pieces of you would reach the bottom—an infinitely dense point called a singularity. From there, some physicists believe that those shredded particles that once were you could end up in another universe.

80 planets, and gas clouds. Black holes, it turns out, are a lot more common than you might think. In fact, there are likely trillions[3] of them in the universe.

Viewing the Invisible

However, no one has ever seen a black hole, and
85 no one ever will. A black hole is invisible. It's just a blank spot in space, but scientists are able to deduce its existence by the effect it has on things around it. For example, if a planet or sun comes close to a black hole, it should be possible to see the
90 enormous gravity of the black hole trying to pull the object in. In fact, this is exactly what scientists are planning to do: to **spy on** one while it eats a very large object.

The black hole at the center of the Milky Way
95 galaxy is currently a peaceful one. But it is currently pulling a gas cloud toward itself at about

---

3 One **trillion** is a one followed by twelve zeros: 1,000,000,000,000.

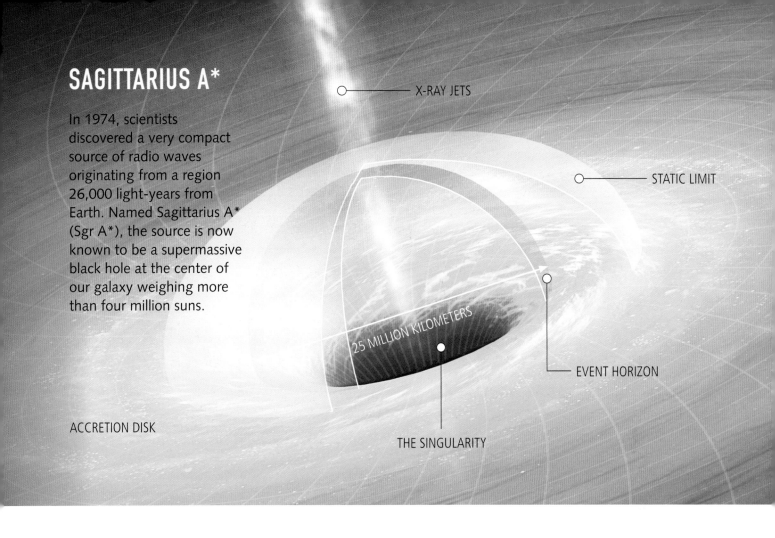

SAGITTARIUS A*

In 1974, scientists discovered a very compact source of radio waves originating from a region 26,000 light-years from Earth. Named Sagittarius A* (Sgr A*), the source is now known to be a supermassive black hole at the center of our galaxy weighing more than four million suns.

X-RAY JETS

STATIC LIMIT

25 MILLION KILOMETERS

EVENT HORIZON

THE SINGULARITY

ACCRETION DISK

2,900 kilometers (1,800 miles) a second. As the gas cloud begins to enter the black hole, telescopes around the world will be able to take
100 a picture of a black hole in action. This will be the best proof so far that black holes certainly exist.

A black hole is a messy eater. As objects get nearer and nearer to it, they get hotter and hotter. Black holes also spin, and the extreme
105 heat and spinning break up and throw off large amounts of matter at extremely high temperatures. This heated matter flies through space, away from the hole with unbelievable speed. It can travel millions of light-years[4] straight
110 through a galaxy. The material then cools, comes together, and eventually forms new stars around the galaxy.

Birth of a Universe

In recent years, it has become increasingly
115 accepted that our universe is not everything that exists. We may live, rather, in what's known as

the multiverse—a vast collection of separate universes. This is only a theory, but it seems that to give birth to a new universe, you first need
120 to take a bunch of material from an existing universe, crunch it down, and seal it off in a black hole.

According to this theory, our universe might have been the product of a black hole in another, older
125 universe. 13.8 billion years ago, our universe began when a black hole abruptly exploded. The moment before, everything was packed into a small, massively dense speck—a singularity. Perhaps the multiverse theory can be explained
130 using the example of an oak tree. Once in a while, an acorn is dropped, falls into the soil, and **abruptly sprouts**. So, too, with a singularity— the seed of a new universe.

---

4 A **light-year** is the distance that light travels in one year.

Reading Comprehension

Multiple Choice. Choose the best answer for each question.

Detail

1. Which statement about black holes is NOT true?
   a. They are black because light cannot escape their gravity.
   b. Anything that enters a black hole is lost forever.
   c. Black holes gain weight by eating stars and planets.
   d. The black hole at the center of our galaxy weighs as much as 100 million suns.

Cohesion

2. Where would be the best place in paragraph 2 (lines 11–18) to insert this sentence? *It will die in about five billion years.*
   a. before the first sentence
   b. after the first sentence
   c. after the second sentence
   d. after the fourth sentence

Inference

3. Will there ever be a black hole in our solar system?
   a. Yes. Every star eventually becomes a black hole.
   b. Perhaps, but not for another 5 billion years.
   c. Perhaps, but only if our sun collapses.
   d. No. Our sun is too small.

Cause and Effect

4. What caused people in the scientific community to start to think about black holes in a new way?
   a. Albert Einstein presented his theory of relativity.
   b. New telescopes began to be widely used.
   c. Astronauts in the 1960s brought back new information.
   d. Advances in physics proved black holes existed.

Fact vs. Theory

5. Which statement is a theory, and not a proven fact?
   a. Black holes are extremely common.
   b. There are more than 100 billion galaxies in the universe.
   c. The black hole in our galaxy is pulling a gas cloud toward itself.
   d. Our universe is the product of a black hole in another, older universe.

Detail

6. Why does the author say no one will ever see a black hole?
   a. Because they probably don't exist.
   b. Because they are invisible.
   c. Because they are too far away.
   d. Because no telescope is strong enough.

Figurative Language

7. Which of the following does the writer NOT use to describe the life cycle of a star or black hole?
   a. become born
   b. eat
   c. marry
   d. die

Critical Thinking

Evaluating: How can scientists claim that black holes exist when, at the same time, they say that no one will ever see one?

Discussion: Are you convinced that black holes exist? Why or why not?

Visualizing from an Author's Description

Descriptive writing is writing that appeals to the senses. It allows you to hear, smell, taste, feel, and especially see what the author is describing. One way to help you visualize something the author describes is to draw a simple diagram or sketch of the object.

A. Visualizing. Use the description below (adapted from the information on pages 172–173) to draw a simple diagram of what would happen to someone who is swallowed by a black hole. Use lines, arrows, labels, or anything else to help make your drawing clear and informative.

What would happen if you fell into a black hole? There is a bottom, but you wouldn't live to see it. Gravity, as you fell, would grow stronger. The pull on your feet, if you were falling feet first, would be so much greater than the pull on your head that you would be stretched until you were ripped apart. Physicists call this being "spaghettified." But pieces of you would reach the bottom. From there, those shredded particles that once were you could end up in another universe.

B. Visualizing. The author provides several other visual descriptions in the reading. Find and sketch another object or situation that the author describes.

Vocabulary Practice

A. Completion. Complete the information with words from the box.
One item is extra.

abruptly   layer   preposterous   spinning   spy on   vice versa

It's a(n) **1.** _____ idea, but imagine getting into a
spaceship and traveling back in time 4.5 billion years. There, far away
from our planet, we **2.** _____ Earth—and wait. We
wait until a Mars-size object called Theia **3.** _____
smashes into it, ripping a large part of our planet away. What have
we just seen? Many would say we have witnessed the birth of our moon.

The moon's large size and low density suggest that it may have emerged
from such an explosion. The impact would have been so huge that material
from the Earth's outer **4.** _____ would have been sent
hurtling into space. This "impact" theory is widely accepted but is still just
one theory. Other theories include that the Earth's gravity
"captured" a passing moon. Another suggests the Earth and moon were
created at exactly the same time. And yet another suggests that the moon
was spit out from the Earth as the Earth was
5. _____ very early in its development.

A total eclipse of
the moon around
mid-totality

B. Definitions. Use the correct form of the words in the box to complete
the definitions. Two words are extra.

abruptly	infinitely	layer	preposterous	squash
sprout	spun	squeeze	spy on	vice versa

1. _____ something causes it to flatten out.

2. If you _____ an orange, you will get orange juice.

3. We use _____ to say the opposite of the statement
is also true.

4. A seed will _____ into a young plant.

5. If you watch something secretly, you _____ it.

6. If something is _____ large (e.g., the universe),
it is endless.

7. When you do something _____, you do it suddenly
and unexpectedly.

8. Something that is _____ is turning around
or rotating.

> **Thesaurus**
> **preposterous**
> Also look up: (*adj.*)
> *ludicrous, nonsensical,
> insane, crazy,
> ridiculous, unreal*

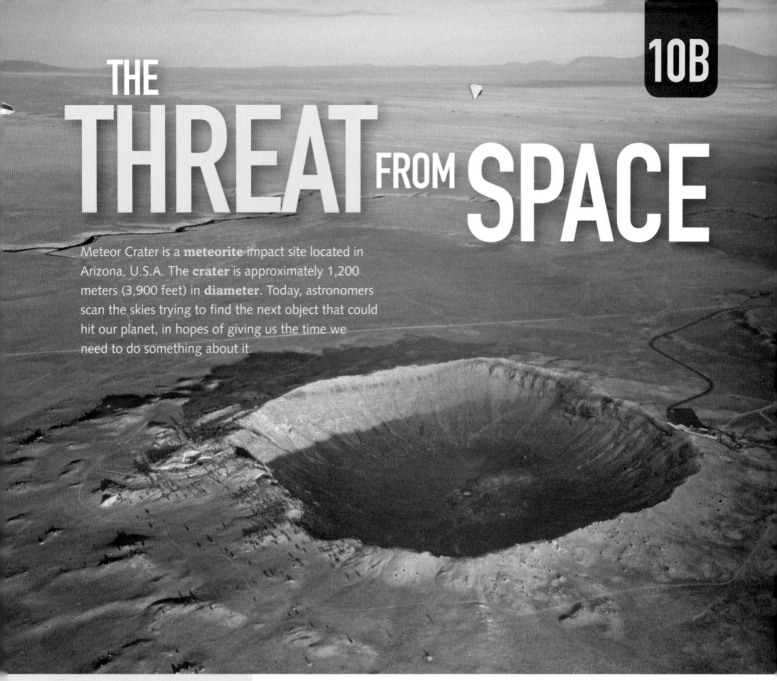

THE THREAT FROM SPACE

Meteor Crater is a **meteorite** impact site located in Arizona, U.S.A. The **crater** is approximately 1,200 meters (3,900 feet) in **diameter**. Today, astronomers scan the skies trying to find the next object that could hit our planet, in hopes of giving us the time we need to do something about it.

Before You Read

A. Definitions. Read the information above and match each word in **bold** with its definition.

1. _____: a large hole in the ground made by something hitting it or by an explosion

2. _____: a piece of rock or metal that has fallen to the ground from outer space

3. _____: a straight line that passes through the middle of a circle

B. Scan. Quickly scan the reading to find the people below. Match each person with a description (**a–d**). Then read the passage to check your answers.

1. _____ David Tholen   **a.** is developing a spaceship to deflect asteroids heading for Earth.
2. _____ Ann Hodges   **b.** noticed an object heading for Earth.
3. _____ Ed Lu   **c.** thinks nuclear bombs could be the solution.
4. _____ Vadim Simonenko   **d.** was hit by a meteorite.

SUDBURY
248 kilometers (155 miles) wide
1.9 billion years ago

METEOR CRATER
1.17 kilometers (0.73 miles) wide
50,000 years ago

CHESAPEAKE BAY
85 kilometers (53 miles) wide
35 million years ago

CHICXULUB
170 kilometers (106 miles) wide
65 million years ago

The 174 colored dots in these images of Earth are places where meteorites have struck our planet and left a crater as evidence. These craters vary in diameter from less than 8 kilometers (5 miles) across to nearly 300 kilometers (186 miles) across.

1 **IT WAS JUST AFTER 9 P.M.** on June 18, 2004, at an observatory[1] in Arizona, U.S.A. David Tholen, an astronomer from the University of Hawaii, was scanning the sky for asteroids[2]
5 when he noticed an object headed in the direction of Earth. He and his colleagues hoped to take a closer look later that week but were unfortunately prevented by rain. By the time astronomers finally got another look at it in
10 December of that year, they realized they had a problem. The object was a large asteroid, which they named Apophis after the Egyptian god of evil. Bigger than a sports arena, it comes frighteningly close to our planet every few
15 years. By Christmas, Tholen had calculated that the chance Apophis would smash into Earth on April 13, 2029, was one in 40.

Alarm about the threat started to spread to the public. Then, on December 26, 2004, a real
20 **catastrophe** struck: the Indian Ocean tsunami, which claimed hundreds of thousands of lives. The public forgot about Apophis. Meanwhile, astronomers had found earlier images of the asteroid. The extra data enabled the scientists
25 to calculate its orbit, and they discovered that it would actually fly safely by Earth in 2029.

---

1 An **observatory** is a building with a large telescope from which you can study the stars and planets.

2 An **asteroid** is a large rock moving through outer space.

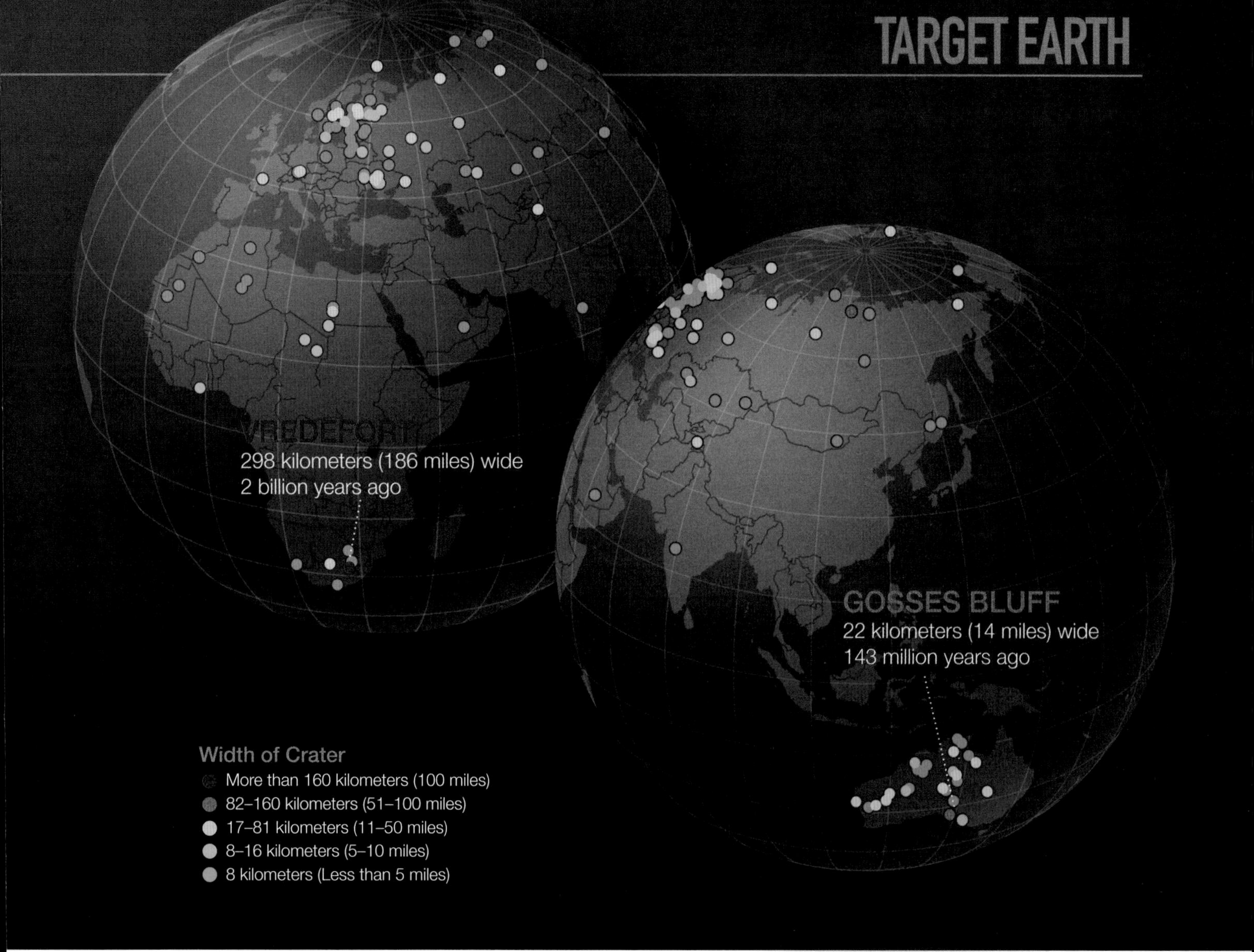

VREDEFORT
298 kilometers (186 miles) wide
2 billion years ago

GOSSES BLUFF
22 kilometers (14 miles) wide
143 million years ago

Width of Crater
- More than 160 kilometers (100 miles)
- 82–160 kilometers (51–100 miles)
- 17–81 kilometers (11–50 miles)
- 8–16 kilometers (5–10 miles)
- 8 kilometers (Less than 5 miles)

However, this alarming **scenario** started a race among scientists to find solutions to the threat of large objects striking Earth.

Near Misses

Every day, tons of dust from comets and pieces of asteroids the size of grains of sand burn up in the Earth's upper **atmosphere**. Most days, a piece or two of rock or metal, the size of an apple or bigger, actually makes contact with the Earth. Yet it's unlikely you'll ever see a meteorite hit the ground, let alone be struck by one. Very few meteorites are known to have ever hit a person. In 1954, a grapefruit-sized rock bounced off Ann Hodges's radio and hit her as she lay on her sofa near Sylacauga, Alabama, U.S.A. Somehow, she escaped with only a bruised hip and wrist.

Since then, there have been some spectacular near misses. On August 10, 1972, an object the length of a car and weighing 150 tons traveled through the upper atmosphere. Hundreds of people saw its bright trail that sunny afternoon as it crossed the sky from Utah, U.S.A., to Alberta, Canada, before flying back out into space. On March 22, 1989, a rock as big as 300 meters across came within several hundred thousand kilometers of Earth, which, in astronomical terms, is uncomfortably close.

Smash Hits

There is evidence that, in the past, massive comets[3] or asteroids have struck Earth's surface. Thirty-five million years ago, a three-kilometer-wide (two-mile-wide) rock smashed into the ocean floor, 160 kilometers (100 miles) from what is now Washington, D.C., leaving an 85-kilometer-wide (50-mile-wide) crater buried beneath Chesapeake Bay. Another giant rock, called Titan, ten kilometers (six miles) in diameter smashed into the Gulf of Mexico around 65 million years ago, unleashing thousands of times more energy than all the nuclear weapons on the planet combined. "The whole Earth burned that day," says Ed Lu, a physicist and former astronaut. The chaos and devastation were unimaginable. Three-quarters of all life forms, including the dinosaurs, went extinct.

Astronomers have identified numerous asteroids big enough to cause a catastrophe for the entire planet. None is on course to do so in our lifetimes, but there are many smaller asteroids that could strike in the near future, with devastating effects. On June 30, 1908, an object as big as a 15-story building fell in Tunguska, a remote part of Siberia. The object—an asteroid or a small comet—exploded several kilometers before impact, burning and blowing down trees across 2,000 square kilometers (800 square miles). Clouds of tiny particles of dust and ice filled the sky. The particles reflected the sun's light onto the Earth, and for days people in Europe could read newspapers outdoors at night. More recently, in 2013, a 20-meter (65-foot) meteor exploded over Chelyabinsk Oblast, Russia, injuring dozens of people on the ground. It was the largest object to enter the Earth's atmosphere since Tunguska.

The next time a large object falls out of the sky, we may be taken by surprise—currently, there is no early-warning system for near-Earth objects. However, over the next decade, sky surveys, like the one being done by Tholen, should begin filling that gap. Astronomers are compiling a list of thousands of asteroids to help us anticipate the next strike. "Every couple of weeks," says Lu,

"we're going to be finding another asteroid with, like, a one-in-a-thousand chance of hitting the Earth."

What Can Be Done?

Within decades, the world's leaders may be faced with a **dilemma**: what to do about an incoming object. Few experts are giving this much thought, according to NASA astronomer David Morrison "The number would roughly staff a couple of shifts[4] at McDonald's," he says. Ed Lu is one of them.

Lu is working on a plan that employs a spaceship to **deflect** asteroids headed for Earth. "We were originally thinking about how you would land on an asteroid and push it," he says. "But that doesn't work well." If the surface isn't solid, you have trouble landing or keeping anything on it. Moreover, asteroids are always rotating. "If you're

---

3 A **comet** is a bright object with a long tail that travels around the sun.

4 A **shift** is a group of workers who work together for a set time before being replaced by another group.

On February 15, 2013, a meteor crashed into Chebarkul Lake in Russia.

pushing and the thing is **rotating**, the pushing just cancels out,"[5] Lu says.

120 Pulling the asteroid along would be much easier. "Rather than having a physical line between you and the thing you're towing,[6] you're just using the force of gravity between them," Lu says. A nearby spacecraft would pull the asteroid
125 off course very slowly but steadily, using only gravity. And over the long distances of space, just a slight change in course could mean missing Earth by tens of thousands of kilometers.

An Asteroid Bomb?

130 The **drawback** to Lu's plan is that it would work only for asteroids up to a few hundred meters across that could be **engaged** far from Earth. If the rock is small, we could try hitting it with a spacecraft. When all else fails, and for large
135 asteroids and comets, only one strategy has a chance of working: nuclear bombs. Russian scientist Vadim Simonenko and his colleagues concluded that the best way to deflect an asteroid up to 1.5 kilometers (one mile) or so
140 wide would be to explode a nuclear bomb nearby. The explosion would destroy smaller rocks. For larger ones, the explosion would burn a layer of rock off the asteroid's surface. The expanding gas would act as a rocket **motor**,
145 pushing the asteroid onto a new course.

Apophis may pose a great challenge for world leaders. As it swings past Earth in 2029, there's a slim chance that Earth's gravity will deflect the asteroid just enough to put it on a certain
150 **collision** course with our planet on the next pass, in 2036. The odds are currently estimated at one in 45,000, so a strike is very unlikely. Meanwhile, astronomers will continue to track Apophis to learn if it will merely taunt us again,
155 or actually strike.

---

5 If one thing **cancels out** another thing, the two things have opposite effects so that when they are combined, no real effect is produced.

6 If a vehicle **tows** something, it pulls it along behind it.

Reading Comprehension

Multiple Choice. Choose the best answer for each question.

Purpose

1. What is the purpose of this reading?
   a. to explain the problem of objects hitting Earth and to explore solutions
   b. to give reasons that an impact from space is very unlikely
   c. to convince the reader that Apophis will probably strike the Earth
   d. to encourage the reader to get involved in saving the Earth

Cause and Effect

2. Why did the public forget about Apophis in 2004?
   a. The Indian Ocean tsunami struck.
   b. There was a huge explosion over Russia.
   c. Some scientists doubted its existence.
   d. No one ever saw the asteroid again.

Sequence

3. Which of the following impacts is the oldest?
   a. Chesapeake Bay
   b. the Gulf of Mexico
   c. Tunguska
   d. Sylacauga

Vocabulary

4. In line 97, *filling that gap* means _____.
   a. covering the space between the sun and the Earth
   b. adding to our knowledge about objects that could strike the Earth
   c. measuring the gap between the ground and a falling object
   d. completing our understanding of why objects explode above the Earth

Detail

5. According to the passage, what are astronomers doing so we are better prepared for a possible asteroid strike?
   a. building early-warning systems
   b. equipping rockets with nuclear bombs
   c. compiling a list of asteroids
   d. studying the craters created by asteroids

Detail

6. Which method of deflection wouldn't work well on a rotating asteroid?
   a. exploding a nuclear bomb nearby
   b. hitting it with a spacecraft
   c. pulling it using gravity
   d. landing on it and pushing it

Detail

7. What might change the course of Apophis so that it hits the Earth within the next 30 years?
   a. its own gravity
   b. a spacecraft's gravity
   c. the Earth's gravity
   d. a comet's gravity

Critical Thinking

Discussion: Why do you think so few scientists are working on the threat of an asteroid hitting Earth?

Analyzing: Which of the methods suggested in the passage do you think would be most effective in preventing a catastrophe? Can you think of any other options?

Understanding References to Things Beyond the Text

Writers sometimes make references to things outside the text, assuming that the reader will understand these references. For example, instead of stating the exact weight or length of something, the writer might say *weighs as much as an elephant* or *is longer than a soccer field*. They do this to give an approximation, to avoid using too many numbers, and to make the text more interesting

In the text, the writer states that few astronomers are concerned about objects hitting the Earth, adding that "the number would roughly staff a couple of shifts at McDonald's." The writer assumes the reader knows McDonald's is a restaurant where roughly five to fifteen people work a single shift.

A. **Multiple Choice.** Choose the description that is closest to the underlined approximation.

1. Sputnik, the first satellite in space, <u>weighed less than a refrigerator</u>.

    a. less than 85 kilograms (190 pounds)   b. less than 170 kilograms (370 pounds)

2. The number of people in space right now <u>can be counted on one hand</u>.

    a. 5 or less   b. more than 5

3. The Hubble Telescope <u>is about as long as a school bus</u>.

    a. 13 meters (40 feet)   b. about 25 meters (80 feet)

4. Astronauts can now fly to the International Space Station <u>in the time it takes to watch three movies</u>.

    a. around two hours   b. around six hours

B. **Ranking.** These phrases from the text describe the size of objects in space. Rank them from **1** (smallest) to **6** (largest).

_____ bigger than a sports arena

_____ grapefruit-sized

_____ the length of a car

_____ the size of an apple

_____ the size of grains of sand

_____ as big as a 15-story building

Vocabulary Practice

A. Completion. Complete the information with the correct form of words from the box. One word is extra.

atmosphere	**catastrophe**	**collide**
deflect	**drawback**	**scenario**

How did the Earth's moon form? As you learned on page 176, four main theories have been proposed over the years:

1 The moon is a piece of the Earth that broke off long ago.

2 The Earth's gravity captured the moon as it traveled by.

3 The Earth and moon simply formed together from the same cloud of material.

4 The moon was formed when another object **1.** _____ with the Earth.

The first three theories were once each taken seriously, but, one by one, they have became unpopular as researchers exposed their **2.** _____. Today, the fourth theory is the most widely accepted. In this **3.** _____, another planet struck Earth, and pieces of rocky material were **4.** _____ into space. That material became our moon.

Thanks to powerful, new computers, scientists have been able to learn the size of the planet that struck the Earth, and exactly how the resulting **5.** _____ crash could have helped form the moon. They hypothesize that in order to create an object that has the size and speed of our moon, the object that smashed into Earth 4.5 billion years ago would have had to have been about the size of Mars.

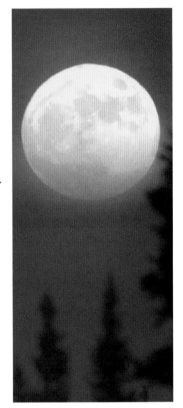

∧ Full moon rising over Alaska, U.S.A.

B. Completion. Complete the sentences below using the correct form of words from the box. One word is extra.

atmosphere	**catastrophe**	**dilemma**	**engage**	**motor**	**rotate**

1. Our Earth _____ once every 24 hours.

2. In many science fiction novels, spaceships are sent to _____ enemy aliens before they reach Earth.

3. Governments face a(n) _____: whether to spend money on a space program or to use the money to improve life here on Earth.

4. Without enough gravity, a planet or moon cannot hold on to gases that could form its _____.

5. To help robot vehicles navigate the rough surface of Mars, each of their six wheels has its own _____.

> **Word Link**
> The prefix **di** can have the meaning of "two" in certain words, e.g., *dilemma*—a situation involving a difficult choice between two or more things; *dialog*—a conversation between two people; *diatomic*—involving two atoms.

VIEWING Solar System

Before You Watch

A. Labeling. Label the planets in order from their distance from the sun.

a. Earth   b. Jupiter   c. Mars   d. Mercury

e. Neptune   f. Saturn   g. Uranus   h. Venus

1. _____
2. _____
3. _____
4. _____
5. _____
6. _____
8. _____
7. _____

B. Discussion. What do you know about our solar system? Can you think of one fact about each planet?

While You Watch

A. Matching. Match each planet to its description.

1. _____ Earth   **a.** same size as Venus
2. _____ Jupiter   **b.** rotates on its side
3. _____ Mars   **c.** contains polar ice
4. _____ Mercury   **d.** known for its extreme temperatures
5. _____ Neptune   **e.** famous for its massive rings
6. _____ Saturn   **f.** the windiest place in the solar system
7. _____ Uranus   **g.** atmosphere mostly of carbon dioxide
8. _____ Venus   **h.** has a huge red spot

B. Completion. Work with a partner. Try to complete the sentences with the correct numbers from the box. Then watch the video and check your answers.

1	4	27	70	99	150
480	1,200	1,300	4.5 billion	7 billion	billions

1. Our solar system formed _____ years ago.
2. The sun accounts for _____ percent of all the solar system's mass.
3. On Mercury, it can get as cold as minus _____ degrees Celsius at night.
4. The surface temperature of Venus can be _____ degrees Celsius.
5. More than _____ percent of Earth's surface is covered in water.
6. Mars has canyons that are _____ times deeper than the Grand Canyon.
7. Jupiter is so big, it can hold _____ Earths.
8. Only _____ planet is larger than Saturn.
9. Uranus has at least _____ moons.
10. Neptune has winds of over _____ miles per hour.
11. The former planet of Pluto is more than _____ kilometers from the sun.
12. Beyond our solar system are _____ more stars and galaxies.

After You Watch

A. Discussion. Read about how the planets got their names. Do you know what they mean in your language? If astronomers discover another planet, what do you think they should call it?

Mercury: named for the winged Roman god of travel because it appears to move fast
Venus: named for the Roman god of love because it's the brightest planet
Earth: comes from an old word *er* which eventually became the English word *earth*
Mars: named for the Roman god of war because of its red, bloodlike color
Jupiter: named Jupiter because he was the most important god to the Romans
Saturn: named for the Roman god of farming (Saturn was the father of Jupiter)
Uranus: named for the Greek god of the sky (Uranus was the grandfather of Jupiter)
Neptune: named for the Roman god of the sea because of its blue color
Pluto: now a "dwarf" planet, was named after the Roman god of the underworld because he could make himself invisible

11

GREEN CONCERNS

A farmer tends to his crops during a drought in Bangladesh.

Warm Up

Discuss these questions with a partner.

1. Do you think you use more or less water than the average person where you live?

2. Think about items you own. What will happen to them when you no longer need them?

3. What do you think the expression "Waste not, want not" means?

A man fills up huge barrels with fresh water. These barrels will be distributed to residents of Mexico City.

Before You Read

A. Quiz. How much do you know about water? Complete this quiz.
Check your answers on page 204.

1. Of all the Earth's water, **2.5** / **10** / **25** percent is freshwater.
2. Of that amount, **10** / **30** / **50** percent is in rivers and lakes.
3. Most of the world's freshwater is used for **drinking** / **farming** / **industry**.
4. Freshwater animals are disappearing **faster** / **more slowly** than land or sea animals.
5. It takes **500** / **5,000** / **50,000** liters of water to produce one kilogram of rice.
6. Compared to 100,000,000 years ago, the world today has **less** / **the same amount of** / **more** water.

B. Scan and Predict. What three parts of the world does the reading focus on? What kinds of water problems do you think each region faces? Read the passage to check your ideas.

WATER WORRIES

1 **IN THE CASTILE-LA MANCHA REGION** of south central Spain,
Julio Escudero, a 74-year-old former fisherman, fondly[1] recalls
an area on the Guadiana River called Los Ojos—"the eyes."
Large underground springs bubbled up into the river, where
5 Escudero and his community fished for carp and crayfish.
"I would sit in my boat six or seven meters away and just watch
the water coming up," Escudero says. "Now it looks like the
moon." Los Ojos doesn't exist anymore: That stretch of the
river dried up in 1984. Additionally, 186 square kilometers
10 (46,000 acres) of surrounding wetlands[2] —vital not only to the
local people but also to countless species of plants and wildlife—
have disappeared.

As farming in the region has increased, La Mancha has witnessed
an explosion of well digging in the past 40 years that has lowered
15 the water table and **diverted** water from rivers and streams.
The number of wells has grown from 1,500 in 1960 to an official
count of 21,000 today, and some experts say the real number,
including illegal wells, could **surpass** 50,000.

A Global Problem

not enough

20 La Mancha is just one of many places facing water **shortages**.
This century, many countries will face the same dilemma that
has confronted the people of Spain: how to balance human
needs with the requirements of natural systems that are vital for
sustaining life on Earth. The United Nations recently outlined
25 the extent of the problem, saying that 2.7 billion people would
face severe water shortages by 2025 if consumption continues at
current rates. Today, an estimated 1.2 billion people drink unclean
water, and about 2.5 billion lack proper toilets or waste disposal
systems. More than 5 million people die each year from diseases
30 related to unclean water. All over the globe, humans are pumping
water out of the ground faster than it can be **replenished**. In this
difficult situation, water conservationists, such as Rajendra Singh
in India and Neil Macleod in South Africa, are working to find
solutions to the water crisis. Both have found innovative ways to
35 improve their local water situations.

crisis = big problem

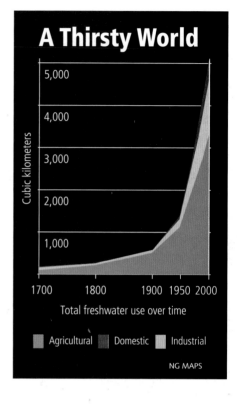

A Thirsty World

Cubic kilometers

5,000
4,000
3,000
2,000
1,000

1700   1800   1900 1950 2000

Total freshwater use over time

■ Agricultural ■ Domestic ■ Industrial

NG MAPS

Because of irrigated agriculture,
the Industrial Revolution, and a
population explosion, humans
use 45 times as much water as
they did three centuries ago.
Irrigation, which accounts for
70 percent of water use, grows
40 percent of the world's food
and makes it possible to feed the
planet's growing populations.

1 If you remember something
fondly, you remember it
with pleasure.
2 A **wetland** is an area of very
wet, muddy land with wild
plants growing in it.

A Hero in a Thirsty Land

On arriving at the Indian village of Goratalai, Rajendra Singh was greeted by a group of about 50 people. He smiled and addressed the villagers:

40 "How many households[3] do you have?"

"Eighty."

dam = barrier

"It's been four years without much rain," said a woman. "And we don't have a proper **dam** to catch the water."

45 "Do you have any spots where a dam could go?" asked Singh, 43, who has a full head of black hair and a thick beard, both with a touch of gray.

"Yes, two spots."

"Will the whole village be willing to work there?"

50 "Yes," they all replied together.

"I would like to help you," Singh told them, "but the work has to be done by you. You will have to provide one-third of the project through your labor, and the remaining two-thirds I
55 will arrange."

The villagers clapped, the women started to sing, and the group hiked to a place in the nearby rocky hills. Singh examined the area, and after a few minutes, declared, "This is an ideal site."
60 His organization would provide the engineering advice and materials; the villagers would supply the work. The nine-meter-high (30-foot-high) earthen dam and reservoir,[4] known as a *johad*, could be finished in three months, before the
65 start of the rainy season. If the rains were plentiful, the reservoir would not only provide supplemental surface water for drinking and agriculture, but would also replenish dry wells. "You will not see the results immediately. But
70 soon the dam will begin to raise the water level in your wells," Singh told the villagers.

Soon Singh was gone, heading to a nearby village that had also requested help building a johad. In recent years, Singh's johads have sprung up
75 all over Rajasthan—an estimated 4,500 dams in about 1,000 villages, all built using local labor and native materials. His movement has caught on, he says, because it puts control over water

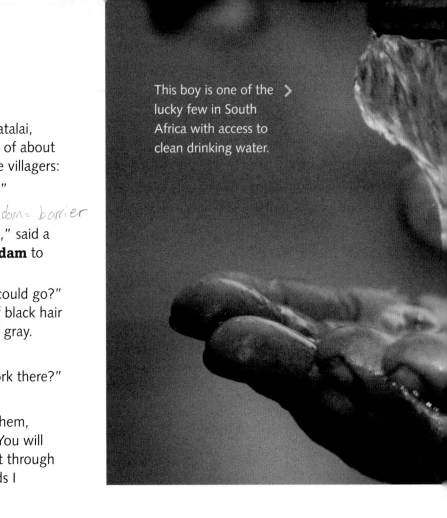

in the hands of villagers. "If they feel a johad is
80 their own, they will maintain it," said Singh. "This is a very sustainable, self-reliant system. I can say confidently that if we can manage rain in India in traditional ways, there will be sufficient water for our growing population."

Waste Not, Want Not

85 In South Africa, Neil Macleod took over as head of Durban Metro Water Services in 1992. The situation he found was a catastrophe. Durban had one million people living in the city and another
90 1.5 million people who lived in poverty just outside it. Macleod and his engineers determined that the entire city was rife[5] with broken water pipes, **leaky** toilets, and faulty plumbing[6]

rife =

---

3 A **household** is all the people in a family or group who live together.
4 A **reservoir** is a lake that is used for storing water before it is supplied to people.
5 If you describe something bad as **rife** in a place, it is very common.
6 The **plumbing** in a building consists of the water and drainage pipes, bathtubs, and toilets in it.

whereby 42 percent of the region's water was simply being wasted. "We **inherited** 700 reported leaks and bursts. The water literally just ran down the streets. Demand for water was growing four percent a year, and we thought we'd have to build another dam by 2000," recalled Macleod.

Macleod's crew began repairing and replacing water pipes. They put water meters on residences, replaced eight-liter toilets with four-liter models, and changed wasteful showers and water faucets. To ensure that the poor would receive a basic supply of water, Macleod installed tanks in homes and apartments to provide 190 liters (50 gallons) of water a day free to each household. Water consumption in the city of Durban is now less than it was in 1996, even as 800,000 more people have received service. Through sensible water use, Durban's conservation measures paid for themselves within a year. Macleod has assured the city that no new dams will be needed in the coming decades, despite the expected addition of about 300,000 inhabitants.

In Durban, Macleod has also turned to water recycling. At the water recycling plant, wastewater is turned into clean water in just 12 hours. According to Macleod, most people are unable to **discern** a difference between the usual city drinking water and the treated wastewater, although it is actually intended for industrial purposes. Macleod boasts, "Go to many areas of the world, and they're drinking far worse water than this."

Some people still hope that new technology, such as the desalination[7] of seawater, will solve the world's water problems. "But the fact is, water conservation is where the big gains are to be made," says Sandra Postel, a leading authority on freshwater issues and director of the Global Water Policy Project. The **dedication** and resourcefulness of people like Rajendra Singh and Neil Macleod offer inspiration for implementing timely and lasting solutions to the world's water concerns.

---

7 If you **desalinate** seawater, you remove all the salt from it.

Reading Comprehension

Multiple Choice. Choose the best answer for each question.

Gist

1. Another title for this reading could be _____.
   a. Water for the Rich, Not for the Poor
   b. Why We Waste Water: Two Points of View
   c. Water Shortages and Problem Solvers
   d. Politics and Water: Fighting for a Drink

Detail

2. Which of these statements about Castile-La Mancha is NOT true?
   a. Its situation is common to many places around the world.
   b. Overfishing has caused a great deal of environmental damage.
   c. Illegal well digging is a significant problem.
   d. The Los Ojos area has been dry for over 30 years.

Problem and Solution

3. How many people worldwide don't have proper toilets or water disposal systems?
   a. 1.2 billion
   b. 2.5 billion
   c. 2.7 billion
   d. more than 5 billion

Detail

4. What is Rajendra Singh's solution to water shortages?
   a. build dams and reservoirs
   b. pump more groundwater
   c. fix leaky pipes
   d. desalinate seawater

Cause and Effect

5. To what does Singh attribute the success of the *johads*?
   a. their cheap price
   b. a higher than normal rainfall
   c. the ability of villagers to sell excess water
   d. giving control of the water to villagers

Detail

6. Which of these methods did Macleod NOT make use of in Durban?
   a. repairing water pipes
   b. replacing toilets
   c. installing water meters
   d. building a new dam

Paraphrase

7. Which of the following did Sandra Postel mean by "water conservation is where the big gains are to be made" (lines 130–132)?
   a. Water conservation is an opportunity for large profits for businesses.
   b. Water conservation is the most effective method to address water shortages.
   c. Water conservation technology is still in need of many improvements.
   d. Water conservation is required by law in order to ensure large gains.

Critical Thinking

Evaluating: The writer uses an anecdote to illustrate the work of Rajendra Singh. Why do you think the writer does this?

_____

Discussion: Which of the water conservation strategies in the reading do you think would be most effective in your country? Why?

Identifying Sources of Information

Writers often present material from a variety of sources to inform or persuade the reader. They may cite the source to support the information they are presenting. It is important to be able to identify the sources of this information to see how credible the claims are. In some cases, a writer may not provide a source. Ask yourself why. The information may be obvious and not need a source, but it may also be because the source is less credible or even unknown.

A. Multiple Choice. Look back at the reading on pages 189–191. Choose the correct source for each statement. In some cases, no source is given.

1. There are 21,000 wells in La Mancha. (line 17)
   a. an official count   b. an expert   c. no source given

2. There may be 50,000 or more wells in La Mancha. (line 18)
   a. an official count   b. some experts   c. no source given

3. If consumption continues at current rates, 2.7 billion people will face severe water shortages by 2025. (lines 25–27)
   a. a health organization   b. the United Nations   c. no source given

4. More than 5 million people die each year from diseases related to unclean water. (lines 29–30)
   a. a health organization   b. a leading authority   c. no source given

5. There hasn't been much rain in Goratalai in four years. (line 42)
   a. a first-hand account   b. a scientific journal   c. no source given

6. Water consumption in the city of Durban is now less than it was in 1996. (lines 109–111)
   a. a government study   b. a leading authority   c. no source given

7. Most people can't tell the difference between city drinking water and the treated wastewater. (lines 121–123)
   a. a community group   b. a water conservationist   c. no source given

8. Water conservation holds the most promise for solving the world's water problems. (lines 130–132)
   a. a website   b. a leading authority   c. no source given

B. Discussion. What do you think are the most credible sources of information in the text? Which are less credible? Why? Share your ideas with a partner.

Vocabulary Practice

A. Completion. Complete the information with the correct form of words from the box. Four words are extra.

dam	dedicated	discern *to see and recognize*	divert	inherit
leak	replenish *to fill up again*	shortage	surpass	whereby

By the year 2025, the world population will **1.** ___surpass___ 8 billion, 3 billion of whom could face chronic water **2.** ___shortages___. Some scientists say that success or failure of water conservation efforts will depend on whether people can recognize the seriousness of the situation and are willing to take action to use less water.

One problem is that when water is cheap, people don't see the need to conserve. The European Environment Agency found that 75 percent of the water that households in Albania pay for is wasted because of **3.** ___leaks___ in their pipes. If water becomes more expensive, people might use water more efficiently. During the 1993 droughts in California, farmers paid about ten cents a ton for water, compared to three cents a ton after rain had **4.** ___replenished___ the supply. At ten cents, many farmers in California started growing crops that require less water. When the price of water was raised in Chile, the average amount of water **5.** ___divert___ into fields for use in irrigation decreased by nearly 26 percent. One notable success story is the Working for Water program in South Africa. The program has changed the way individuals are charged for water, instituting a system **6.** ___whereby___ people who conserve water pay less.

water shortage
drought
جفاف
leak of rain

If water becomes more expensive, people will think twice before wasting it.

B. Definitions. Match the definitions to words from the box in **A**.

1. ___discern___ : to be aware of something and know what it is
2. ___shortage___ : a state in which there is not enough of something
3. ___replenish___ : to make something full or complete again
4. ___inherit___ : to receive something from someone who has died
5. ___leak___ : a crack or hole that a substance such as a liquid or gas can pass through
6. ___surpass___ : to be better than or have more of a particular quality than others
7. ___dam___ : a wall that is built across a river in order to make a lake
8. ___dedication___ : giving a lot of time and effort to something important

> **Thesaurus leak**
> Also look up: (*v.*) *drip, ooze, seep, trickle*; (*n.*) *crack, hole, opening*

TECHNOLOGY AS TRASH

Before You Read

A. Understanding Infographics. Look at the infographic on page 199 and answer the questions. (1) Leed ⇒ nerve kidney (2) plastic ⟶ make cancer (3) Mercury ⟶ brain, kidney

  1. What are three substances in everyday electronics that can become toxic?

  2. What percentage of laptops in the U.S. are recycled? 26.1 %

B. Discussion. Discuss these questions with a partner. Check your ideas as you read the passage.

  1. In what ways do you think electronic products can be dangerous to your health?

  2. What do you think happens to old phones, TVs, or computers when they are thrown away?

Cables from computers and other electronics are burned to recover copper, near the Agbogbloshie slum in Accra, Ghana

1 | An Electronic Wasteland

As the morning rain stops in Accra, the capital city of Ghana, and the sun heats the humid air, a terrible-smelling black smoke begins to rise above the vast Agbogbloshie Market.

5 Past the vegetable and tire merchants is a scrap[1] market filled with **piles** of old and broken electronics waste. This waste, consisting of broken TVs, computers, and monitors, is known as "e-waste." Further beyond the scrap market are many small fires, fueled by old automobile tires, which

10 are burning away the plastic covering from valuable wire in the e-waste. People walk through the smoke—a highly poisonous mixture of chemicals—with their arms full of brightly colored computer wire. Many of them are children.

Israel Mensah, 20, explains how he makes his living here.

15 Each day, scrap sellers bring loads of old electronics. Mensah's friends and family buy a few computers or TVs. They break them apart to remove valuable metals and wires, as well as any parts that can be resold. Then they burn the plastic covering off the wire and sell it to replenish their

20 supply of e-waste. The key to making money is speed, not safety. "The gas goes to your nose, and you feel something in your head," Mensah says as he knocks his fist against the back of his head. "Then you get sick in your head and your chest." Broken computer and monitor cases are unwanted

25 and thrown in a nearby lagoon.[2] The next day, the rain will wash them into the ocean.

The Problem of E-waste

E-waste is being produced on a scale never seen before. Computers and other electronic equipment become

30 **obsolete** in just a few years, leaving customers with little [*out of date*] choice but to buy newer ones to keep up. Tens of millions of tons of computers, TVs, DVD players, monitors, cell phones, and other equipment are **discarded** each year.

Sadly, in most of the world, the bulk of all this waste ends

35 up in landfills.[3] Here, it poisons the environment; e-waste contains a variety of toxic **substances** such as lead, mercury, and arsenic that leak into the ground. Recycling is in many ways the ideal solution to the problem. E-waste contains significant amounts of valuable metals such as silver, gold,

---

1 **Scrap** is material from old, damaged cars or machines.
2 A **lagoon** is an area of calm seawater that is separated from the ocean by a line of rock or sand.
3 A **landfill** is a large, deep hole in which huge amounts of garbage are buried.

A boy carries copper wires from old electronic devices at a market in Ghana.

and copper that make it attractive to recycle. In theory, recycling gold from old computers is far more efficient—and less environmentally destructive—than digging it from the earth. The problem is that a large percentage of e-waste that is dropped off for recycling in wealthy countries is sold and diverted to the developing world—to countries like Ghana. As quantities of e-waste increase worldwide, it poses an increasing threat to the health of people living in the developing world.

To address the problem of the international trade in e-waste, 170 nations signed the 1989 Basel Convention, an agreement that requires developed nations to **notify** developing nations of **hazardous** waste shipments coming into the country. Then, in 1995, after pressure from environmental groups and developing nations, the Basel Convention was modified to ban hazardous waste shipments to poor countries completely. Although the ban hasn't yet taken effect, the European Union, where recycling **infrastructure** is well developed, has already written it into their laws. One law holds manufacturers responsible for the safe disposal of electronics they produce.

David and Goliath

Companies like Creative Recycling Systems in Tampa, Florida, are hoping to profit from clean e-waste recycling. The key to their business is a **colossal**, building-size machine that is able to separate electronic products into their component[4] materials. Company president Jon Yob called his project "David," because it has to do battle with a "Goliath"[5] in the form of the huge quantity of e-waste in the United States.

David is able to avoid the contamination occurring in places like the market in Accra. As the machine's steel teeth break up computers, TVs, and other e-waste, toxic substances are naturally released, but there are machines installed inside David whereby all the toxic dust is removed from the process. "The air that comes out is cleaner than the ambient[6] air in the building," explains vice president Joe Yob, Jon's brother.

David can handle some 70,000 tons of electronics a year. Although this is only a fraction of the total, it wouldn't take many more machines like David to process the entire United States' output of high-tech trash. Unfortunately, under current policies, domestic processing of e-waste is not compulsory, and while shipping waste abroad is ethically questionable, it is still more profitable than processing it safely in the United States. "We can't compete economically with people who do it wrong, who ship it overseas," says Joe Yob. The company is hoping that the U.S. government will, sometime in the near future, create laws **deterring** people from sending e-waste overseas.

Ultimately, shipping e-waste overseas may actually come back to harm the developed world. Jeffrey Weidenhamer, a chemist at Ashland University in Ohio, bought some jewelry made in a developing country for his class to analyze. It was **distressing** that the jewelry contained high amounts of lead, but not a great surprise, as jewelry with lead has turned up before in U.S. stores. More revealing were the quantities of metals such as copper and tin mixed in with the lead. Weidenhamer argued in a scientific paper that the proportions of these metals suggest that the jewelry was made from recycled computer parts.

Since the developed world is sending large quantities of materials containing lead to developing nations, it's to be expected that those countries will make use of them in their manufacturing processes. "It's not at all surprising things are coming full circle and now we're getting contaminated products back," says Weidenhamer. In a global economy, it's no longer possible to get rid of something by sending it to other countries. As the old saying goes, "What goes around comes around."

---

4 The **components** of something are the parts from which it is made.

5 In a well-known story from the Bible, a small, young man named **David** fights a very large, strong man named **Goliath**. Surprisingly, David defeats Goliath.

6 **Ambient** air is air that surrounds you.

An employee arranges discarded computers at an electronic waste recycling factory in Wuhan, China.

TVs, computers, cell phones, and other electronics contain parts that pose no danger in daily use but become toxic without proper disposal. These electronics contain dangerous toxins.

Lead, for example, can harm the nerves, kidneys, and reproductive system. Plastic, when burned, releases chemicals that can cause cancer. Mercury, a liquid metal, has been linked to brain and kidney damage.

Most electronics thrown away in the U.S. end up in landfills, while some are incinerated (burnt). Generally, less than a quarter are recycled.

	Thousands of tons (2005)	Percent recycled
TVs (CRT)	759.1	13.4%
Monitors (CRT)	389.8	24.5%
Printers, keyboards, computer mice	324.9	26.1%
Desktops	259.5	26.1%
TVs (projection)	132.8	13.4%
Laptops	30.8	26.1%
Cell phones	11.7	19.2%
Monitors (LCD)	4.9	24.5%

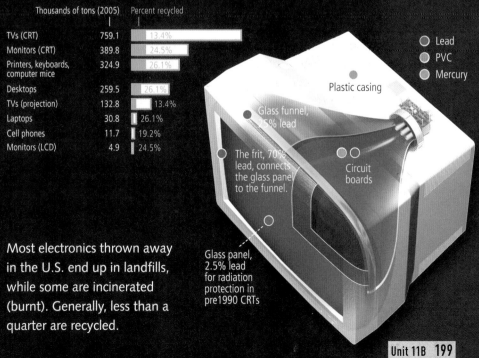

○ Lead
○ PVC
○ Mercury

Plastic casing

Glass funnel, 25% lead

The frit, 70% lead, connects the glass panel to the funnel.

Circuit boards

Glass panel, 2.5% lead for radiation protection in pre1990 CRTs

Reading Comprehension

Multiple Choice. Choose the best answer for each question.

Main Idea

1. What is the main idea of the reading?
   a. E-waste provides business opportunities for many people.
   b. E-waste is enriching the developing world.
   c. The world is facing a serious e-waste problem.
   d. Recycling of e-waste should be stopped.

Detail

2. Why are there fires at the Agbogbloshie Market?
   a. to burn unwanted computer and monitor cases
   b. to burn off the covering from metal wires
   c. to keep people warm as they recycle e-waste
   d. to signal to scrap sellers that e-waste is available

Vocabulary

3. In line 31, what does the phrase *keep up* mean?
   a. to keep the computer they already have
   b. to get educated about computers currently sold
   c. to maintain a positive attitude toward computers
   d. to obtain the latest, best-performing computers

Detail

4. What was the Basel Convention modified to do in 1995?
   a. remove hazardous chemicals from e-waste
   b. stop hazardous waste shipments to poor countries
   c. set up safer recycling centers in developing countries
   d. notify developing countries of dangerous shipments

Inference

5. Which problem does Creative Recycling Systems have?
   a. It takes too long to build large recycling machines.
   b. They can't handle all the e-waste produced in the U.S.
   c. It costs more to use their service than to ship e-waste abroad.
   d. They are breaking current laws by shipping e-waste overseas.

Detail

6. Why does Jeffrey Weidenhamer think that the jewelry he bought was made from recycled computer parts?
   a. Because the jewelry came from Ghana.
   b. Because the jewelry came from a developing country.
   c. Because the metal contained large amounts of lead.
   d. Because the metal contained certain proportions of copper and tin mixed with lead.

Paraphrase

7. In line 123 it says, "What goes around comes around." What does this mean?
   a. Your actions have consequences that will eventually affect you.
   b. Whether or not your actions are correct, bad things will happen to you.
   c. No matter how unfairly you are treated, continue to treat others fairly.
   d. Don't worry about the actions of others, because you can't control them.

Critical Thinking

Evaluating: Do you think the writer is critical of the fact that some people in Ghana make their living from e-waste? If so, why? If not, do you think the writer blames anyone?

Discussion: What steps not mentioned in the passage can people or governments take to address the problem of e-waste in the world?

Reading Skill

Understanding a Writer's Attitude and Bias

Writers use language in different ways to express a range of feelings and attitudes, such as agreement, disapproval, and judgment. As you read, look for words and phrases that indicate how the writer feels about a topic.

Positive or negative adjectives: *worthy, impressive, shameful, overrated*
Positive or negative adverbs: *importantly, notably, unfortunately, regrettably*
Transition words and phrases: *but, however, nevertheless, in any event*

In some cases, a writer's feelings may not be indicated explicitly, and must be inferred.

A. Classifying. Do these words indicate a positive, neutral, or negative attitude? Add them in the correct column in the chart below.

manipulate = to arrange, control
"handle

| arrogantly | attractive | fortunately | ideal | sadly |
| secretly | selfish | typical | ultimately | well-earned |

Positive	Neutral	Negative
attractive	secretly	sadly
fortunately	typical	selfish
ideal	ultimately = eventually	arrogantly = proud
well-earned		

B. Determining Attitude. Look back at the reading and find this information.
Mark (+) if the writer approves or feels positively about the statement.
Mark (−) if the writer disapproves or feels negatively. Underline the words in the text that helped you decide.

ethical = moral

sadly **1.** ___−___ In most of the world, the bulk of e-waste ends up in landfills. (paragraph 4)

idea **2.** ___+___ In many ways, the solution to the problem is recycling. (paragraph 4)

problem **3.** ___−___ A large percentage of e-waste that is dropped off for recycling in wealthy countries is sold and diverted to the developing world. (paragraph 4)

4. ___−___ Under current policies, domestic processing of e-waste is not compulsory. (paragraph 8) *unfortunatly*

5. ___−___ Shipping waste abroad is more profitable than processing it safely in the United States. (paragraph 8) *is ethically questionable*

6. ___+___ Jewelry sold back to the United States contains high amounts of lead. (paragraph 9) *distressing = worry*

Vocabulary Practice

A. Completion. Complete the information below using the correct form of words from the box. One word is extra.

discard	hazardous	infrastructure	notify	pile	substance

throw away, reject

Reuse and recycle: These well-known ideas for dealing with trash are being employed to handle e-waste such as old computers, cell phones, and televisions. Many companies send used electronic items from the United States and the European Union to developing nations. They claim to be recycling, and also helping the developing world so that it can modernize its economy and **1.** _infrastructur_ However, the reality may be quite different.

The Basel Action Network of Seattle, Washington, recently reported that three-quarters of the supposedly reusable electronics shipped to Lagos, Nigeria, are in fact broken. Consequently, large **2.** _piles_ of e-waste end up being **3.** _discarded_ along rivers and roads. Often it's picked apart by the desperately poor, who come in contact with toxic **4.** _substance_ such as lead. Lead is known to be especially **5.** _hazardous_ to the health of growing children.

Richard Gutierrez of the Basel Action Network believes many companies in developed nations pay lip service[1] to recycling while actually disposing of their e-waste as cheaply as possible, leaving the developing world to deal with the problems it causes.

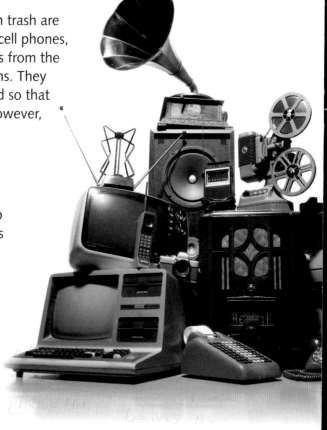

⌃ Old electronics contain high levels of toxic substances that can be hazardous to our health if not discarded properly.

---

1 **Paying lip service** is agreeing with or supporting something using words, but not really meaning it.

B. Words in Context. Complete each sentence with the correct answer.

1. A computer described as **colossal** must be extremely _____.
   - a. large
   - b. small

2. The word **distressing** is commonly used to describe _____.
   - a. problems
   - b. gifts

3. One way to **deter** a burglar is to leave your lights _____.
   - a. off
   - b. on

4. If you are **notified** about something, you are _____ about it.
   - a. told
   - b. angry

5. Technology that is **obsolete** is _____.
   - a. very new
   - b. no longer useful

Word Partnership
Use **substance**
with: (adj.)
banned substance,
chemical substance,
natural substance.

VIEWING Your Water Footprint

Before You Watch

A. Quiz. What do you know about cotton? Take this quiz with a partner.

1. Cotton is the **most popular** / **second most popular** fabric in the world.
2. About **30** / **70** countries in the world grow cotton.
3. The highest quality cotton comes from **Australia and Egypt** / **the U.S. and Mexico**.
4. The first Chinese **paper** / **clothing** was made of cotton.
5. The world's largest cotton producer and importer is **China** / **India**.
6. Cotton has been grown as a crop for over **4,000** / **7,000** years.
7. The average American owns **17** / **27** cotton T-shirts.

∧ A field of cotton ready for harvesting, in Juliette, U.S.A.

B. Discussion. Discuss these questions with a partner.

1. What are you wearing or using now that is made from cotton?
2. What advantages does cotton have over other fabrics used for clothing?
3. Besides clothing, what else can cotton be used for?

While You Watch

A. Noticing. You are going to watch a video about cotton and T-shirts, and the effect they have on the environment. Check (✓) the claims that are made in the video.

☐ Cotton is used in food.

☐ Cotton has a major impact on the planet.

☐ It takes very little energy to grow cotton.

☐ It takes a lot of energy to manufacture and transport cotton.

☐ Most fresh water is used for drinking.

☐ To save water and energy, it's suggested that we not buy cotton.

B. Completion. Work with a partner. Try to complete the sentences with the correct numbers from the box. Then watch the video and check your answers. There is one extra number.

$\frac{1}{3}$	1	2	5	40
70	97	900	2,700	250,000

It takes **1.** _____ liters of water to make one T-shirt. That amount is enough for one person to drink for **2.** _____ days. One load of drying uses **3.** _____ times more energy than washing. One load of washing uses **4.** _____ gallons of water.

Don't we have plenty of resources? Plenty of water? Yes, but **5.** _____% is salty. Nearly **6.** _____% is locked in snow and ice. That leaves less than **7.** _____% that we can access, and **8.** _____% of that grows our crops.

Skip the drying and ironing and save **9.** _____ of your T-shirt's carbon footprint.

After You Watch

A. Discussion. Discuss these questions with a partner.

1. How many T-shirts do you own? Do you consider that a lot?
2. How difficult would it be for you to make some of the changes suggested in the video?
3. What else could you do to reduce your water footprint?

Answers to the Quiz on page 188:
1. 2.5; **2.** 10; **3.** farming; **4.** faster;
5. 5,000; **6.** the same amount of

LIVING LONGER

12

An elderly man ice-skating
at the Galleria Mall, Dallas,
Texas, U.S.A.

Warm Up

Discuss these questions with a partner.

1. Where in the world do you think people
   have the highest quality of life?

2. Do you think your lifestyle is better or
   worse than your grandparents'?
   In what way?

3. Who is the oldest person you've met?
   Why do you think some people can
   live to a very old age?

205

Before You Read

A. Definitions. Read the caption and complete the definitions below with the words in **bold**.

1. A(n) ___isolated___ place is a long way from large towns and is difficult to reach.
2. A(n) ___gene___ is a tiny part of a living thing that controls its growth and development.
3. People who live to be 100 years old or older are called ___centenarians___
4. A(n) ___syndrome___ is a medical condition that is not normal but also not a disease.
5. ___diabetes___ is a medical condition in which a person has too much sugar in his or her blood.

B. Discussion. Which is more important for a long and healthy life: genes or behavior? Discuss your opinions and give examples. Then read the passage to check your ideas.

Norman Apolo Ramirez, age 51, with his family. He has Laron **syndrome**, a condition caused by a **gene** that makes him unusually short, but that also protects him from cancer and **diabetes**. Research on such genes, found in **isolated** groups of people, may one day help others avoid disease and live to be **centenarians**.

GENES, HEALTH, AND LIFESPAN

1   **Now in his 90s,** billionaire businessman David Murdock looks much younger than his age. His advice to others is this: "It is never too late to change the way you eat—once you do, your body will thank you with a longer and healthier life." But when it

5   comes to longer **lifespans**, could genes play a more important role than diet and exercise? Scientists have begun looking at the genes of small, isolated communities to better understand the illnesses of old age and how they might be avoided. In Italy, Ecuador, and the United States, studies are revealing [*to show*] information related to genes

10   that may one day help everyone reach their old age in good health.

Taste for Life

On a cool January morning, Giuseppe Passarino drove on a mountain road through orange trees into Calabria, in the far south of Italy. Passarino, a geneticist at the University of Calabria, was headed for

15   the small village of Molochio, a town with four centenarians and four 99-year-olds among its 2,000 inhabitants. [*resident*]

Soon after, he found 106-year-old Salvatore Caruso in his home. Caruso told the researcher that he was in good health, and his memory seemed excellent. He recalled the death of his father in 1913, when

20   Salvatore was a schoolboy; how his mother and brother had nearly died during the great flu **epidemic** of 1918–19; and how he'd been dismissed from the army in 1925 after accidentally falling and breaking his leg in two places. Asked about the reasons for his long life, the centenarian smiled and said in Italian, "No drinking, no smoking,

25   no women." He added that he'd eaten mostly figs and beans while growing up and hardly ever any red meat. Passarino heard much the same from 103-year-old Domenico Romeo, who described his diet as "a little bit, but of everything."

Passarino is working to understand the reasons that Calabrians like

30   these live such long lives. In the dim, cool hallway outside his university office stand several freezers full of blood taken from elderly Calabrians.

⌃ Figs—believed to be among the world's healthiest foods— are soft, sweet fruit that grow in Italy and other warm countries.

Calabria, Italy

dim = not bright or distinct

The DNA from this blood has revealed that people who live into their 90s and beyond may have such long lives because of a gene that affects their sense of taste. This gene gives people a taste for bitter foods like broccoli and field greens, vegetables that promote cellular[1] health and assist digestion.

Size Matters

Nicolas Añazco is known as "Pajarito"—Little Bird in Spanish. Nicolas, 17, said he became aware of the reason for his name at age six, when he looked around at his classmates: "I realized that I was going to be smaller than them." Because of a single gene, Nicolas looks like an eight-year-old and is 115 centimeters (three feet nine inches) tall. That gene causes a condition called Laron syndrome, the reason Nicolas is so small.

Nicolas is one of the Laron people of Ecuador. Researchers have found that they are related to people who traveled from Europe to Ecuador in the 15th century. These travelers carried a gene that sometimes causes problems with growth. The same problem has been discovered in other places where they **relocated**.

Ecuador—

In Ecuador, the Laron people **settled** in small towns and villages across 200 square kilometers (75 square miles) of the Ecuadorian countryside. Due to a lack of roads, phones, and electricity until the 1980s, the area remained isolated. Over the centuries, their gene problem was **passed down** from parents to children through the generations.

39-year-old Freddy Salazar, who also has Laron syndrome, is 117 centimeters (three feet ten inches) tall. He even had the seat of his car raised since he couldn't see through the windshield. Victor Rivera, 23 years old and **slightly** taller than Salazar, was the subject of a famous photograph shown at many scientific meetings, taken when he was four. He was so small that the ear of corn he was holding was a little larger than his arm. Luis Sanchez, at 43, is an elder[2] among the Laron syndrome group, laughed along with his friends when someone asked if they knew about the

latest scientific reports about their condition. "We are laughing," he explained, "because we know we are **immune** to cancer and diabetes." Indeed, he is partly right. People with Laron syndrome are especially healthy into their old age. The same gene that causes their growth problems may also protect them from disease.

The Gene Hunt

Oahu, Hawaii, U.S.A.

Protective genes have also attracted the attention of researchers in the United States. In one study of an isolated, **homogeneous** population, University of Hawaii researchers have found a gene related to long life in Japanese-American men on the island of Oahu. In yet another study, in La Jolla, California, physician Eric Topol and colleagues are searching through the DNA of about a thousand people they call "the wellderly," people over the age of 80 who have no **chronic** diseases such as high blood pressure, heart disease, or diabetes, and have never taken prescription drugs for them. "There must be modifying genes that explain why these individuals are protected from the deleterious[3] genes that affect the aging process," Topol says. "The hunt is on."

But genes alone are unlikely to explain all the secrets of living to 100. As geneticist Passarino explains, "It's not that there are good genes and bad genes . . . It's certain genes at certain times. And in the end, genes are probably responsible for only 25 percent of living a long and healthy life. It's the environment, too, but that doesn't explain all of it either. And don't forget chance."

This brought to mind Salvatore Caruso, still going strong at 106 years old. Because he broke his leg 88 years ago, it wasn't **mandatory** that he go to Russia with the other soldiers and fight in the war. "Not a single one of them came back," he said. It's another reminder that while genes may be a primary factor in living longer, a little luck doesn't hurt.

---

1 **Cellular** means relating to the cells of animals or plants.

2 An **elder** is a person who has authority in a tribe or community because of his age and experience.

3 Something that is **deleterious** or has a **deleterious** effect is harmful.

‹ Aged 106, Salvatore Caruso still walks on his own, does not need glasses, and enjoys singing with his grandsons.

Irving Kahn holds a world record as the oldest active investment professional at the age of 108.

Reading Comprehension

Multiple Choice. Choose the best answer for each question.

Gist

1. What is this reading mainly about?
   a. the role that genes may play in living a long life
   b. how a healthy diet can increase your lifespan
   c. how centenarians are helping the scientific community
   d. healthy ways to avoid getting older

Detail

2. What is true about all three of the communities described in the reading?
   a. The people there all avoid red meat.
   b. The people there were all relocated.
   c. They are all small and isolated.
   d. They have the most centenarians in the world.

Detail

3. What does the gene that Giuseppe Passarino discovered in older Calabrians do?
   a. It allows them to taste things more than other people.
   b. It gives them a taste for bitter, healthy foods.
   c. It lets them eat large amounts of food and still be healthy.
   d. It makes it difficult to digest certain unhealthy foods.

Detail

4. What is NOT true about the Laron people?
   a. They originally lived in Europe.
   b. Most of them came to Ecuador in the 1980s.
   c. They have a gene that makes some of the population smaller in size.
   d. They have a gene that helps protect them from some diseases.

Cohesion

5. The following sentence would best be placed at the end of which paragraph? *But it may also protect him from serious diseases as he ages.*
   a. paragraph 5 (starting line 39)
   b. paragraph 6 (starting line 48)
   c. paragraph 7 (starting line 57)
   d. paragraph 8 (starting line 64)

Detail

6. Which best describes the "wellderly"?
   a. any older Hawaiian who lives a healthy life without disease
   b. Japanese men and women in California who are never sick
   c. elderly Japanese-American men on Oahu who have no chronic diseases
   d. older Japanese in the U.S. who no longer need to take prescription drugs

Inference

7. Which statement would Passarino probably agree with the most?
   a. The answer to why people live longer lies in genetics.
   b. Scientists need to find the good genes and the bad genes.
   c. There will be fewer centenarians in Calabria in the future.
   d. Genetics, the environment, and luck all affect longevity.

Critical Thinking

Evaluating: Which of the three regions mentioned produces the strongest evidence for the importance of genes for longevity?

_____

Discussion: If you wanted to live to a very old age, would you need to make any changes in how you live your life? What would they be?

Identifying Reasons

A reading text may contain one or more reasons **why** an action happens. Identifying why things happen helps you understand the relationship between actions in the text. The reason may come before or after an action. Words that signal reasons include *because* (*of*), *since*, *due to*, and *the reason*. In the following examples, the reason is underlined.

Because / Since <u>he never exercises,</u> he's started to put on weight.

The reason he has put on weight is (**that**) <u>he never exercises.</u>

He's started to put on weight **due to** / **because of** <u>a lack of exercise.</u>

A. Analyzing. Answer these questions with reasons from the reading.

1. According to Salvatore Caruso, why has he had such a long life? (starting line 17)

   23   <u>The reasons for his long life are no drinking no smoking no women</u>

2. According to Giuseppe Passarino, why do Calabrians live such long lives? (starting line 29)

   33   <u>They've had such a long life because of gene the effect of sens of</u> taste

3. Why is Nicolas Añazco shorter than others his age? (starting line 39)

   43   <u>because he has single gene that they called Laron syndrome</u>

4. Why did the area that the Laron people settled in remain isolated for so long? (starting line 57)

   <u>because of lack of roads, phones, and electricity</u> until the 1980

5. Why did Freddy Salazar have the seat of his car raised? (starting line 64)

   <u>because he couldn't see through the windshied</u>

6. Why did Luis Sanchez and his friends laugh when they were asked about the latest reports about Laron syndrome? (starting line 64)

   <u>because they know they are immune to cancer and diabetes</u>

7. Why didn't Salvatore Caruso go to Russia 88 years ago? (starting line 109)

   <u>because he broke his leg 88 years ago</u>

B. Scanning. Look back at the reading. Circle the words that signal the reasons in **A**.

Vocabulary Practice

A. Completion. Complete the information with words from the box. Three words are extra.

relocated	chronic	lifespan
mandatory	passed down	slightly

lifetime
to a small extent

Living longer is not something most people want to just leave to chance. New research on the tiny worm *Caenorhabditis elegans* may hold promise for humans, say scientists. They say they have extended the lives of these worms, and they might be able to do the same for humans.

U.S. researchers have altered two genetic pathways in the worm—changes that get **1.** _passed down_ to the next generation. In doing so, they increased the worm's **2.** _lifespan_, claims lead scientist Dr. Pankaj Kapahi, from the Buck Institute of Age Research in Novato, California. "Basically, these worms lived to the human equivalent of 400 to 500 years," he says. Each of these alterations extended the worms' lives **3.** _slightly_. What is remarkable is that when they are added together, the combined impact turned out to be much greater.

The research may explain why it has been difficult to identify single genes that are responsible for the long lives enjoyed by centenarians. "It's quite probable that interactions between genes are critical in those fortunate enough to live very long, healthy lives," says Dr. Kapahi.

∧ *Caenorhabditis elegans,* a transparent nematode (roundworm), about 1 mm in length

B. Words in Context. Complete each sentence with the correct answer.

1. A flu **epidemic** would affect a _____ number of people.
   a. small   b. large ✓

2. People who **settled** in an area _____ it.
   a. left   b. moved into ✓

3. A **homogeneous** group is made of _____ of people.
   a. the same kind ✓   b. different kinds

4. If you are **immune** to a disease, you most likely _____ it.
   a. will get   b. won't get ✓

5. A **chronic** disease is one that _____.
   a. lasts for a long time ✓   b. you have for a short time

6. If something is **mandatory**, you _____ do it.
   a. have to ✓   b. don't have to

7. If someone **relocates**, they _____ location.
   a. stay in the same   b. move to a new ✓

> **Word Link**
> The word root **gen** means "race," "kind," or "type," e.g., *genetics, homogeneous, indigenous, generic, genre.*

IN SEARCH OF LONGEVITY

Okinawa, Japan

Before You Read

A. Discussion. Read the caption. What healthy habits do you think Okinawans and other long-lived seniors have that help them live longer? For each of the categories below, write down one or two healthy habits.

Food and Drink	
Family and Social Life	
Hobbies and Activities	

Squatting effortlessly, Kame Ogido, 89, inspects a pinch of seaweed, part of a low-calorie, plant-based diet that may help give Okinawans an average life expectancy of 82 years, among the longest in the world. These "super seniors," and others in Italy and California, share a number of habits that may be the secrets of living longer.

B. Scan. Read the passage. Does the information match your ideas? Add in any other information you find from the passage.

1 **A LONG, HEALTHY LIFE** is no accident. It begins with good genes inherited from your family, but it also depends on good habits. So what's the formula for success? In a recent study, funded
5 in part by the U.S. National Institute on Aging, scientists have focused on groups living in several regions where exceptional **longevity** is the norm: Sardinia, Italy; Loma Linda, California; and the islands of Okinawa, Japan. Groups
10 living in these three areas of longevity offer three sets of **guidelines** to follow.

A 103-year-old **>** Sardinian man dines with his extended family.

Sardinians

Taking a break from farm work in the village of Silanus, 75-year-old Tonino Tola tickles the
15 chin of his five-month-old grandson, Filippo, who watches from his mother's arms. "Goochi, goochi, goo," Tonino whispers. For this strong, healthy, 1.8-meter-tall (six-foot-tall) man, these two things—hard work and family—form the
20 foundation of his life. They may also help explain why Tonino and his neighbors live so long.

Sardinia,
Italy

A community of 2,400 people, Silanus is located on the edge of a mountainous region in central Sardinia, where dry fields rise suddenly into mountains of stone. In a group of villages in the heart of the region, which scientists call a "Blue Zone," 91 of the 17,865 people born between 1880 and 1900 have lived to their hundredth birthday—a rate more than twice as high as the average for Italy.

Why do they live so long? **Lifestyle** is part of the answer. By 11:00 A.M. on this particular day, the industrious Tonino has already milked four cows, chopped wood, slaughtered[1] a calf, and walked over six kilometers with his sheep. Now, taking the day's first break, he gathers his grown children, grandson, and visitors around the kitchen table. Giovanna, his wife, unties a handkerchief containing a paper-thin flatbread called *carta da musica*, pours some red wine, and cuts slices of homemade pecorino cheese.

These Sardinians also benefit from their genetic history. According to Paolo Francalacci of the University of Sassari, 80 percent of them are directly related to the first Sardinians, who arrived in the area 11,000 years ago. Genetic traits made stronger over generations may favor longevity. Nutrition, too, is a factor. The Sardinians' diet is loaded with fruits and vegetables, milk and milk products, fish, and wine. Most of these items are homegrown.

Adventists

It's Friday morning, and Marge Jetton is speeding down the highway in her purple Cadillac.[2] She wears dark sunglasses to protect her eyes from the sun's glare, though her head is **barely** higher than the steering wheel. Marge, who turned 101 in September, is late for one of several volunteer commitments she has today. Already this morning she's eaten breakfast, walked one and a half kilometers (1 mile), and lifted weights. "I don't know why God gave me the **privilege** of living so long," she says, pointing to herself. "But look what he did."

---

1 To **slaughter** animals such as cows and sheep means to kill them for their meat.

2 **Cadillac** is an American brand of car.

Loma Linda, California, U.S.A.

A 101-year-old > Seventh-Day Adventist woman pumps gasoline into her car in Loma Linda, California.

proponent (n) = supporter, defender
consume = to eat or drink, to use, waste

65 Marge, like many other residents of Loma Linda, California, surrounded by orange trees and polluted air, is a Seventh-Day Adventist. The Adventist Church has always practiced and been a proponent of healthy living. It **forbids**

70 smoking, alcohol consumption, and foods forbidden in the Bible, such as pork. The church also **discourages** the consumption of other meat, rich foods, caffeinated drinks, as well as most spices. Adventists also observe a sacred

75 day of the week on Saturday, assembling and socializing with members to **relieve** stress.

A study found that the Adventists' habit of consuming beans, soymilk,[3] tomatoes, and fruit lowered their risk of developing certain cancers.

80 It also suggested that eating whole wheat bread, drinking five glasses of water a day, and, most surprisingly, consuming four servings of nuts a week reduced their risk of heart disease. And it found that not eating red meat had been helpful

85 in avoiding both cancer and heart disease.

In the end, the study reached a surprising conclusion, says Gary Fraser of Loma Linda University: The average Adventist's lifespan surpasses that of the average Californian by four

90 to ten years. That compelling evidence makes the Adventists one of the most-studied cultures of longevity in the United States.

Okinawans

The first thing you notice about Ushi Okushima
95 is her laugh. It fills the room with pure joy. This rainy afternoon, she sits comfortably wrapped in a blue kimono. Her thick hair is combed back from her suntanned[4] face, revealing alert green eyes. Her smooth hands lie folded peacefully

100 in her lap. At her feet sit her friends, Setsuko and Matsu Taira, cross-legged on a tatami mat[5] drinking tea.

Ushi has recently taken a new job. She also tried to run away from home after a dispute with her

105 daughter, Kikue. A relative caught up with her in another town 60 kilometers (40 miles) away and notified her daughter. Not long ago, she started wearing perfume, too. When asked about the perfume, she jokes that she has a new boyfriend.

110 Predictable behavior for a young woman, perhaps, but Ushi is 103.

With an average life expectancy of 78 years for men and 86 years for women, Okinawans are among the world's longest-lived people. This is

115 undoubtedly due in part to Okinawa's warm and inviting climate and scenic beauty. Senior citizens living in these islands tend to enjoy years free from disabilities. Okinawans have very low rates of cancer and heart disease compared to seniors

120 in the United States. They are also less likely to develop dementia[6] in old age, says Craig Wilcox of the Okinawa Centenarian Study.

A **lean** diet of food grown on the island and a philosophy of moderation—"eat until your

125 stomach is 80 percent full"—may also be factors. **Ironically**, this healthy way of eating was born of hardship. Ushi Okushima grew up barefoot[7] and poor; her family grew sweet potatoes, which formed the core of every meal. During World

130 War II, when the men of the island joined the army, Ushi and her friend Setsuko fled to the center of the island with their children. "We experienced terrible hunger," Setsuko recalls.

Many older Okinawans belong to a *moai*, a
135 mutual support network that provides financial, emotional, and social help throughout life. *Ikigai* may be another key to their success. The word translates roughly to "that which makes one's life worth living," and it is something that is different

140 for each person. "My *ikigai* is right here," says Ushi with a slow sweep of her hand that indicates her friends Setsuko and Matsu. "If they die, I will wonder why I am living."

---

3 **Soymilk** is a drink made from soybeans.
4 If you are **suntanned**, the sun has turned your skin an attractive brown color.
5 **Tatami mats**, made of woven straw, are the traditional material for floors in Japanese homes.
6 **Dementia** is a serious illness of the mind.
7 Someone who is **barefoot** is not wearing anything on their feet.

Yoga every morning helps this elderly Japanese man stay in shape.

"*Ikigai*. . . that which makes one's life worth living."

Reading Comprehension

Multiple Choice. Choose the best answer for each question.

Purpose

1. What is the purpose of the reading?
   a. to revise the lifespan estimates for three cultures with high longevity
   b. to compare three cultures and rank them in terms of longevity
   c. to investigate three cultures with high longevity and discover their habits
   d. to expose the myths about three famous cultures with high longevity

Cause and Effect

2. Which of the following is NOT mentioned as a factor in Sardinians' longevity?
   a. quality of medical treatment
   b. nutrition
   c. lifestyle
   d. genetic history

Detail

3. Which of the following statements about Marge Jetton is true?
   a. She smokes occasionally.
   b. She regularly eats rich, spicy food.
   c. She has an active social life.
   d. She is unable to do physical exercise.

Reference

4. In line 90, *that compelling evidence* refers to _____.
   a. Adventists' reduced rates of heart disease
   b. Adventists' lifespan compared to average Californians
   c. Adventists' avoidance of red meat
   d. Adventists' reduced risk of certain cancers

Cause and Effect

5. Which of the following is NOT mentioned as a reason for the Okinawans' longevity?
   a. their social relationships
   b. their diet
   c. their religious beliefs
   d. their natural environment

Inference

6. Which advice would Ushi Okushima and her friends probably agree with most?
   a. Don't have a man in your life.
   b. Retire from work as early as possible.
   c. Act young and you will feel young.
   d. Don't have children.

Synthesis

7. Which statement is true about Sardinians, Adventists, and Okinawans?
   a. Religion is an important factor in their longevity.
   b. Most of their food is homegrown.
   c. They have strong friendships and family relationships.
   d. They drink red wine and eat cheese.

Critical Thinking

Relating: The reading presents a variety of guidelines to help in living longer. Which do you think would work best for you? Why?

_____

Discussion: Some countries are experiencing an aging population. What problems could this cause? What can these countries do to prepare for this change?

Understanding Quantitative and Qualitative Data

> Writers usually need to support their ideas, theories, or hypotheses with data. The data can take two forms—quantitative and qualitative. A well-balanced article will include both types.
>
> Quantitative data is based on numbers and patterns. It is statistical. Researchers use quantitative data to make generalizations from a sample population or to measure the responses in a survey. For example:
>
> *Eighty percent of the women said they ate mushrooms as part of their diet.*
>
> Qualitative data relies more on observation and interpretation. It is non-statistical. Researchers use qualitative data to describe behavior or to make observations about a trend. For example:
>
> *The women got up early every morning to collect wild mushrooms for their lunch.*

A. Completion. Look back at the reading and complete these notes. Use one word for each blank

Sardinians	Adventists	Okinawans
hard work and 1. _family_ form foundation for life	active lifestyle, *for example* e.g., driving, volunteering, exercising	stay busy and stay positive—laugh! lifespan of 78 (men) and 7. _86_ (women)
91 of 17,865 people born between 1880 and 1900 have lived to 100	healthy 4. _living_ (lifestyle) e.g., no smoking or drinking, or eating pork, discourages red meat, caffeine, spices	8. warm and inviting _climate_ and scenic beauty
rate is 2. _twice_ as high as average Italian		lower cancer and heart disease rates than Americans
active lifestyle, e.g., milk cows, chop wood, kill calf, walk	to reduce heart disease, study suggests drinking 5 glasses of water a day and eating 5. _four_ servings of nuts each week	diet—lean foods, locally-produced
genetics—80% directly related to first Sardinians		moai: support 9. _network_
healthy, homegrown 3. _diet_	live 4-10 years longer than average 6. _California_	ikigai = "what makes life worth living"

B. Analyzing. Underline the quantitative data in the chart. Circle the qualitative data.

Vocabulary Practice

A. Matching. Read the information below and match each word in **red** with its definition.

Food is necessary for all living things. The body requires good nutrition to function well. Therefore, it seems quite **ironic** that starving animals that eat **barely** enough to survive are the ones that live the longest. For more than 70 years, scientists have known that animals such as dogs and mice show increased **longevity** with decreased food intake. In other words, mice fed 40 percent fewer calories[1] than what is considered to be a healthy diet will live, on average, 40 percent longer than mice fed normal diets.

Could eating less food be a useful **guideline** to help slow the aging process in humans as well? Donald Ingram at the National Institute of Aging investigates the effects of a **lean** diet (which is 30 percent reduced in calories) on monkeys. It's too soon to tell if the animals will live longer; the study began in 1987, and the monkeys typically live for 40 years, but so far, the animals do seem to be somewhat healthier. "But we just don't know enough yet about how much longer large animals might live on a calorie-restricted diet," Ingram said.

1 **Calories** are units used to measure the energy value of food.

1. ___longevity___ : long life
2. ___lean___ : low in fat
3. ___barely___ : only just
4. ___guideline___ : advice about how to do something
5. ___ironic___ : odd because it is the opposite of what one might think

∧ Rhesus monkeys fed a lean diet seem healthier than those fed a normal diet. Scientists are still waiting to fully analyze the results of this study.

B. Words in Context. Complete each sentence with the correct answer.

1. If your doctor **forbids** you to eat fish, you _____ eat it.
   a. should
   b. shouldn't

2. It's always **discouraging** when you _____ a test.
   a. fail
   b. pass

3. After you _____, your **lifestyle** usually changes.
   a. get married
   b. go shopping

4. An employee might be given a **privilege** as a form of _____.
   a. punishment
   b. reward

5. You may feel **relief** when something bad _____.
   a. happens
   b. doesn't happen

> **Word Partnership**
> Use *relief* with: (*v.*)
> **express** relief, **feel** relief, **bring** relief, **provide** relief; (*n.*)
> **sense of** relief, **sigh of** relief, **pain** relief, relief **from symptoms**, **disaster** relief.

VIEWING The Science of Stress

Before You Watch

A. Definitions. Read the information below and match the correct form of each word in **bold** with a definition. You will hear these words in the video.

It is important to exercise daily as it helps improve our psychological and **physiological** functions. For example, running on a **treadmill** is a great way to **boost** your mood. This is because the "happy hormones" produced by your brain **kick in** even though your energy is being **depleted**.

1. _depleted_ : to reduce the amount or supply of something
2. _kick in_ : to begin to take effect
3. _treadmill_ : an exercise machine that allows you to run while staying in one place
4. _boost_ : to help to increase, improve, or be more successful
5. _physiological_ : having to do with the way the body works physically

< Exercise produces hormones that boost your mood and relieve stress.

B. Discussion. Discuss these questions with a partner.

1. Do you have much stress in your life? Do you think you have more or less than the average person your age? Why?

2. Which age group do you feel probably has the most stress: preteens, teenagers, young adults, adults, or the elderly? Why?

3. Should we aim to have zero stress in our lives? Why or why not?

While You Watch

A. Noticing. Check (✓) the topics that are discussed.

- ☐ medicine to reduce stress levels
- ☑ what adrenaline does to our body
- ☑ two different types of stress
- ☐ the fuel you need to take in to reduce stress
- ☑ tests that show the effects of stress on the body
- ☐ stress in older people vs. younger people

B. Completion. Complete these notes on the stress study's conclusions using the words in the box. Two words are extra.

body	breathing	burn	chemicals	exercise
kick in	levels	longevity	physical	stress

Physical test

- heart rate and 1. ___breathing___ increase
- increased 2. ___levels___ of adrenaline and cortisol
- heart rate and oxygen levels show release of 3. ___stress___ hormones
- also exploiting energy they create
- conclusion: body deals with 4. ___physical___ stress well

Mental stress

- heart rate and blood pressure increase
- increased levels of adrenaline and cortisol
- 5. ___chemicals___ not compatible with situation
- releases cortisol but doesn't 6. ___burn___ extra fuel
- can lead to bone density and 7. ___longevity___ problems
- conclusion: body doesn't deal with mental stress as well, but 8. ___exercise___ helps

After You Watch

A. Discussion. Discuss these questions in a group.

1. These are some of the most stressful situations we face. Which have you experienced?

relationship issues	money concerns	job or school pressure
poor nutrition	media overload	health issues

2. These are some of the physical and mental symptoms of stressed people. Have you experienced any of these? Which one(s)?

Physical symptoms: fatigue, headache, upset stomach, a change in appetite
Mental symptoms: feeling nervous, feeling angry, not having energy, wanting to cry

3. What are some creative or unusual ways you relieve stress?

Photo Credits

1 Ray Chui/Your Shot/NGC, 3 Michael Nichols/NGC, 4–5 Mark A. Garlick/NGC, 7 Bobby Modey/NGC, 8–9 Geoff Ridenour/NGC, 10–14 Will Van Overbeek/NGC, 14 (cr) Eduardo Munoz/Reuters, 15 Annie Griffiths/NGC, 16 Annie Griffiths/NGC, 17 Annie Griffiths Belt/NGC, 19–22 Annie Griffiths/NGC, 22 (cr) Xinhua/Photoshot/Newscom, 23 (tl) (tr) National Geographic, 23 (cl) (cr) Annie Griffiths/NGC, 25 Laura Goetz/NGC, 26–27 China Daily Information Corp – CDIC/Reuters, 29, 30–32 (t) Ankit Narang, 32 (tr) Zvonimir Atletic/Shutterstock.com, 33 Tim Laman/NGC, 35 Tim Laman/NGC, 36–37, 38–40 (t) Tim Laman/NGC, 40 (tr) Tim Laman/National Geographic Image Collection/Alamy, 41 Emilia Stasiak/Shutterstock.com, 42 (tl) (tr) (cl) (cr) National Geographic, 43 Jim Holmes/Design Pics/Corbis, 44–45, 48–50 Cultura Creative (RF)/Alamy, 47 Jim Richardson/Corbis, 50 (tr) Christian Jung/Shutterstock.com, 51, 56–58 (t) Pallava Bagla/Corbis, 52–53 Jim Richardson/NGC, 54 Pallava Bagla/NGC, 58 (tr) Martin Harvey/Alamy, 59 (tr) 33333/Shutterstock.com, (cl) Humannet/Shutterstock.com, (bl) Nobuhiro Asada/Shutterstock.com, (bc) Gregory Gerber/Shutterstock.com, (br) Kai–Uwe Och/Colouria Media/Alamy, 61 AP Images/Rob Griffith, 62–63 Robert Clark/NGC, 64 Scott Camazine/Alamy, 65, 67–69 (t) Wanted Collection/Shotshop GmbH/Alamy, 66 (t) Aamod Zambre/ephotocorp/Alamy, (b) James Leynse/Corbis, 69 (tr) David Liittschwager/NGC, 70 Matthias Schrader/dpa/Corbis, 71 Tim Laman/NGC, 72, 74–76 (t) Cary Wolinsky/NGC, 76 (tr) Shawn Ehlers/WireImage/Getty Images, 77 (cl) (cr) (bl) (br) National Geographic, 78 (tc) (cl) (bl) National Geographic, 79 Asia Photopress/Alamy, 80–81, 84–86 Ollyy/Shutterstock.com, 86 (tr) James W Porter/Bridge/Corbis, 87, 92–94 (t) Herbert Kane/NGC, 88 Stephen Alvarez/NGC, 89 Stephen Alvarez/NGC, 92 (tr) Michael Dodge/Getty Images, 93 (cr) Jim Richardson/NGC, 94 (cr) Kenneth Garrett/NGC, 95 (cl) (cr) (bl) (br) National Geographic, 97 Joel Sartore/NGC, 98, 102–104 Joel Sartore/NGC, 99 Joel Sartore/NGC, 100 Joel Sartore/NGC, 104 (tr) Holger Ehlers/Alamy, 105, 110–112 Michael Nichols/NGC, 108 Michael Nichols/NGC, 112 AfriPics/Alamy, 113 National Geographic, 114 (tl) (tr) (cl) (cr) National Geographic, 115 Danish Siddiqui/Reuters, 116–117, 120–122 Nicolas Reynard/NGC, 119 Fredrik Renander/Alamy, 122 (tr) Marin Gray/NGC, 123 Reza/NGC, 124 Chris Johns/NGC, 125 Joel Sartore/NGC, 126 Sam Abell/NGC, 127, 128–130 Jason Edwards/NGC, 130 (tr) Steve Hamblin/Alamy, 131 Lori Epstein/NGC, 132 (tl) (tr) (cl) (cr) National Geographic, 133 Pablo Paul/Alamy, 134–135, 139–141 EA/J. L. Charmet/De Agostini/Getty Images, 136 Cary Wolinsky/NGC, 137 Active Museum/Alamy, 138 Laurent Maous/Gamma–Rapho/Getty Images, 141 (cr) Joe Scherschel/NGC, 142–143 (t) Cary Wolinsky/NGC, 142–143 (b) natsukashi/Alamy, 143 (br) Joel Sartore/NGC, 145, 146–148 The food passionates/Corbis, 148 (tr) Cary Wolinsky/NGC, 149 (r) Rebecca Hale/NGC, 150 (tl) (cl) (bl) National Geographic, 151 Jim Richardson/NGC, 152–153, 156–158 NGM Staff/NGC, 154 JeremyRichards/Shutterstock.com, 158 (tr) Kenneth Garrett/NGC, 159 Erik Jepsen/Calit2, 160–161 William H. Bond/NGC, 162–166 National Geographic, 163 (tr) Mark Thiessen/NGC, 166 (tr) RGB Ventures/SuperStock/Alamy, 167 Gray Martin/NGC, 169, 182–184 Andrzej Wojcicki/Science Photo Library/Getty Images, 170–171, 174–176 Mark A. Garlick/NGC, 172–173 Mark A. Garlick/NGC, 176 (tr) Steven and Donna O'Meara/NGC, 177 Stephen Alvarez/NGC, 180–181 AP Images/Kyodo, 184 (cr) Michael S. Quinton/NGC, 185 Space/NASA Sites, 187 Dick Durrance II/NGC, 188 Peter Essick/NGC, 190–191 Peter Essick/NGC, 192–194 Eduardo Munoz/Reuters, 194 (cr) age fotostock Spain, S.L./Alamy, 195 Friedrich Stark/Alamy, 196–197 Peter Essick/NGC, 199, 200–202 (t) Stringer Shanghai/Reuters, 199 (b) Don Foley/NGC, 202 (tr) PM Images/Getty Images, 203 Amy White & Al Petteway/NGC, 205 David Alan Harvey/NGC, 206 Fritz Hoffmann/NGC, 207 (t) John Glover/Alamy, 209–212 (t) Fritz Hoffmann/NGC, 209 (b) Fritz Hoffmann/NGC, 212 (tr) Heiti Paves/Shutterstock.com, 213 David McLain/NGC, 214 David McLain/NGC, 215 David McLain/NGC, 217–220 David McLain/NGC, 220 (tr) Oleg Senkov/Shutterstock.com, 221 Blend Images/Alamy

NGC = National Geographic Creative

Illustration Credits

34–35 NGM Art/NGC, 34, 82, 101, 107, 149, 154, 207, 208, 213, 214, 215 National Geographic Maps, 90–91 John T. Burgoyne/NGC, 109 Dittemore M. Brody/NGC, 178–179 Sean McNaughton/NGC

Text Credits

9–11 Adapted from "The Visual Village," by James Estrin: NGM October 2013, 16–19 Adapted from "A Camera, Two Kids and a Camel," by Annie Griffiths: National Geographic Books 2008, 27–29 Adapted from "True Love," by Lauren Slater: NGM February 2006, 34–37 Adapted from "Birds Gone Wild," by Jennifer S. Holland: NGM July 2007, 45–47 Adapted from "Food: How Safe?" by Jennifer Ackerman: NGM May 2002, 52–55 Adapted from "Food: How Altered?" by Jennifer Ackerman: NGM May 2002, 63–66 Adapted from "Designs from Nature: Biomimetics," by Tom Mueller: NGM April 2008, 71–73 Adapted from "Dreamweavers," by Cathy Newman: NGM January 2003, 81–83 Adapted from "Human Journey," by James Shreeve: NGM March 2006, 88–91 Adapted from "Pioneers of the Pacific," by Roff Smith: NGM March 2008, 99–101 Adapted from "Racing to Rescue Koalas," by Mark Jenkins: NGM May 2012, 106–109 Adapted from "Family Ties: The Elephants of Samburu," by David Quammen: NGM September 2008, 117–119 Adapted from "Karma of the Crowd," by Laura Spinney: NGM February 2014, 124–127 Adapted from "Live, Laugh, Celebrate," by Ferdinand Protzman: National Geographic Books 2009, 135–138, 143–145 Adapted from "Pick Your Poison," by Cathy Newman: NGM May 2005, 153–155 Adapted from "Laser Archaeology," by George Johnson: NGM December 2013, 160–163 Adapted from "Conjuring Genghis Khan," by Luke Dittrich: NGA December 2009/January 2010, 171–173 Adapted from "Black Holes," by Michael Finkel: NGM March 2014, 178–181 Adapted from "Target Earth," by Richard Stone: NGM August 2008, 189–191 Adapted from "Water Pressure," by Fen Montaigne: NGM September 2002, 196–199 Adapted from "High Tech Trash," by Chris Carroll: NGM January 2008, 207–209 Adapted from "Longevity," by Stephen S. Hall: NGM May 2013, 214–217 Adapted from "New Wrinkles on Aging," by Dan Buettner: NGM November 2005

National Geographic Magazine = NGM
National Geographic Adventure = NGA

Acknowledgments

The Authors and Publisher would like to thank the following teaching professionals for their valuable feedback during the development of this series:

Ahmed Mohamed Motala, University of Sharjah; **Ana Laura Gandini**, Richard Anderson School; **Andrew T. Om**, YBM PINE R&D; **Dr. Asmaa Awad**, University of Sharjah; **Atsuko Takase**, Kinki University, Osaka; **Bogdan Pavliy**, Toyama University of International Studies; **Brigitte Maronde**, Harold Washington College, Chicago; **Bunleap Heap**, American Intercon Institute; **Carey Bray**, Columbus State University; **Carmella Lieske**, Shimane University; **Choppie Tsann Tsang Yang**, National Taipei University; **Cynthia Ross**, State College of Florida; **David Schneer**, ACS International, Singapore; **Dawn Shimura**, St. Norbert College; **David Barrett**, Goldenwest College, CA; **Dax Thomas**, Keio University; **Deborah E. Wilson**, American University of Sharjah; **Elizabeth Rodacker**, Bakersfield College; **Emma Tamaianu-Morita**, Akita University; **Fu-Dong Chiou**, National Taiwan University; **Gavin Young**, Iwate University; **George Galamba**, Woodland Community College; **Gigi Santos**, American Intercon Institute; **Gursharan Kandola**, Language and Culture Center, University of Houston, TX; **Heidi Bundschoks**, ITESM, Sinaloa Mexico; **Helen E. Roland**, ESL/FL Miami-Dade College-Kendall Campus; **Hiroyo Yoshida**, Toyo University; **Hisayo Murase**, Doshisha Women's College of Liberal Arts; **Ikuko Kashiwabara**, Osaka Electro-Communication University; **J. Lorne Spry**, Contracting University Lecturer; **Jamie Ahn**, English Coach, Seoul; **Jane Bergmann**, The University of Texas at San Antonio; **Jennie Farnell**, University of Connecticut; **José Olavo de Amorim**, Colegio Bandeirantes, Sao Paulo; **Kyoungnam Shon**, Avalon English; **Luningning C. Landingin**, American Intercon Institute; **Mae-Ran Park**, Pukyong National University, Busan; **Mai Minh Tiên**, Vietnam Australia International School; **Marina Gonzalez**, Instituto Universitario de Lenguas Modernas Pte., Buenos Aires; **Mark Rau**, American River College, Sacramento CA; **Max Heineck**, Academic Coordinator/Lecturer, King Fahd University of Petroleum & Minerals; **Dr. Melanie Gobert**, Higher Colleges of Technology; **Michael C. Cheng**, National Chengchi University; **Michael Johnson**, Muroran Institute of Technology; **Michael McGuire**, Kansai Gaidai University; **Muriel Fujii**, University of Hawaii; **Patrick Kiernan**, Meiji University; **Philip Suthons**, Aichi Shukutoku University; **Renata Bobakova**, English Programs for Internationals, Columbia, SC; **Rhonda Tolhurst**, Kanazawa University; **Rodney Johnson**, Kansai Gaidai University; **Rosa Enilda Vásquez Fernandez**, John F. Kennedy Institute of Languages, Inc.; **Sandra Kern**, New Teacher Coach, School District of Philadelphia; **Shaofang Wu**, National Cheng Kung University; **Sovathey Tim**, American Intercon Institute; **Stephen Shrader**, Notre Dame Seishin Women's University; **Sudeepa Gulati**, Long Beach City College; **Susan Orias**, Broward College; **Thays Ladosky**, Colegio Damas, Recife; **Thea Chan**, American Intercon Institute; **Tom Justice**, North Shore Community College; **Tony J.C. Carnerie**, UCSD English Language Institute; **Tsung-Yuan Hsiao**, National Taiwan Ocean University, Keelung; **Virginia Christopher**, University of Calgary-Qatar; **Vuthy Lorn**, American Intercon Institute; **Wm Troy Tucker**, Edison State College; **Yohei Murayama**, Kagoshima University; **Yoko Sakurai**, Aichi University; **Yoko Sato**, Tokyo University of Agriculture and Technology